# WH~~

# TO SELL

## INSIDE STRATEGIES FOR
## STOCK-MARKET PROFITS

# JUSTIN MAMIS
### AND
# ROBERT MAMIS

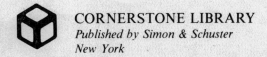

CORNERSTONE LIBRARY
*Published by Simon & Schuster*
*New York*

Published by Cornerstone Library
A Simon & Schuster Division of
Gulf & Western Corporation

Simon & Schuster Building
1230 Avenue of the Americas
New York, New York 10020

CORNERSTONE LIBRARY and colophon are trademarks of Simon & Schuster,
registered in the United States Patent and Trademark Office.

Manufactured in the United States of America

ISBN 346-12340-2

# *Contents*

1  THE NEUROTIC INVESTOR    6

    Selling: The Irrational Fear    8
    How Do I Know When to Sell?    10
    A Professional View    12
    Public Misconceptions    14
    The Psychological Factor    15
    Tomorrow and Tomorrow . . .    18

2  RIGHT IS WRONG    19

    Mental Mistakes    26
    The Market vs. Individual Stocks    27
    The Law of Supply and Demand    31

3  MARKET CYCLES AND SELLING    35

    The Theory of Market Cycles    40
    Long-Term Waves    43
    Short-Term Swings    49
    Intermediate-Term Waves    52

4  PROTECTING AGAINST LOSSES    58

    "They" vs. You    61
    How Professionals Minimize Losses    64
    Using "Stop-Loss" Orders to Minimize Losses    67
    Using "Stop-Loss" Orders to Lock In Gains    78
    Recognizing Realities    80
    Using the Dow    83
    What Doesn't Go Up Must Come Down    87

5  WHEN TO SELL (I)    90

    The High/Low Differential    92
    In Defense of Technical Analysis    95

iv    *Contents*

A Contrary Indicator    97
The Advance/Decline Line    100
The Advance/Decline Ratio    103
The Odd-Lot Index and Odd-Lot Short-Sales Ratio    106
Believing the Indicators    109

6  WHEN TO SELL (II)    113

An "Average" Average    114
Indicators Using Other Dow Averages    118
Volume Indicators    120
Indicators Based on the Most-Active List    123
Other Useful Indicators    125
Indicators Based on Fundamentals    131
Three Monthly Indicators    133

7  THE SPECIALISTS    138

Good News, Bad News    142
Using the Book    146

8  A BASIC SELLING STRATEGY    151

The Market Order    153
Limited-Price and Other Types of Orders    156
Entering the Order before the Opening    157
How the Opening Is Arranged    159
Why You Can Get a Better Price    161
But Suppose There Is News    165
The Professional's Pet    172
Back to Basics    174

9  INDIVIDUAL STOCKS    176

Analyzing Rally Action    177
The Second Correction    181
Using Waves    182
A Few Rules    186
Analyzing Tops    187
The Triangle    194
The Point & Figure Method    196
Choosing Charts    199
Case Histories    202

10 SELLING SHORT 214

Some Elementary Notions of Short Selling 215
Not So Speculative 216
The Practical Side 217
Timing the Short Sale 220
Additional Precautions 222
The Inevitability of Being Early 224
Shorting at Primary Tops 227
On the Way Down 235
The Jones Boys' Philosophy 238
Another Warning 240
Yes, but . . . 241
A Brief Summary 245

11 SELF-RELIANCE 247

Patience, Perspective, Failure 249
A Last Word 253

# 1

## The Neurotic Investor

Dozens of books have been published on how to buy stocks. Perhaps the reason there are so few on the subject of how to sell them —deciding whether, when, and at what price—is that selling techniques are far more complicated, and subject to considerably more emotional pressure, than those of buying.

If you simply throw darts at the stock tables, you can hit any one of the thousands of stocks listed on the exchanges or traded over-the-counter, phone your broker, and tell him to buy it. Should you hesitate for some reason or other, and miss the opportunity, you've lost nothing; your cash, your purchasing power, is still available until another choice appears. To take the same approach to selling is obviously absurd. The situation is no longer casual or random; now the rest of the 3,490 or so stocks that the dart missed are someone else's concern and, for better or worse, you're obliged to confront exclusively and continually the stocks you own.

This problem wouldn't be too severe if you could merely turn the buying process upside down and operate on the simple basis that whatever influenced you to spend your money in the first place will, in reverse, indicate the time and price at which to cash in your stock. That, unfortunately, is a quick way to losses. The law of opposites may be a plausible scientific concept, but stock-market analysis is only a pseudo-science, dressed in the trappings of rationality while operating under rules which are consistent only in their treachery. So while, say, the chart pattern of a top when turned around may resemble a bottom pattern, quite different influences are at work both in the marketplace and in your mind. Different decisions about whether to sell and when to sell are required.

Indeed, if the techniques of selling were but the mirror images of buying, one would expect that at least the "professional" money managers, who are paid huge salaries to buy and sell for mutual funds, pension funds, bank trust departments, and the like, would have learned by now how to execute sales with skill and dispatch. But this is not the case, as the only widely available statistics from this sector (on mutual-fund activities, to be discussed in detail later) consistently prove. One erstwhile hot-shot manager of a supposedly venturesome mutual fund admitted that his firm had chalked up substantial paper profits in the wildly speculative period prior to the 1969–70 bear market, but that "we weren't aggressive enough in selling and lost perhaps 90 percent (!) of the gains we had accumulated." Obviously, he was venturesome only on the buy side but didn't know when—or how—to sell. Indeed, he didn't even learn his lesson; after recouping some of those losses during the next bull phase, and vowing not to make the same mistakes again, he made different ones as the 1973–4 bear market unfolded, and sadly acknowledged later that he'd not only lost those profits but some of the underlying capital as well.

By dint of their allegedly superior knowledge and skills, their access to huge funds which enable them to diversify more broadly than the public investor, plus their advantage of getting first call on brokerage firm analysis and research (and being able to relax, too, because it isn't their money at stake), money managers ought to do better than the market even in adverse times. Yet, if 1974 was a bad year for the market, it was an abysmal year for mutual funds. Whereas one out of every eight listed stocks was able to close out the year with a gain, only one out of every fifty mutual funds had a positive record. In other words, at the outset of 1974 you'd have had six times better odds using a dart than entrusting your money to a professional fund manager.

What these and other equally appalling statistics show is that even the experienced and reputable have trouble when it comes to selling. Had the mutual funds, non-profit foundations, college-endowment funds, and other similar institutions known how to sell properly, they would have cut their losses early in the decline and held a substantial amount of cash in reserve for a later buying opportunity. Instead, despite full-time concentration, Harvard Business School degrees, Brooks Brothers suits, and carpets on the floor, they rode the devastating 1973–4 bear market down with virtually fully invested positions. How do highly paid professionals succeed in chalking up a record no better than the most amateurish man in the street? The inability to sell when one should, repeated time and again by amateur and Wall Streeter alike, has all the earmarks of neurotic behavior.

## Selling: The Irrational Fear

Stocks are bought not in fear but in hope. No matter what the stock did in the past, it assumes a new life once a purchaser owns it, and he looks forward to a rosy future—after all, that's why he singled it out in the first place. But these simple expectations become complicated by what actually happens. The stock acquires a new past, beginning from the moment of purchase, and with that past come new doubts, new concerns, new conflicts. The purchaser's stock portfolio quickly becomes a portfolio of psychic dilemmas, with ego, id, superego, and reality in a state of constant battle.

Consider these nagging questions: Happily, the stock has gone up, but will it go up more, or is this the time to sell? Or it has gone down, will it slide some more or turn around and go up at last? Should I take a small loss now? Could I swallow such a huge loss, or should I at least wait for a rally? Now that it is finally rallying, should I hold until I'm even? Now that I'm even, shouldn't I reward my patience by aiming for a gain? The decision *not* to sell maintains hope, thereby preserving a future. Indeed, the thought of selling a stock and thus abruptly ending the dream is so paralyzing that for every conceivable market situation there are ready-made excuses for holding on at least a little while longer. And these excuses invariably are based on the desire to believe that the future will be better than the present. Any excuse, however absurd, becomes convenient as long as it postpones indefinitely the necessity to act.

You've probably seen brokerage-house reports that admit "the next few quarters are going to be lower" or "the stock could sell off further over the short term," yet these appraisals give absolutely no selling advice in conclusion. Instead, hope is held out for the more distant future, when these real troubles will be past and everything will be glorious. But while the advisor is daydreaming of a better tomorrow, the firm's margin clerk remains unconvinced. All he knows is that the customer's paper loss in following that advice is real enough right now to require more cash in the account. And to show how irrational this "it's only a paper loss until I sell" excuse is, the person getting such a margin call will actually shovel out more of his own money, just to prove to the margin clerk that it *is* only a paper loss, that he, and his dream, are still alive. This neurotic optimism is, unfortunately, abetted by the typical customer's man at the brokerage house who also tends to reject the reality of today for the vague promise of tomorrow. "Let's give it another day" is the last sentence of many a phone conversation when neither customer (whose money is at stake) nor broker (whose ego is equally exposed) can bring himself to admit that the stock in question had better be sold right then and there.

After our earlier description of the selling decision as a "battle," it is not surprising to find a real battleground psychologically described in the same terms. Just transpose these words about Vietnam to the Wall Street arena: "The overwhelming desire for the success of policies to which a strong emotional attachment has been made also leads to an attempt to alter those facts over which one has control, making them consistent with the outcome that is desired. It is as though there is an expectation at a magical level that events over which one has no control will then also fall into the desired pattern."* In short, there's also a light at the end of the stock-market tunnel; we'll win in the future, so long as we don't have to recognize that something negative is happening right now. We develop a magical expectation for the future, rather than utiliz-

*From *Men, Stress, and Vietnam,* by Peter Bourne.

ing something over which we *do* have control: in the stock market, we control by our ability to sell.

## How Do I Know When to Sell?

Is it even possible to know when to sell? Is there some way to separate hopes from real possibilities? It would be nice if there were an easy answer, a ready-made system to spell out. But there isn't. All those "how-to" books on buying stocks conveniently leave out the details of how to sell, unless it's something grandly banal like: "Oh, you sell when the stock has finally stopped doubling, and then you find another supergrowth stock to switch to." Chances are your broker skirts the question, too; neither he nor his firm's market literature advises you when to sell, though both will willingly hound you with buying enticements. That's because there are few moments that cry out for selling, and no simple way to lick the emotions that hinder cutting the cord. When the stock eases slightly below your purchase price, the situation is charged with doubt. Perhaps you *were* wrong, and should accept that small loss. But, then again, maybe it's just a temporary fluctuation: you bought a trifle too soon or a mite too high. And isn't the whole market due for a rally tomorrow? And how about the earnings report to be announced shortly? Or that exciting new product which was the reason you bought the stock in the first place? Such factors should be considered, but not to an unreasonable extent just because the investor won't admit he's made a mistake and should sell instead.

Take the common plight of the recent purchaser who declines the chance to settle for a small loss because it would be too quick an admission of failure. In the scale of things, losing a few hundred bucks isn't nearly the serious defeat that his churning emotions make it out to be. The purchaser, though, would rather hold, nurturing the hope that the stock will come back shortly. But it keeps going down, and before he knows it, the whole list is joining in the decline. As the price sags considerably lower, he shields himself with ignorance: he stops looking at the closing prices in the newspaper; he stops phoning his broker every day. Weeks later, as the crashing prices make the headlines and become the featured news on television, with experts forecasting even more dire developments, hope finally goes down the drain. So, along with thousands of other panic-stricken investors (and those receiving margin calls), our investor dumps his shares into the abyss, and at last releases himself from his torture. He's taken a much bigger loss, but at least he's out!

This is the way major bottoms are often fashioned, leaving these bewildered investors in the lurch as prices turn around and shoot upward through a virtual vacuum. With all the newspapers full of bleak headlines, who would be fool enough to buy stocks at this juncture? Yet someone obviously is, for prices are racing upward on the ticker tape. The buyer is certainly not our investor, who has desperately tried to hold and then finally given up in despair, for he has sworn off the market forever. Nor are the buyers the many other investors who were weeded out by margin calls along the way down, or those few who, with the tenacious courage of Beau Geste, defended their honor throughout and are still holding at substantial paper losses. On the contrary, this tattered group quickly toss their shares into the pot as soon as the rally manifests itself, believing it to be just another bear-market rally designed to trap them; if they get out without a loss, they're delighted and harbor no thoughts of buying, even as they watch their stocks zoom on upward without them. By and large, that leaves as buyers at the bottom only the Exchange specialists (who are required to buy anyway, according to the Exchange rules, whenever there are no other buyers), unemotional professional traders who sense an important change in trend brewing and who are disciplined enough to get right out again if they're wrong, and the fortunate few folk who, having correctly sold long ago, are both emotionally and financially able to join these pros.

Some variation of this vicious cycle is recognizable through each bear market and back up through the next bull. During the rally, as the climate ostensibly improves, the public player, vowing not to repeat his old mistake of selling too late, makes a new one: he sells too soon—as soon as he sees the slightest sign of struggling —because he doesn't believe the rally will continue. When it does persist, he makes amends for that second mistake by making a third: deciding that stocks will come back after a dip, he won't sell at all during the next phase. And then, as noted, he finds himself still holding at the top when that next dip turns into a brand-new bear cycle.

## A Professional View

You can learn from other investors' mistakes. One explanation for why investors make certain mistakes at particular points in the trading cycle was supplied by a professional member-trader whom we'll call Charlie Fisk. "The public is most comfortable," Charlie says, "when they are sitting with losses." This is a judgment born of a dozen years as a customer's man dealing every day with amateur market players, followed by purchase of his own Exchange seat. Now he trades for his own, and his firm's, account, from a seedy office diagonally across the street from the Exchange, with a day's collection of coffee containers on the desk near his only tool—the telephone that links him with the order clerk on the floor. It might be said, as the SEC once tried to insist, that Charlie is a typical member of the "they" club, "they" being that mythical body of money men who the public feels are always on the inside, conspiring to take away its profits. "They" make a stock go up when "they" want to; "they" can always take it back down before the public gets a chance to get out . . . and so on. Before the SEC forced the Exchange to impose stricter trading rules, Charlie spent his day on the Exchange floor and, while there, was a professional's professional, a man whom less nimble traders followed around to see what he was doing. So Charlie knows the market, the people who compose it, and how the game is played.

He has just conveyed to the floor a market order to buy 2,000 shares of Reading & Bates. As he talks, he stares overhead at the ticker tape, which has the very same symbols and numbers flashing by that the public and its brokers also watch. Yet the end results are quite different, since Charlie Fisk makes a lot of money whether the market goes up or down. "Why is the public comfortable with losses?" he reflects, not bothering to relight the cigar jammed in the corner of his mouth; he is literally on the edge of his seat, watching. "Because if their stocks are down from where they bought them, they don't have to worry about selling them. Once he's got a loss, the typical investor is sure he isn't going to sell. He bears the lower price because in his mind it is temporary and ridiculous; it'll eventually go away if he doesn't worry about it. So selling at a loss becomes absolutely out of the question. And since it is out of the question, and his mind is made up for him, the struggle of any potential decision vanishes and he's able to sit comfortably with the loss."

The phone rings as the floor broker reports the details of the RB purchase: 2,000 bought at 30 1/2. By then, of course, Fisk had already surmised which tick on the tape represented his order and had *begun to concentrate on timing his sale from the moment the stock was bought.* The smaller the degree of gain he's after—a point, even half a point—and the briefer the time span, the more significance each tick on the tape assumes. "Get me a fresh size," he snaps back into the mouthpiece. The specialist is obliged to give the size to anyone when asked—information about how many shares are bid for at the current best bid and how many shares are being offered at the lowest asked price.

By then we ourselves can see RB printing at 30 7/8 several times over on the tape overhead. Charlie is concerned; he wants to see a trade at 31, the next round number, to keep the stock's upward momentum going, and it isn't coming up. "I worry about every tick," he mutters. "Don't like that one . . ." as 100 shares prints at 30 3/4. But it is followed by 400 more back at 30 7/8. "Isn't that okay?" we ask. The floor broker comes back with the size, which Charlie scribbles on his pad as he repeats: "Three by two, a half, seven eighths," meaning that the specialist has bids for 300 shares at 30 1/2 and is offering 200 shares at 30 7/8, even after we'd seen over 1,000 traded at that price. Charlie scowls at the tape for a minute, then abruptly seizes the phone again: "Get me out." Then, silent, brooding, he watches the tape until he spots 300 shares of RB printing at 30 1/2, followed by 1,700 more at 30 3/8.

"So I took a little loss." He shrugs. But why did he sell at that exact moment? "My business is trading for fast turns. All of a sudden the stock symbol stopped appearing on the tape and to me that said RB was having trouble eating up the stock offered at 30 7/8, let alone being able to get through 31. To me a stock that can't go up must go down and I don't want to sit around holding it while it does. It could get rolling again this afternoon, but that's a different game."

The public, we remind him, is unable to go in and out on fractions of a point; they've got substantial commissions to pay on every such transaction. "Yes," he replies, "but the principle is the same: sell when the selling is a sound idea, when the stock no longer does what it is supposed to do. My expectations happen to have close tolerances. I take those eighth losses and half-point profits because that's my business. But to the public mind, selling is *never* sound. It always conveys the possibility of being wrong twice: first, admitting that they've made a buying error; second, admitting that they might be wrong in selling out. And if the stock has actually gone up, they're tormented: should they take the profit or hold for a bigger one? That creates anxiety, and anxiety breeds mistakes. But as long as they've got losses, and never have to decide, they can sit back comfortably and dream instead."

## Public Misconceptions

Compare that discussion with a dialogue overheard one day while waiting for a tennis court in New York's Central Park. A couple seated on the next bench was reading the Sunday *Times* when suddenly the man looked up from the financial section. "Say, honey, remember the Jackson-Atlantic I bought at 14, and then it fell to 7?"

"Oh, my God," she exclaimed, "you never told me that!"

"Well, I didn't want to worry you. No need to get upset; it's back up to 14 again, and made the 'most active' list this week."

"Great," his wife said, "now you can sell it and get our money back."

The man looked at her incredulously. "Sell it! Now that it's going up? I waited a whole year for this."

Whether the stock ought to have been sold or not at that point is a matter for guesswork; certainly the facts that it then matched the original purchase price and that a year had elapsed should not have been relevant factors. Note that (1) having endured the loss willingly, he'd never even thought about selling until his wife raised the possibility; (2) he obviously expected her to be proud of him for having successfully stuck it out for a year; and (3) he now felt that he was being challenged to prove that he knew what to do about stocks.

He had willingly tolerated a 50 percent loss in his position on the grounds that "stocks always come back." Yet the manner in which they do, or the length of time it takes, to say nothing of the possibility that they never will come back *enough,* ought to be taken into account. The ranks of once-spectacular star performers that have never come back are legion. Total demise hit the popular darlings National Video and Four Seasons. Memorex fell, in the course of three years in the early 1970's, from a high of 160 to delisting, although it did survive as a company. It took over thirty years for the public's pet, American Telephone, to get back up from its Depression low past its 1929 high. Nor does a company necessarily have to go bankrupt before being thought of as down for the count; if it was bought at 70, and now trades between 5 and 6, it requires a lot of blind faith to believe it should be held because "it'll come back."

## The Psychological Factor

There is evidence that the typical stock-market player not only endures the irrationality of his behavior but actually *relishes* losing, time after time. The repetition of this phenomenon is so reliable that it has long since become one of Wall Street's most dependable indicators, codified in the Theory of Contrary Opinion and expressed in the accurate adage: "The market will do whatever it must to prove the greatest number of investors wrong." With its elements of reward and punishment, the stock market is an ideal arena for one's emotions; the striving to lose, stemming from an investor's subconscious, is a matter for psychoanalysts to define (guilt, sexuality, self-doubt, aggression, etc.). Our concern, as stock analysts, is to recognize the phenomenon, and to use it for our own benefit.

For different reasons at different times in the market cycle, the average investor finds it difficult to accept a small loss or to lock in a profit before it evaporates. The formidable psychic struggle—to sell or not to sell—somehow invariably produces the wrong

decision, selling prematurely when the advance has much further
to go, and, having made that mistake, rebuying and hanging on,
refusing to sell at all after the top has arrived. Every once in a
while, the market tosses in some bait—like the pool hustler who
allows his victim to win a round or two—but for every person who
hangs on to a stock that continues to go up, there are dozens who
lament that they never got around to selling "at 34 and now the
stock is at 8." Naturally, there are innumerable variations on the
loser theme, one of the most frequently applied being the way a
person, subconsciously seeking punishment, manages to sell his
strongest holdings while letting his weaker ones ride on a wing and
a prayer. Taking a fast profit (by selling a stock that's up) to avoid
taking a loss is one way to see stocks that have been sold continue
to rise while the ones that have been kept remain weak. There is
no rule that says a small loss can't become larger, or that a large
loss can't end in bankruptcy rather than a rally. Yet as long as he
doesn't sell, the public player reasons, there's a chance for redemp-
tion. "I learned early that you don't play day by day but year by
year. If someone tells you they don't lose, they don't play. But a
professional keeps losses at minimum." Those words come from a
professional gambler, yet they precisely apply to the game going on
at the corner of Broad and Wall. Just as in poker, a key ingredient
to stock-market profits is knowing when to fold, when to take a
loss, and when to stay out for a while. But the public player,
dreaming only of a more rosy future, has yet to learn that what's
happening right here and now is all that is applicable, all that
counts.

The truth is that even the shrewdest professional on the floor of
the Exchange loses money at one time or another. To paraphrase
the gambler: If you've never lost any money in the market, you've
never played the game. But loss is not only ending up with less than
you put in; loss is also missing a chance—a discernible, objective
chance—to sell at a profit, for then you've given back money that
could have been yours. Public players glibly proceed on the theory
that they are playing with someone else's money, but since it would
be theirs if they had sold at the sensible moment, that, too, is a
rationalization.

It may not be surprising that the stock market, which has been a male province for so long, uses language that abounds with sexual imagery: getting married to a stock; glamour issues; love orders; as well as nicknames like Ma Bell and Bessie. And there are, of course, a number of parallel patterns, too: the frequent mistake of selling too soon can be compared with premature ejaculation, of not being able to sell at all with impotence. Anything that goes up and down, with down being the losing side, certainly has sexual connotations, as does the gaining of money, the male manner of giving birth and proving power.

Too often, selling decisions are dictated by psychological factors rather than by what has been happening on the Exchange floor. Consider the mathematics of the Jackson-Atlantic situation instead of the husband's own needs. Suppose this man sold at 12, when his position started to deteriorate, taking a loss of $200 (plus commissions). When the stock dropped to 7, he wouldn't have cared; having sold long ago, his mind would be clear and he could consider the possibility of buying this, or some other, perhaps more appealing stock. Unlike a holder with a huge loss, whose mind is consumed with getting out when the price comes back, the investor who has already sold is both mentally and financially prepared to buy. That's an edge in itself. But let's suppose he had decided to buy back Jackson-Atlantic as soon as the stock began to show some life again. He might have made that decision around 7; let's say, then, that he bought 150 shares at 8 with the $1,200 he got when he sold at 12. Thus he would own fifty shares *more* than he originally held. The Monday morning after his tennis match he could sell these at 14, the same price at which he stood to break even with his original purchase, and his net profit in this stock would amount to $700 ($900 on this trade less the $200 lost earlier). He would have grossed 50 percent on his original investment, with the commission costs at least partially offset by the interest he would have earned by keeping his $1,200 in the bank for a year. Besides which, and perhaps even more important than the cash gain, add the psychic profit of not having had to rationalize the stock's slipping further from 12 to 7. Yet there he was, wanting to be complimented for having nursed the stock back to the break-even point.

## Tomorrow and Tomorrow . . .

Through the entire market cycle lurks the fear of finalizing the deed, of taking it from dream to reality by selling. This stems from the nature of the market itself—the great American indoor sport, a game which never ends. In a football game, the team that's losing throws a long pass on the outside chance that it might be successful; in hockey, in the last minute, the goalie is pulled out in favor of another forward, in an effort to salvage a score before the final bell rings. But the stock market goes on day after day after day, and never comes to a definitive end. There's always tomorrow, where the unfulfilled dream lies. By not selling, by tightly holding on to his stocks, the investor never has to face reality. Thus the nature of time itself—the actual past, the promise of the future— tempts the typical investor to refuse to deal with the objective situation confronting him.

All this doesn't mean you absolutely *have* to sell to prove yourself. Indeed, there will be plenty of times when the sensible decision is not to be pushed into such action. But you have to pay attention and keep a clear head so that you are ready to sell when the warning signals arrive. You don't have to be on the edge of a chair like Charlie Fisk is every time he makes a commitment, watching every tick every day; once a day, once a week, may be ample when you know what to do. So let's find out how to determine the right time and the right price at which to sell.

appearance. As a result, there is always some way to go wrong in the course of just about every transaction. But it is only hindsight that makes the mistake clear; and we don't, of course, have the luxury of hindsight at the time the decision has to be made.

This means that one important thing to learn at the start is that no matter how hard we try to be right, we are in one way or another bound to be wrong. Assuming that you know what you're doing, that you're experienced, have a feel for what's happening, and have your emotions under reasonable control, the best you can do is be as perceptive and informed as possible for that particular juncture in time, and to act upon your perceptions decisively. Something else might pop up a single tick later, but (1) you can't snatch the act back, and (2) you shouldn't fret about what might have been. With proper discipline and intelligent observation of the information that's available, *you ought to be able to make more money than you lose, and in the stock market, that's the only definition of being right.*

Take the case of an off-floor trader named, let's say, Lesser, who has the reputation of knowing what he is doing. He and his brother comprise Lesser Bros., Inc. One, the Exchange member, works on the New York Stock Exchange floor, while the other sits "upstairs" at an ordinary desk in the middle of an ordinary downtown board room, surrounded on all sides by ordinary retail brokers constantly calling up their customers. But Lesser has no customers; all he does, day in and day out, is trade the firm's capital; it's a job, moving merchandise in and out quickly and profitably, and he has done it well enough over the years to be considered a rich man.

Ignoring the patter of the salesmen around him, he heeds only what the tape is saying and how those transactions relate to the charts of each stock spread out in front of him. In April 1972 Lesser was holding the hot stock of that era, Levitz Furniture. Having paid 50, he was uneasy when he saw that each rally following a normal dip was failing at a successively lower level—first at 54 1/4, then 50 3/4, and again at 50 1/4. That's it, he thought, and on the next rally (which lifted off from 45), he sold out his position at 48 for a small loss. What's more, it became increasingly evident that 45 was an important price level; if broken, LEV could plummet a long way before finding its next level of support. So, at the same time that he liquidated his long position, he went short a like number of shares.

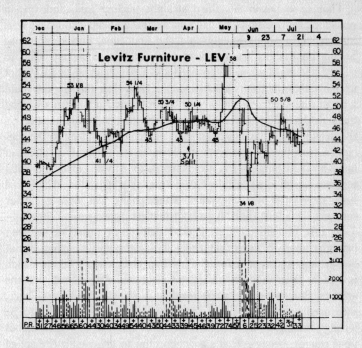

But, as you can see on the chart, LEV refused to break 45 in three straight swats at that level. Then a major brokerage firm recommended purchase and that "expert" confidence in a company whose stock was already up from 10 to 50 in a little over a year induced several big buyers to begin chasing the price up wildly. Seeing the strength materialize, Lesser quickly reversed his reversal, covering the shorts at 51 for his second loss and going long once again. LEV boomed ahead, creating for him a profit large enough to offset both the previous losses. Coming to work one morning, Lesser decided the run-up had been too much too fast and it was time for him to nail down his gain. But when he got to the office, the "broad tape" carried word that the SEC was investigating Levitz and was, consequently, suspending trade in the stock. Once that news was disseminated, and trading resumed, LEV was not to reopen until a torrent of sell orders could be matched with buyers back under 50.

That gave Lesser his third straight trading loss, and yet, in reviewing his decisions, he can't spot a thing he did wrong. He was, in fact, right about having sold the first time, and right about having gone short (particularly as the stock ultimately went to 1 1/2!), and right when he covered and went long, since LEV shot up more than 10 points afterward. Yet each time the market—and a bit of fate—proved him wrong. With hindsight we can see what he might have done differently—namely, kept the short position on the grounds that, as hindsight also made acutely clear to the specialist, furniture in concrete warehouses isn't exactly a glamour industry. But hindsight is not available as a tool. Lesser did what seemed objectively sensible, based on a style of trading which had been successful over the years; although he was wrong, Lesser remains confident that his overall market approach is correct.

In this moralistic-technological culture of ours, we've been brought up to believe that there is a right and a wrong about everything, and that if Judeo-Christian values don't tell us which is which, then modern science can conveniently punch out the answer. But *there is no such absolute in the stock market.* There, measured against a perfect score, one is destined always to be wrong somehow. That fact of Wall Street life must be pasted across your mirror, because that's what coming to grips with the act of selling is all about.

An alert institutional money manager would have sensed, during the great bear market of 1973–4, that the fancy glamour stocks selling at super-high price/earnings ratios were potential disasters, and then he would have seen them actually collapsing all around. If he sold his block of, say, Hewlett-Packard when it broke 80, he would have slept well as it plunged into the low 50's. Look at how right that selling was—until, during the first upwave of the new bull market, HWP not only recovered that lost ground but quickly went up to a new all-time high well over 100. He could have held, he thinks in hindsight, because it turns out that HWP, virtually alone among the glamour stocks, staged a remarkable performance: last to break down, best on the upside (a not untypical sequence). So he was both right and wrong and the quasi-scientific test might well have produced a third decision, instead . . . Did he put the money from the sale to good use thereafter?

The history of Memorex illustrates right and wrong in reverse. If you finally got around to selling MRX at 30, or even 20, long after it was sliding from its record peak around 160, you sure looked wrong to have been so slow-witted, but not so wrong when the stock plunged under 3 and then off the board entirely. Subsequent action made even that laggardly sale at least relatively right. And yet, here is MRX reborn on the ticker tape, as final proof that there is no flawless stock-market decision.

In each of these examples it is easy to see what the perfect path would have been, just as Lesser could see, afterward, where absolute rightness lay in Levitz. But he knows he did what needed to be done *at the moment.* "I did it based on all the evidence available at the time," Lesser says, "and I'd do it the same way again. The only way to win at this game is to be consistent."

Since, indeed, the stock market is nothing but a game, with players on both sides of each transaction, with a score in money-points, and with eventual winners and losers, it is often revealing to compare it to more familiar games. Take baseball: the manager who orders a sacrifice bunt whenever nobody's out and the tying run is on first base knows it won't work every time. The batter might pop up, a fielder could pull off a brilliant play, or the runner might die on second anyhow. But he knows that the law of averages, developed over similar past situations, is on his side, and he can, based on his own experience and insight, refine the odds by considering other factors, such as the bunting ability of the batter, the speed of the base runner, the skill of the next batter, and so on.

Strangely, the same fan who appreciates that the manager is playing percentage baseball is unable to translate that approach from baseball to the game he is playing—the stock market. Instead of looking back over his own record of success and failure to see which technique worked and which didn't, or what frame of mind affected each decision or failure to decide, he tends, in the market, to repeat his errors time and again. "Next time," he insists, after striking out again with the winning run on third, "it will be different."

Next time he ought to keep his eye on the ball that's being

pitched and not stand there visualizing the adulation that will come from his game-winning hit. Sheer hope that it'll be different next time, instead of learning from experience, is changing a reasoned decision into a sheer gamble. To be sure, this gamble can always be rationalized; the stock market offers infinite opportunity for making excuses. A good reason is the sugar coating that makes emotion easier to swallow; if you don't want to sell, can't bring yourself to sell, why, then, it's simple enough to find a reasonable excuse for that non-act. Here's one for you: the classic "I'm locked in" heard so often from the investor who insists he can't sell now because the stock has already fallen. Of course he could pick up the phone and sell in a second, but he's created that concept of being "locked in" as the reason behind his emotional inability to accept an already very real loss.

Not all emotions are misplaced in the market; after all, we're not entirely crazy and many times our feelings may parallel stock action; our instincts may be perceptive. But we'll bet those insights usually come when you have no personal stake in the matter. "Levitz looks like it's topping out up there," you can wisely tell your neighbor, but if you already owned LEV, could you be so blithe about it? Rather than being an evaluation of any supposed (and impossible to ascertain) value, the price of a stock at any given time is essentially a bet on what the price will be sometime in the future, so both the buyer and the seller have an emotional stake in being proven right. That's when all those reasons can be conjured up from the Wall Street culture.

If you want to make profits on balance, year in and year out, you can't afford to be taken in by such self-serving phantoms. You have to learn to recognize them for the excuses that they are. Nor can you trust that somehow you'll survive simply because you deserve to; if the market were that compassionate, would so many upstanding citizens have lost so much money to it?

Because everyone has his own style of becoming a victim, it is difficult to establish definitive guidelines which will rein in emotions. Confronting your own stock portfolio will require some hard study and, probably, some painful facing up to facts. Try withdrawing from the market for a while, and thus unburdened, sit down and analyze your decisions over a period of time. A convenient way to do this is to use your income tax Schedule D reports for the past several years, since these represent an unarguable situation. Then honestly detail all the factors you can think of which affected your selling judgment—both when you didn't sell and when you finally did—with particular attention to non-market factors (a marital spat, a job change, etc.), as well as to market influences (too quickly snatching that two-point profit). We'll bet that a pattern emerges which you'll find both startling and, we hope, edifying.

One person who did precisely this sort of self-analysis was a floor trader on the New York Stock Exchange. He was compelled to make a choice between being a trader full time or merely being a floor broker representing orders for others. In the course of reviewing his records to see which activity was the more profitable, he perceived that his trading on the long side was only mediocre but that he made a mint whenever the bear took hold. He decided to forgo working for commission dollars, and he also made it a policy to tread very carefully when the market was bubbling bullishly. But when he caught a whiff of an impending top, and could start selling short aggressively, he knew just what to do and milked declines for all he could.

With experience, and with some grasp of what has consistently affected your judgment in the past, you should be able to determine at which times and under what conditions you function best . . . and when you should be extra-careful, or even stay away entirely. One important thing every professional knows, because it is his business to know, is that he doesn't have to play the game every single minute of every day. But the public, playing a game, betting, if you will, has a predilection for continually being in the market in one way or another. "Isn't there *one* stock worth buying?" was a common question during the massive 1973–4 bear market. *There is no rule that says you always have to have action;* yet that is perhaps the most disastrous of all the common errors we've noticed. Rather than continually confronting the market on its own often inscrutable terms, stop and ask yourself what you know, whether what you know is enough to act upon and how *you* are relating to it. Maybe it is a period when the market's personality conflicts with yours, or something in your extra-market life is hampering your ability to view stock action objectively, or, simply, perhaps it's a time when the market's course isn't clear to anyone. Then it is best to step aside. You owe it to yourself to find out exactly how ready and able you are to play, because it's yourself you end up playing against.

## Mental Mistakes

What has all this to do with knowing when to sell? Well, if there is no perfect time to sell, no absolutely right end-of-the-rainbow moment, *the important task is to avoid the wrong time.* None of us can ever get rid of our extra-market dispositions entirely, but we can identify them, recognize them when they attempt to interfere, devise individual rules of play in advance to keep them at bay, use them when they can be of service (such as knowing when to become aggressive), and, if we lose our concentration and make a mistake, understand how to get back into gear with what's happening instead of perpetually berating ourselves.

The classic Wall Street fable that illustrates this is about the man who, back in the 1920's, was so invariably wrong that his friends secretly arranged with his broker to be called whenever he placed an order, so they could do the opposite. In September 1929, he sold, and they all rushed in to buy. Battered thereafter, they asked him how he had managed to come up with a sensible order. "Oh," he answered blithely, "I realized that every time I did something, I should have done the opposite, so this time, when I picked up the phone to place a buy order, I forced myself to sell."

Without attempting to be all-encompassing—the variations are infinite—here are a few examples of potentially harmful mental attitudes to keep in mind and perhaps to uncover within yourself:

One of the more significant is the tendency to view the market as if it weren't played with real money. There's no contract to sign when making a transaction, Wall Street being one of the last bastions of the belief that a man's word is his bond, so it is easy to spend tens of thousands of dollars, sometimes simply as part of what seems like a casual conversation with one's broker. Besides, you can "charge" it, inasmuch as you are not required to settle the deal for five business days. And even then no cash changes hands;

writing out a check to pay for a purchase is less wrenching than pulling dollar bills out of a wallet. If you are using margin, the paper-money effect is even more pronounced; borrowing automatically from a brokerage house doesn't seem at all like going to a bank and taking out a loan (although it *is* much like it) and so the reality of any loss becomes postponed and blurred. Wrong decisions thus become readily tolerated.

Another mental diversion is using the stock market as if it had totemic powers. The children's game of "step on a crack, break your mother's back" is not much different from selling a stock (or refusing to) to teach your wife a lesson. Then there's the "last of the ninth" fantasy, in which the game is won with a home run just when a loss seems inevitable. Men have seen a basket swish through the hoop at the buzzer enough times to project the belief that adversity in the stock market can be reversed in the same way. "Why sell when there's still a chance" is the rationalization then expressed. (Without this history of gamesmanship, women seem to come to Wall Street with a more open mind, learning to play the market by its own rules, thus often doing better than men.) Once you've become more aware of your need to use the market for your own nefarious ends, you'll be in much better mental shape to see what is actually happening.

## The Market vs. Individual Stocks

Even as you come to feel comfortable with the ebb and flow of the averages, you're bound to be frustrated that no matter how easy it is to foretell their direction, your individual stocks are still giving you headaches. The averages are merely the backdrop of the game; the real contests are waged over stocks themselves. Even in its broadest consensus, the market is never completely unanimous. Certain stocks will invariably be out of phase, either still going up (as many glamours were until late in both the 1969–70 and 1973–4 bear markets) or topping out ahead of the Dow Jones industrial average (as "hot" stocks like Levitz and Bausch & Lomb did in 1972). By the time the blue-chip average hit its bottom in late May 1970, DuPont was already starting to rise emphatically in defiance. And from May 1971 through November of that year, the market underwent a severe intermediate-term correction, although you wouldn't have known it from the action of the mobile-home stocks, which kept going up and up and up. Obviously, you cannot be alone in your opinion—not when millions of shares trade—and hope to survive for long. Nor do you have the millions of dollars needed to hold a stock up by yourself. The question always comes down to the unrepealable law of supply and demand: *Who is more prevalent, buyers or sellers?*

There are two aspects of this law: current and potential. As for the current battle, that is what you see on the ticker tape and read about in the newspaper stock tables, both the price changes and the degree of volume needed to produce those changes. You've got to learn to recognize the times when the tide of battle has shifted, with sellers first stemming a rally and then beginning to press their advantage and sending the stock tumbling back down.

Potential supply and demand is more familiarly described as support and resistance. These are price levels which were developed during the past action. If, for example, a lot of people bought Polaroid between 38 and 44 on its way down from 150, thinking it was by then a bargain, and then stuck with it miserably down to 15, you could look at that 38–44 area as a potential resistance area, a price level where many of those sufferers would be likely to sell their shares as soon as they could get even. And, of course, this potential source of sellers becomes an actual one as the current stock price closes in on the prior area of activity. Therefore, if you bought Polaroid at 15, you would be alert for problems as the stock neared 38 again.

Once we were invited to attend, as observers, a typical brokerage house Monday-morning salesmen's meeting, this one composed of a number of institutional salesmen gathered to hear what their firm's fancy research department had to say. They can have quite an effect on the market, since institutions (mutual funds, insurance companies, pension funds, bank trust departments, and the like) are the largest influence on supply and demand these days. The salesmen, on this particular morning, were anxiously hoping for a "story" they could sell, something exciting from the researchers that they could get on the phone with and use to generate a buy order from one of their institutional customers. As it happened, the analyst had only a mediocre story about a textile company to deliver, but since he'd been scrutinizing the company for months and was being paid an unusually large salary to come up with ideas, he had to deliver a report on something.

The salesmen around the table swallowed this story hard, particularly since the analyst admitted that he had recommended the same stock previously some five or six points higher. This, he rationalized, made it an even better bet at its current 27, a frequently heard line of reasoning that can cost investors fortunes. His analysis was that the stock's price drop had discounted the industry's, and the company's, hard times. (This is the kind of rationalization we spoke of previously.) Despite the cliché that "the market never discounts the same thing twice," the reality is that it often does. Tobaccos, for example, got pummeled with fresh waves of selling every time the cancer story made the headlines, discounting the same thing, by our count, seven times. But salesmen, after all, need commission income more than they need to ask questions, and so we watched this group rise from the meeting, march to their desks, and start dialing assiduously.

This illustrates one way demand can be created. For even though the textile story was, shall we say, thin, salesmanship brought in some buy orders and the stock started to go up. At first the advance was relatively uncomplicated; almost all those holders who had wanted to get out as the price dropped had done so already, and any given institutional buy order would be able to gobble up all the stock offered for sale from 27 to 28 and still be looking for more. Indeed, the salesmen managed to give this stock enough of a push to get the price up over 30 in a few days, a bullish jiggle which seemed to justify the earning of commissions. But just a glance at the past history of this particular stock, as recorded on a chart, showed that there was a large area of potential supply in the 32–36 area, where the stock had traded for many weeks before breaking down again. As a result, it was not hard to predict that by the time the stock got back up near 32 most of the salesmen-generated buying would already have taken place and a lot more sellers would show up. At that point, therefore, supply became stronger and the tide of battle shifted; indeed, as sellers spotted the weakness of the buying, they pounded into the breach in their haste to get out, driving the price down sharply the next day.

Typically, the way institutions buy their stock is to try to accumulate it bit by bit. Unless they happen to run smack into a large block for sale in a stock they've decided to acquire, the order on the Exchange floor is usually filled over a period of time, as they gather in the desired number of shares while trying to keep the price from leaping until they're done. But when they do their selling, they are not so patient; having accumulated those thousands of shares, institutions usually want out promptly, as soon as the decision to sell is made. This desire to flee involves a rapid search, via telephone and/or a computerized system into which big block requests are fed, for someone on the buy side who'll be interested in their shares. Lacking that easy out, the block to be sold will be sent to the Exchange floor, where the floor broker handling the order will take the specialist aside and see if anything can be quickly worked out to get such a big block sold near the current price.

Let's suppose that there's no handy alternative but to rely on the marketplace itself. The floor broker stands at the trading post with his 100,000-share order to sell written on a deceptively tiny scrap of paper. He may not want to overly influence what is happening, so if another broker were to come along with a mere 100 shares to buy, he'd let the order go right past him for someone else to sell to. But an order for 500 or 1,000 shares to buy would be a different story; he'd step forward, sell, scratch out his running total on the scrap of paper, and scribble in the new number of shares he has left to sell. Thus, even though the price of the stock might be staying up there unchanged, or even advancing slightly, a close observer could note that there was a lot of selling volume in the stock. Indeed, the balance between buyer-initiated trades and seller-initiated trades could be calculated by adding up the number of shares traded at an "up" tick (a price higher than the last sale price) or a "zero plus" tick (a price higher than the last different sale price), which would be trades initiated by buyers, and compare the total to the number of shares sold (those which traded on "down" ticks or "zero minus" ticks). A sequence of 100 shares at 52 . . . 100 shares at 52 1/8 . . . another 300 shares at 52 1/8 . . . 200 shares at 52 1/4 . . . followed by three lots of 100 shares each, also at 52 1/4, would take the stock up one quarter of a point on 1,000 shares. If the next tick on the tape were 1,000 shares at 52 1/8, the broker would have done his job well, selling 1,000 shares without disturbing the price of the stock for future sales. This action on the ticker tape then gets summarized in the newspaper, and finally is translated graphically (for use by the technically minded) to a chart of the price fluctuation.

## The Law of Supply and Demand

Take a look at the Eastman Kodak charts for mid-1972 here and on the following page.

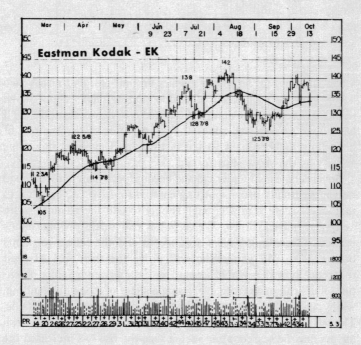

Suppose our broker is trying to unload 100,000 shares of EK but, with the market rising and Kodak having just made a new all-time high, he doesn't feel the need to hurry. Initially, near the end of July (on the daily chart), he sells 5,000 shares just to get his feet wet, and then steps aside to let the stock drift up to the 140 level, where he is a more active seller of bigger pieces while letting small orders keep EK up. Indeed, it even straggles up to

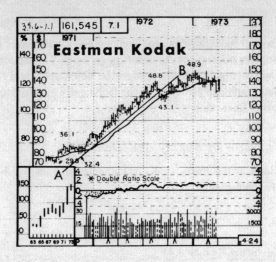

a new high at 142; he's been a seller around 140, and nearly two weeks later, he's disposed of 90,000 shares. That's about it, he thinks. Even if he just dumps the last 10,000 shares abruptly, he'll have done his job well, since the falling price makes the rest of his selling look brilliant to the institution. The chart shows his activity as the stock slips to 135.

Buyers come in at under 130 and become persistent in the 126–130 range, eventually proving strong enough to drive EK back up to 140, where there is now enough supply to halt the advance again and turn it back down. We've got a real tussle on our hands between the willing buyers around 130 and the sellers 10 points higher. Who will win? Who will prove the stronger? At least theoretically, sellers would seem to have the advantage since potential sellers can arise from every single share of stock outstanding, while potential buyers must come with money from the outside. The sell side has yet another advantage: motivation, for while fresh buyers may be scarcer after such a rise, the rise has increased the number of potential profit takers (both long-term and those who bought a few days earlier near 130).

The truth is, however, you don't really know who will win at this point. But you *do* know certain details: (1) that for the first time in nearly a year, EK has failed to go on to a new high after a normal correction; (2) that the stock is moving sideways for the first time in that entire span; (3) that any uptrend line drawn (for example, A–B on the weekly chart) has now been broken by this action; (4) that the same is true for the long-term Moving Average line, identified on the weekly chart as the heavy black line (Moving Averages will be discussed in detail in a later chapter); (5) that even if buyers were to emerge triumphant from this tug-of-war (by taking EK up to another new high), it wouldn't alter the evidence of a loss of momentum taking place; and (6) that you can recognize that sellers will have won if the 126–130 support area, where buyers had been strong enough before, gives way.

Thus although you don't know "right" or "wrong," you can see that there is certain objective evidence in the market. The basic law of supply and demand is the best objective counterweight to all those emotional reasons that otherwise create losses. No rule said Eastman Kodak at this time was worth 140, no more, no less, that it became a bargain at 130 or deserved to sell at 160 eventually. But there are certain details that can be ascertained.

Even so, the market doesn't make it easy. A new high, for example, may be a sign of renewed strength, or it may, with hindsight, turn out to be the top. A judgment has to be made somewhere along the line. You may want to ask, at this point, if you should be looking for all those chart patterns you've heard about —head-and-shoulders, diamonds, triangles, rising wedges, *et al.* Because the mannerisms of buyers vs. sellers often repeat themselves, certain chart patterns also reappear consistently. If you want to get into this aspect of the market, we strongly recommend *Technical Analysis of Stock Trends* by Robert D. Edwards and John Magee. But remember: all chart patterns are no more than individual peculiarities in the way a stock signals the underlying changes in supply and demand. You could keep it all in your head, as many professional traders do. A chart is history, helpful as a reference to where potential support and resistance can be expected, and even more so in portraying the action objectively so you can resist taking the bait which might look tasty to your emotions. "Look! the stock is going up again," you may cry, and buy at 131. Think of how comfortable it would have been to stay with Eastman Kodak when the company reported a 21 percent jump in earnings, surely a good reason to continue to be bullish. But it just so happened that *that* report came the week the stock failed to make a new high, and instead sold off 5 percent.

Many investors become confused because they try to link corporate developments with market action. (And it isn't just the public; all those analysts singling out so-called growth companies wind up with losses the same way.) One says: "Eastman Kodak has been a great stock to own during the bull market because the company is doing so well." But the stock's performance has nothing to do with that reason, except insofar as the strength of the company's balance sheet creates a group of people willing and anxious to buy stock. A stock goes up in price because of the *buyers,* not because of the balance sheet; if we see their buying on the tape we don't need to know their motivation, just their numbers. Furthermore, the willingness to act upon whatever reason the buyers may have is boosted because, if you will, there *is* a bull market in progress. When the bull starts to fade and is toppled, so too does Kodak join the decline; then, even though earnings may continue to grow, even though the balance sheet may be just as robust, that reason is no longer valid. The law of supply and demand has asserted itself. The question "Why does a chicken cross the road?" is no joke on the Street; when someone says, "Why is that stock going down?" the *objective* answer is, "More sellers than buyers."

Therefore, if the law of supply and demand—the one thing you can keep track of objectively, the one tool that is devoid of emotion —tells you you're wrong, it's wise to accept it. You may think Kodak is going still higher for all those "becauses," but if that support level gives way in the marketplace and the price falls to 125, don't fight it. "Can I bear to take yet another loss?" "Suppose I sell and the stock goes back up?" "How can I sell such a nice company?" Can't you just hear those echoes? But the rule is as applicable to the stock market as it is to real life: *Do not rationalize failure.*

If you root for stocks in the market game, there is nothing wrong with being a fair-weather fan. The decisive act of selling may turn out, with hindsight, to be a mistake, but the indecisive act of *not* selling can turn out to be a disaster.

# 3

## Market Cycles and Selling

Ever since the first corporate share was purchased, it has been a credo of American culture that the road to wealth is the patient accumulation of stocks in growing corporations. As the country expanded, steel, oil, mining, and railroad ventures paid off handsomely. For years, railroad shares were considered the premier investment for those who'd made their pile and wanted to keep it safe and sound. More than one will of the pre-Depression era specified in unbreakable terms that the heirs were to entrust the family fortune only to railroad shares. As it turned out, railroads were safer than buggy-whip or streetcar companies, but by the time the country's massive industrial growth began to produce a comparable boom in the stock market, railroads weren't the thing to be in. Industry—products—became the fashionable investment; railroads, especially as disaster struck in the thirties, lost their respectability and became speculative. One generation's gilt became the dross of the next.

Despite such shifts in fashion, it may seem, in that era of extraordinary growth, that *any* investor who bought into the market was bound to have profited on the trip upward. Not so; someone who bought the Dow Jones industrial average (of the thirty leading industrial giants) prior to the 1929 crash and held on to them through thick, thin, and thunder would have had a net loss twenty years later of over 52 percent and would not have gotten even until 1954, a quarter of a century later. Going from 161.60 in 1949, when rising prices began to bail out the pre-Crash investor, the Dow moved to 679.36 in 1959, for a decade's gain of 320 percent. That was a great decade, but it was *not,* as so many took it to be, testament to the ultimate virtue of squirreling stocks away. The next ten years (1959 to 1969) also contained a prolonged and benign bull market, yet when it was over the DJI had advanced a grand total of 120 points, an average of only 12 points per year! And 12 points is a move the DJI often makes in a single day.

If, bewitched by how marvelous everything seemed to be in the early sixties, an investor bought the Dow industrial average at the outset of 1966 (at 995), he would have taken an immediate loss, but would have gotten almost even by the end of 1968. Then a third of his capital would have been rapidly snatched away. By the end of 1972, he'd have struggled back to being even, and after actually getting ahead for a couple of weeks in January 1973, he'd have been taken on a roller-coaster ride scarier than any at Coney Island, ending that October back at the original level. (Of course, none of these ups and downs takes inflation into account; were the paper holdings converted back into real dollars, far fewer goods would have been purchasable.) But the worst was yet to come for those who assumed they had bought good stocks and who confidently put them away. Less than a year later, by the fall of 1974, the Dow toppled back down below all its achievements of the entire decade of the sixties and was even impinging on 1958 levels! To complete the examination of this decade: by January 1976 the Dow managed to return to the level of January 1966, but during that ten-year span inflation had stripped away about one third of the real value of the investments, for an actual loss of 33 percent in buying power.

The same sad story is true of individual stocks, even the bluest of blue chips. Consider having locked 100 shares of U.S. Steel in a safe-deposit box in the early forties (original cost about $1,000). By 1959 the virtue of believing in this country's economic growth would seem to be confirmed, with those shares being valued at $10,900. Little more than ten years later, though, locking those shares up wouldn't have seemed so wise, for they'd fallen back to a value of $2,500—still a gain, but a far cry from the peak value.

Even though the strongbox approach may in the end yield gains, especially on paper, *maximum* profits are seldom taken. Certainly U.S. Steel is a quality company, not likely to go bankrupt and decimate one's entire investment, but its stock has ups and downs like every other. And for every "buy it and put it away" investment in a company like U.S. Steel, there are a hundred others bought because they seem to have had vast potential at the time of purchase—perhaps as the current favorite blue chip or the exciting name that is being touted as a blue chip of the future. Remember that old favorite Cinerama, the concern reputedly destined, in 1961, to revolutionize the motion-picture industry? Up the stock shot to 22 1/2; down it went to 2. Another widely ballyhooed stock of its time was Kalvar, the photocopier fledgling which was to outstrip Xerox. It went to over 300 on that promise, and down to under 3 on the reality. Then there was National Video, bought on the thesis that it would carry color television to new heights; its own height was near 125, but those shares are now just so much fancy wallpaper. Nor should we omit such a solid citizen as Penn Central, surely locked up in many strongboxes when up near 70; how sad those certificates must look in the same boxes nowadays.

To be sure, over the years the market has gone up, and just as surely there have been profits to be made and kept. In earlier times, stock-market wealth typically came from being on the inside of shenanigans. It was not nearly as important to ride the cycles as to ride the coattails of the great manipulators of the nineteenth century. This was true even through the Roaring Twenties, when pool operators and their buddies were the adventurers to follow. The SEC has since put a damper on such conduct, and the theory of investing is a nobler activity. Without such intrigue, it has become essential to pay attention to the cyclical nature of the market.

Whereas the 1929–49 period would have resulted in an overall loss of 58 percent to those who believed in the "lock 'em up and leave 'em alone" approach to investing, had you bought at the bottom and sold at the top of each of the three major bull markets that occurred within that twenty-year span and stayed out of the market completely the rest of the time, your *gain,* not including dividends, would have been 1,700 percent! (And, having sold, you should really include some mental profit for not having to suffer during the down periods, plus some added true profit of interest earned with your capital while out of the stock market.) Similarly, though buying in 1949 at a supercyclical trough and holding until that cycle peaked in 1966 would have produced a quintupling of funds, the investor who swung with the shorter but still major tides, selling out in 1956, 1962, and 1966, when the market reached important tops, and buying back at subsequent bottoms, would have done nearly *four times* as well! Nor does any of this include taking advantage of the bear via short selling for further capital protection and enhancement (to be discussed in a subsequent chapter).

Similar comparisons can be applied to individual stocks, though with far more varied results. Each bull market has had its own hot stock; clearly, anyone who bought this winner in its time and sold it at the top would have been best off. But that's perfection; let's study one example of a strongbox stock—International Business Machines—to see what would have happened had it been traded in and out at major tops and bottoms, rather than tucked away throughout the cycles.

We're not talking about the kind of in-and-out trading a member on the Exchange floor does, but something more long-term. In 1949, brokers were aggressively recommending Alcoa and Du Pont, rather than IBM, as the growth blue chips. By 1959 IBM was much more the leading light, and you could have bought in at around 80 (adjusted for subsequent splits). If you sold ten years later, at its top of 370 in 1968, that would have been a profit of over 360 percent. But if you'd traded in and out a mere three times during this period, here's what would have happened: bought around 80 in 1959 and sold at the 1961 top around 160; back in at the 1962 bottom around 90 and out again at the 1966 top near 180; in again at the 1966 low at 150 and out again at the 1968 top close to 370. Adding it up, that's 100 extra points—125 percent more on the original investment—and a hefty reward merely for paying attention.

Moreover, in this context you must also consider that the country's economic fertility is rapidly becoming exhausted after two hundred years of growth. No longer do acorns drop from the tree of free enterprise and immediately sprout in rich native soil. The sudden surge in conglomeration in the late sixties, by which additional paper money was created out of existing corporations that were already fully capitalized, showed as much as anything else how little prospect is left for fresh growth. It can be done, of course. Clever financiers and novel ideas can still pull millions out of a hat. Recent examples, such as Diners Club, McDonald's, and Electronic Data Systems, which all sell convenience, exploit the periphery of an economy of plenty. As long as the country will pay for it, ingenious entrepreneurs can be expected to keep inventing some such industry along the way. But there's a big difference between a hunch that some new concept will catch on and endure and investing your money in continued, vital, and basic growth, such as steel, mining, oil, or railroads.

The investor who squirrels away his stock certificates because it worked in the past is betting on the future in a highly dangerous way. He must believe that each company he selects is going to participate fully in whatever growth lies ahead, and that such future growth is inevitable and will continue unchecked and undepressed. Yet the United States itself has already become, in a manner of speaking, a mature company; what used to be growth pains are now middle-aged aches and bureaucratic signs of arthritis. Were it a common stock, one wonders who would buy "America" (ticker symbol: USA; earnings: negative; management: questionable; long-term debt: enormous; potential for bankruptcy: likely) on the grounds that it still merited a growth stock's price/earnings ratio.

*Not to sell, therefore, is perhaps the riskiest investment approach of all.* Nevertheless, it is surprising how many naïve investors still venture their capital on the assumption that there's indiscriminate growth ahead. As growth itself becomes a struggle—and for every company that flourishes, scores of others have only one season in the sun—it will be all the more difficult to pick the few companies that will survive with their earlier promise intact. It is far better and easier to learn to sell at the sensible time, a time predicated not so much on earnings growth as on the market's and the stock's "natural" fluctuations.

## The Theory of Market Cycles

That word "natural" is placed in quotation marks because the ebb and flow of securities prices is obviously a man-made phenomenon, even though it gives the impression of responding to a higher order. So prevalent is this impression, in fact, that a number of observers have spent years earnestly trying to calculate the periodicity of market fluctuations, like so many astronomers puzzling over the universe. One vast cyclical concept was developed by a Russian economist named Nikolai Kondratev, who, early in this century, isolated a sequence of wars, types of governments, and economic activity that, as it turned out, had demonstrable pertinence to the stock market. If the United States slides into another deep depression somewhere around 1980–1, you'll know that Kondratev's approximate fifty-year cycle was in force again.

Another cycle student, R. N. Elliott, applied his studies solely to the stock market and came up with something known as the Elliott wave-cycle theory. The theory is like something out of *Alice in Wonderland*: at any given time it is of little direct use; only *afterward* can it be applied with any degree of certainty. But a relatively clear notion of where the market has been is rare enough information in itself. The basis of the theory can be traced back to the thirteenth-century mathematician Leonardo Fibonacci, who determined that the ancient Egyptian architects of the Great Pyramid at Giza had followed a specific arithmetic progression in the pyramid's design. The series starts with the numbers 1 and 2 and continues with the sum of the previous two numbers: 1, 2, 3, 5, 8, 13, 21, 34, 55, etc. One characteristic of this series is that the numbers bear an approximate ratio, one to the next, of 1.62 and, reciprocally, of .62. These are, as it happens, relationships also found in nature. Limbs branching out from a tree are said to increase by Fibonacci numbers, as do the diameters of the spirals in sea shells, the number of rings on an elephant's tusk, etc. The Western musical octave also is comprised of Fibonacci numbers: 13 keys on a piano, with five black and eight white.

In 1939 Mr. Elliott published articles in which he applied the Fibonacci series to stock-market movements, showing that what appeared in nature and at Giza could also be found in the market, although sometimes a bit of shoving and squeezing was needed to make the cyclical terms fit. Elliott defined market movements by stating that there is always one large overall cycle in effect, consisting of a bull and bear market within that cycle, and, further, that the bear market will have two downswings and one upswing, while the bull market will have three upswings and two intervening downswings. In turn, those waves would, if examined closely, be found to break down into lesser waves of Fibonacci numbers: 3, 5, 8, as they got progressively smaller, 13 yet smaller, etc. Elliott and his followers came up with extraordinarily arcane variations on this theme, market phenomena they called "flats," "inverted flats," and "reverse inverted flats," to name a few of the esoterica. Often these terms are applied to the sheer confusion of the applier. For our purposes, however, the fundamental theory of three or five waves comprising important cyclical swings is empirically consistent and hence worth paying attention to.

This is especially so since some remarkable forecasts have been made by Elliott disciples. In 1961, Hamilton Bolton, publisher of *The Bank Credit Analyst,* analyzed the then-prevailing market as follows: "The advance from 1949 should be complete when 583 points (161.8 percent of the 361 points of the 1949–1956 rise) have been added to the 1957 low of 416, or a total of 999 DJIA." This target, of course, was hit squarely on the nose five years later in 1966, coincident with what appeared to be the required number of waves for the entire upcycle, which began in 1949! (We say "appeared" because there was, in late 1968, a return to that approximate level in the Dow, while at the same time the unweighted averages registered a much higher peak; you'll see how this minor disparity affects the count later on.)

Considering that the end of the fifth wave (third upwave) of a bull market within a larger five-wave bull cycle marks the end of that entire cycle, it was time, according to the theory, for a new super-bear cycle. Sure enough, along came the 1966 smash (the first bear market), followed by a bull market of speculative dimensions (wave two, up), and then a second and much more severe bear market (wave three, down). Elliott's theory provided the needed perspective to warn many investors that the worst wasn't over simply because there had been a bear market in 1966; it wasn't going to be just another interruption in a constantly rising market, as so many thought and later regretted. What's more, the theory indicated that the 1969–70 bear market was sure to go lower than the 1966 bottom, as indeed it did. And along the way, if you were to scrutinize each of these swings, you'd find that Elliott's requirements had been met in simple fashion. During the 1969–70 slide, for example, there were the requisite three waves down and two intervening waves up, with each, in turn, displaying the lesser waves in approximate Fibonacci harmony.

The problem is that *at the time* it wasn't absolutely clear whether to measure by the 1966 or the 1968 top. The former seemed slightly more valid, and, if so, an orthodox conclusion would have been that the low in 1970 completed that super-bear cycle. But it didn't look very complete by other measurements, so an Elliott devotee would then have been faced with (1) deciding the top was really 1968 for the prior super-bull cycle, or (2) insisting that the super-bear then in power would be yet another five-wave sequence. The answer, unfortunately, didn't become known until later. In this case, when the bear market of 1973–4 crashed below the prior 1970 low, it was evident that this was but a continuation, at its virulent worst, of the entire super-bear structure. In hindsight, then, it didn't matter, except to theoreticians, which of the options was deemed correct; in practical terms it was enough to know that the big bear still lived on to the bottom in late 1974. In turn, this suggests that, if an entire super-bear cycle died at that point, *three* bull markets should follow over the rest of the decade. A similar problem in counting the requisite number of waves occurred when one school of Elliott's theory called the top in December 1968 and another insisted on using May 1969. While those in the latter camp got the number of waves they wanted for the top, they didn't have enough to call for an end to that particular bear market in May 1970 and were waiting for yet another wave down. It never came, and they were caught short, literally.

On the evidence, it is good to know just about where Elliott's wave theory says the market is within a super-cycle and even within a major wave, but clearly it is not a system to bet the rent money on. What it does prove emphatically is that the stock market does not go straight up or straight down. One wave is never enough; stocks move in a *pattern* of waves, and these flows eventually and inevitably reverse in like degree. That is a vital perspective to maintain.

## Long-Term Waves

Just as a surfer picks certain waves to ride in preference to others, an investor, knowing that stock-market waves come in all shapes and sizes, should analyze which ones are likely to give him the best ride for his money. There are four basic types, each with its own advantages and disadvantages. *Super-waves* last for many years (e.g., the super-bull cycle of 1949 to 1966/68), encompassing lesser, though major to us, bull and bear waves. Next are *long-term waves,* what we'd call a *primary trend* or a *major bull or major bear market* (e.g., the bull market that ran from 1962 to its top at the outset of 1966, or, in turn, the bear market of 1966). *Intermediate-term waves* usually last several months, like the intermediate-term uptrend within the major bull market which lasted from December 1970 until the end of April 1971, followed by an intermediate-term correction, or downtrend, from that point until Thanksgiving 1971. Finally, there are *short-term* swings within intermediate-term waves; for example, that 1971 correction consisted of a drop of over 100 Dow points from May to early August, when an interruption, fed by Nixon's game plan, caused a short-term swing upward for several weeks, followed by a decline of 130 points from that intervening rally—all, we remind you, as part of an intermediate-term downtrend within a major bull market, which hindsight tells us, existed within a super-bear cycle.

Each such wave, big or little, offers its own buying and selling opportunities. Our task is to determine which, according to its own characteristics, is most productive to follow. First, however, we must dismiss the strongbox approach, for that hides even from super-cycles, and anyone who doesn't want to sell his stocks before a super-bear cycle is launched is too self-destructive to save.

Riding super-waves is, as we briefly demonstrated in discussing Elliott's theory, an enormously difficult predictive task. Such an investor, thinking the worst had passed in the summer of 1970, would have been clobbered in 1973–4 (as, indeed, many of the bank trust departments and huge university endowment funds were, having created a theory that they would own only "one-decision" stocks, stocks so good that they could be bought and held through anything). Super-cycles cannot be accurately defined, and so are useless as timing tools; there are much more useful waves.

The primary trend, at least, is discernible to a considerable degree; certain indicators, which we'll discuss in later chapters, speak at the tops and bottoms of such waves, and the length of time involved in a primary trend—a couple of years or so: 1962–6, 1967–8, 1970–2—is not so long that you are likely to lose track of the overall context (bullish or bearish) in which you are dealing. Certainly it is sensible to try to buy near the bottom of a major bear market and to sell near the top of the ensuing bull market.

But it is hard to stay sensible when watching primary trends. It's been a long, profitable ride upward, and toward the end comes the most excitement. Speculative stocks start zooming, new issues crackle, good economic news abounds, and optimism becomes pervasive in the media and on the Street. It's tough not to be swept up in that sort of climate, particularly when, as in 1972, the speculative fever is in blue-chip stocks. Even if one is sophisticated enough to realize there'll be a piper to pay sooner or later, the strong temptation is to keep a finger in the pie while hot tips, booming prices, and tales of quick fortunes pour in. In such an atmosphere, it takes the slide itself to provide evidence that the end has arrived. By then a lot of losses have piled up and a lot of those easy bull-market profits have gone down the drain.

Not only is an ebullient state of mind hard to deal with at such tops, but the technical evidence of the demise of a primary trend is, by its nature, often late, coming after the top has been completed and the decline has started. After all, the first downward whack looks like just another temporary correction, no different from the one that had previously interrupted the bull market. Not until the next rally also fails, is it clear that the primary trend is over. One example of how this delay affects long-term technical analysis can be seen in the fact that the venerable Dow theory requires two signals to show that a primary uptrend has ended: not only that the Dow industrial average fails to make a new high and then breaches a prior support level (obviously, therefore, *after* the peak has been seen), but the Dow theory also requires confirmation from the Dow transportation average, thus further delaying the signal. The investor who prefers to ride out intermediate corrections and hopes to swing only with the primary trend must wait for such signals to appear, and then, because he's caught in the midst of a sharp decline, feels he needs to wait for the next rally before selling. Many such investors become trapped in a destructive bear market.

Trying to identify the top of a bull market in the averages, such as the Dow industrials, is hard enough, but many times the averages will not be consistent with what your own individual holdings are doing. For instance, Bausch & Lomb, a huge winner in the early seventies, started falling apart many weeks before the Dow hit its own top in January 1973. With the averages still advancing, it would have been tempting for a holder of BOL to persuade himself to stay with it as it tumbled, arguing that the continuing bull market would bring it back up to the high he'd missed. Perhaps such a holder would have recalled how the beginnings of the 1969–70 bear market were totally ignored by a dozen or so of the Street's flossiest glamours, which waltzed upward virtually by themselves throughout 1969, oblivious that the music had long since stopped and, in fact, that the ballroom was on fire. If you'd held on to Bausch & Lomb through 1972 because you were watching the behavior of the Dow for the sign to start selling, and because similar high-fliers had kept going well past the Dow's peak on the previous bull-market top, you'd have tossed an awful lot of your own money back into the pot.

Thus, another impediment to tracking the primary trend is that *no general market move encompasses every stock simultaneously.* The discrepancy between your stock and the average (and the need to make a decision about yours while eyeing the average) is one of the most constantly frustrating elements of the market, particularly as you probably will be holding a portfolio of several different issues, each one out of phase with the others *and* the averages. Adding to the confusion is that it isn't this way at bottoms, where stocks tend to start going up as one big happy family; at tops they expire one by one. Most bottoms are made when the market tumbles as a whole, as it did in the avalanche that ended in December

1974. During such phases, signs of a bottom tell you to start buying just about anything from Abbott Labs to Zurn. That's why the dart-throwing system actually seems to work: at major bottoms it's hard to miss a big winner unless you miss the page entirely.

What goes on at bottoms is not even remotely applicable to having to judge individual stocks as each in turn forms a major top and then starts down. Over the years we've observed that about one third of all stocks register their bull-market tops ahead of the averages, another third at approximately the same time, and the remaining third after (sometimes long after) the averages have already turned down. So your chances of being right in regard to your own portfolio, even if you correctly identify a major top in the Dow to the exact day, are apt to be no better than one in three.

*It is vital to be able to convince yourself to sell a stock regardless of how the averages look.* Continuing to hold while it is already on its way down could cancel out any advantage gained by correctly holding other stocks that are still in gear with the averages, especially since stocks have a way of going down much faster than they go up. By the same token, you don't want to liquidate so completely that you dump the very stock that moves ahead in defiance of the overall market. A classic example of such action was American Research and Development (since merged into Textron), which was actually a tremendously profitable *buy* when the extensive 1969–70 bear market got underway. The DJI started rolling over and going down, while ARD was breaking out on the upside for a rapid doubling in price! A lot of people who sold that stock in late 1968 and early 1969 were dead right about the market and dead wrong about the stock.

The opposite situation is illustrated by another popular issue of the late sixties, University Computing, which hit its all-time high in 1967 well before an overall bull market had completed its cycle; as the bull went roaring ahead, UCX went the other way in its own private, long-term, bearish cycle. There were, however, swings of *intermediate-term* duration in which UCX actually doubled (and more) on the upside; while it worked its way inexorably down from a peak 185 to under 5, it experienced rallies from 55 to 110 and again from 14 to 38. While others hope and pray that such rallies will keep going up until they get even, the reality is that these rebounds must be recognized as selling opportunities for anyone holding such a weak stock, regardless of the action of the averages at those times.

Obviously, the anomalies of the marketplace are enough to drive anyone to an early grave in potter's field. One views the long-term action of the averages and of individual stocks, but there's no apparent way to link the two consistently. Besides, the emotional pressures created along the way by intermediate-term waves sorely disrupt the equanimity of the investor who is trying to follow the major trend.

To illustrate the bewilderment that can arise when you deal strictly in primary trends, let's go back to the turbulent spring of 1971. You've just had a rousing rally that has emphatically confirmed a new bull market so, in accord with the market's primary trend, you elect to hold on to your stocks that spring. You reason that, while a correction is due, that's about all it should be. Why get involved with taxes and steep commission costs by going in and out? And then there is the very real difficulty of trying to catch the next bottom. Indeed, your judgment seems to be right when the market slides from the Dow 950 level to nearly 840; that, you think, is enough. Then along comes Nixon with the first of his economic game plans, which gives the market quite a boost. But another downleg soon sets in. At first, you can accept this as evidence of a more severe correction than you expected—one in keeping with an Elliott pattern of two downwaves and one intervening upwave—but suddenly, with prices tumbling, a reason for the decline becomes apparent: by November there is a severe international monetary crisis, generating headlines and driving stocks even lower. The 840 level has cracked as if it were no support at all; there is talk of worldwide disaster. Would you retain last April's confidence, holding on to your stocks in the belief that "it's just an intermediate-term correction; the primary trend will reassert itself soon"? Actually, that's all it turned out to be, but our point is that it is extremely difficult to maintain perspective in the midst of collapsing prices and a churning stomach. Too many investors lose track of their original decision and panic in exactly such situations. *The risk of an emotional defeat after an objective decision is a serious problem for those who follow primary-trend moves.*

The goal, clearly, is to place oneself in a market position in which the least risk is assumed for the most potential reward. But this is a delicate balance at best. Trying to catch tops at their very peak might yield maximum reward, but the risk is increased considerably. On the other hand, surrendering the possibility of a large reward for the calm of risklessness is better accomplished in a savings bank. To make good money in equities, one is obliged to take risks, but these risks should be based on as much information as possible. When the situation becomes diffuse, as it does when you are trying to devote yourself to a trend that might well last a couple of years or more, it becomes more difficult to be decisive and more likely that emotional squalls will batter your judgment. Sometimes you'll jump and dump; at others you'll procrastinate. Waiting one day, and then another, for enough evidence is like continually swearing that your next cigarette will be your last. Indecision is habit-forming, and can be injurious to your wealth.

In sum, there are a number of complications when you invest in primary uptrends. First, a substantial portion of profits probably will have to be given up before it's proved that the uptrend is over and that many stocks should long since have been sold. Second, once the decline has set in, the belated arrival of long-term reversal signals generates a desire to put off getting out until the next rally, and a feeling of being locked into the very stocks you wanted to profit from near the end of the primary uptrend. In turn, this increases the chance that when the rally does come you'll be convinced that the uptrend has been renewed and thus will compound the mistake by doing nothing. Third, there's the perplexing problem of trying to time your particular holdings to the action of the overall market, because there is no such animal as the average stock. Fourth, you waive the opportunity to greatly enhance total profits by selling before intermediate-term corrections set in and buying back later at lower prices. Finally, trying to peg decision-making to a judgment of primary trends can leave you exceptionally vulnerable to having the wrong emotions at the wrong times: gloom, despair, and hopelessness traditionally mark the time when bottoms are formed; blinding optimism and Lourdes-like faith in the future, at tops. Since *no* stock goes from A to Z without first stopping at H, retracing to D, bouncing on to N, coming back to

F, or even A, the simple appeal of the primary trend is, in fact, highly problematic. Indeed, it is almost as risky—speculative, if you will—as betting that you never have to sell at all.

## Short-Term Swings

Given the problems of following primary trends, it might seem feasible to take the opposite tack and to get out at the first hint of weakness and back in as soon as strength returns. In this short-term way, the future can be shrunk to a few days, or, at most, a couple of weeks, so even if you're wrong, you're never *that* wrong. Many amateur players believe they're protecting themselves against big problems by dealing strictly in short-term swings. Indeed, they may have taken a bath in a Levitz or University Computing before, so they swear it'll never happen to them again, because they're going to take those profits as soon as they're made and then get out. But once you buy a stock in the afternoon at 20 and sell it the next morning at 23, you're apt to get hooked on a very dangerous game, best left to professionals . . . and best suited for lining your broker's pockets with a steady stream of commissions.

Just as long-term investors pooh-pooh market swings as not affecting *them,* short-term traders exaggerate the significance of every little twitch, convinced that looking at the market through a microscope will disclose its secrets. Each downtick triggers apprehension; each uptick may be the last chance to sell out; every minute the stock is not on view on the tape heightens anxiety. What will happen next? And next? "Better grab that profit while I can," the novice mutters, unable to let a potentially big winner develop comfortably. In this Lilliputian world, every eighth of a point is a milestone. The uneasiness is incessant and may even be exactly what such a speculator subconsciously desires. The short-term trader is obliged to keep close and constant watch—during his lunch hour, at business meetings, even while he's incommunicado in the dentist's chair. Stock-market injury seems to take place repeatedly at just those moments when he has his back turned. (This paranoia is not totally without foundation. Spurred by professionals, the market often moves decisively on partial holidays when bank trust departments and insurance companies are closed, and on those odd days, such as the Friday after Thanksgiving, when few people are paying attention.)

His anxiety is compounded by compulsiveness, for an amateur short-term trader is driven to have a bet down even when the market is dull or perilous. Most professional traders, however, like most professional gamblers, recognize that there are stretches when the game isn't worth the risk. They may not know what the market is going to do next—and they'll admit it! They are quite willing to step aside to wait for better odds. Many times a professional trader will leave the Exchange floor early, just to keep away from temptation after he has decided he doesn't want to do anything more that day, preferring to wait for more substantial clues before choosing the next direction and/or a lower-risk time to play.

A revealing parallel comes from a professional gambler, whose work consists of studying the entries each day at race tracks around the country. He is employed by a number of big bookies as a handicapper (an "investment" analyst) and supplements this income with his own astuteness in betting. There are days when he personally doesn't make a single wager, even though he keeps feeding advice to his clients. In the vast majority of races, he explains, there simply is no clear-cut choice. Although one horse might handicap out as a shade more promising than the rest, that isn't good enough for him. Nor does he bet if two horses look much better than the rest of the field, or when the odds on a horse he favors aren't high enough. He bets *only* when all the aspects come together favorably; as a professional, he tries to reduce chance as much as possible and realizes that there will always be another race. Yet the public throngs to the track and feels compelled to bet on every race, with the daily double, exacta, trifecta, and all else thrown in for good measure.

So, too, in the stock market, where the gamble is the same, although the atmosphere is more polite. Short-term traders think they should always have a bet going on some ticker symbol or other, a need that is encouraged by customer's men who stand to capitalize on the easy commissions generated by such gamblers. Even in a bear market, short-term traders will hope they've found the one stock that will beat the odds. For the public trader, the hope is too often just that.

A professional trader on the Exchange can take short-term losses with equanimity because, as a member, he pays no commissions. (Taking into account transfer taxes, clearance costs, and other small items, the cost usually comes to about an eighth of a point, meaning that if he buys 100 shares at 20 and sells at 19 7/8, his loss is approximately $25.) But to amateurs, a small loss is compounded by the additional cost of the round-trip commission —perhaps $100 to $200. So the person with a slight loss tends to hold until he's offered stronger proof that the situation is bad, which leads him to lose two or three more points while waiting for that proof. Thus, even when played close to the vest, the typical short-term loss can easily turn out to be a hefty $500 or $600, about four points down plus commission costs. But that's only half the bad news. To recover that four-point loss, the trader has to chalk up an eight-point gain, because profitable transactions, too, get clipped for two-way commissions. He has to hit two winners as big as his small loss *just to stay even.*

The hard truth is that a short-term trader cannot do what an Exchange member can do. Not only are a member's transactions commission-free, but he has the added advantage of being in direct touch with the floor, either in person or on the phone to a friendly broker who is handling his orders and is familiar with his style. It is not that he gains any time advantage (your orders can get executed just about as promptly), but his questions get answered, and salient bits of trading information flow back to him. He is geared, and poised to act decisively, which is less taxing when there is little extra penalty for being wrong. And, of course, it's his job, and that gives him the psychological advantage.

Because the professional appears to fare better, some public traders who have the instinct, need, and greed, but not the time, turn their accounts over to registered representatives who have built up a reputation for such trading. In that way, they get the thrills and emotional involvement without the burden of personal decision-making. Sooner or later, though, even the most red-hot broker handling such an account is bound to find himself in a jam. He'll buy a stock for his customer's account that looks ready to make a quick move, but the stock doesn't produce immediately. There's nothing wrong yet and it still appears ready, so he decides to give it a further chance. To pay for it, though, he has to sell something else from his client's fully invested portfolio. Not wanting to show losses in the account if he can help it (*his* vanity and *his* guilt feelings are also at stake), he opts to sell a stock which shows a profit, regardless of whether that position is ripe to be sold or not. It takes only a few such switches before the customer finds himself no longer a free-swinging trader but an involuntary holder of weak positions, bereft of those stronger stocks which had been (and probably still are) going up. Often, a surrogate's emotional involvement in buying ("Got to make that loss back before the account gets taken away") and in selling ("Can't take another loss or he'll murder me") is as destructive as your own. Instead of the inner anguish of being able to blame yourself, you now have a handy scapegoat: *he* did it to me. But the losses are the same!

We might add that there are some people who are only part-time gamblers, akin to those who blow their bankroll only when they visit Las Vegas but are otherwise solid citizens. These traders get caught up late in the game, when excitement and a lot of action lure them in; they take a flyer here and there, lose, and withdraw, swearing never to play the market again . . . until the gambling itch comes back during the next cycle. There's probably no way we can convince a compulsive short-term gambler to find a better strategy, short of recommending Gamblers Anonymous. Our warning is directed at the less neurotic. Playing short-term swings is, for a non-member of the Exchange, a sure way to losses. There will be profits during some phases, and small losses, which, taken singly, won't seem like much; but over a period of time such in-and-out activity will leave your capital in tatters and your nerves a wreck.

## Intermediate-Term Waves

Between the two extremes of short-term, in-and-out trading and the blurred, long-term investment view lie intermediate-term waves. Though sometimes obscured by the peculiarities of the averages or the quirks of the marketplace, they are always there, and are always discernible, as moves in the market which last from several weeks to several months before exhaustion sets in and a countermove ensues. An intermediate-term wave can be in gear with, or contrary to, the primary trend. On the next page is a chart of the Dow Jones industrial average from December 1968 to mid-1974 with each of the intermediate-term waves identified.

A number of intermediate-term waves are readily apparent, starting with the final intermediate-wave onslaught of the 1969–70 bear market (labeled A on chart). You can see, within this, a total of five short-term waves, three down and two up, with the final slide the longest as that bear market came to an end. Once the base for the new bull market was complete, the first intermediate-term upwave (labeled B) was inaugurated; it is a particularly fine example of an intermediate-term rally sustained for several months without real concern (except by anxious holders) before suffering a reversal. Indeed, all three uplegs of this bull market are similar (with the moves in 1970–1 and again in 1971–2, each from the end of November to the end of April, virtually identical), crisply defined, recognizable for what they are, and, as we'll discuss later, clearly foreseeable at their outsets via technical indicators. So, too, were the corrections against the primary trend which intervened: Note how this totaled five intermediate waves—three up and two down—within the long-term bull market, just as the intermediate-term waves themselves had three or five shorter-term waves, in keeping with the Elliott wave-cycle theory. Unlike long-term and short-term moves, intermediate-term waves are relatively precise in form; they last long enough and are sufficiently identifiable to be outstandingly adaptable moves for selling purposes.

Consider, for example, the first rise in the new bull market: once the move is launched—in this case on a decisive upside breakout across the 790 level in December 1970—one can be reasonably confident that it isn't going to collapse abruptly. Instead, the first minor reversal can be presumed to be nothing more than a short-term reaction, during which some early profits are taken by nervous traders. In 1971, this phase occurred in February, lasted five days, and retraced a mere 1.3 percent, the market equivalent of blinking one's eyes while speeding through a small town and missing it. In 1972, the comparable initial correction lasted less than two weeks and declined about 3 percent. The quantitative difference

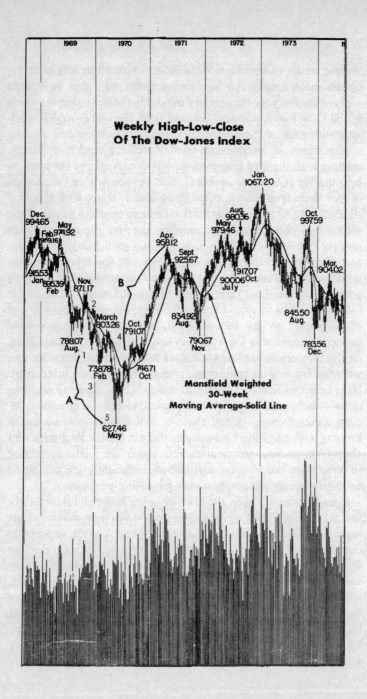

**Weekly High-Low-Close
Of The Dow-Jones Index**

1969    1970    1971    1972    1973

Dec. 994.65
Feb 974.92
969.16 May
915.53
Jan 896.39 Feb
871.17 Nov.
2
788.07 Aug.
803.26 March
1
738.78 Feb.
3
A
5
627.46 May

B
Apr. 958.12
Sept. 925.67
Oct. 791.07
4
834.92 Aug.
746.71 Oct.
790.67 Nov.

May 979.46
Aug. 980.36
Jan. 1067.20
917.07 Oct.
900.06 July

**Mansfield Weighted
30-Week
Moving Average-Solid Line**

Oct. 997.59
Mar. 904.02
845.50 Aug.
783.56 Dec.

between the two reflected the fact that the second came much later in the overall bull cycle and hence the market was not as powerful or broad. Such tidbits of deduced information are, to the practiced eye, subtle but highly significant clues about the market's future. Having witnessed a brief short-term correction, you can expect the second, as it comes, to be somewhat more extensive, but still merely contrary to the intermediate-term uptrend in force, *not* the beginning of a serious reversal. (In 1971, the second correction came in March.)

Consistently, intermediate-term uptrends in a primary uptrend flow through those five short-term waves (three up, two down). Investors following this course must become alert after the second minor correction to the potential end of the cycle and be prepared to sell into the third and final portion of the rally. (However, intermediate-term moves *against* the primary trend—up in bear markets, down during bull—usually encompass only three short-term waves. As an example, see the swings from April 1971 through November of that year.) This third upleg in an intermediate-term upwave is when smart money starts to get out while naïve newcomers, finally convinced the rally is going to endure forever, start buying in.

Thus, selling into the strength of this last short-term wave up of an intermediate-term rise is an efficient way to get out at good prices. But that is not the sole advantage provided. Most useful is the fact that the stock market's various technical indicators work best as an intermediate-term top is approached during that last wave. For the most part, extreme emotional and fundamental factors underlie major-trend reversals; the end of a cycle requires Wall Street to be so hysterically keyed up for a *continuation* of the trend that the stage is set for a refusal to recognize the turn, when it comes, as valid. Anyone looking for evidence of a shift in the long-term trend will, therefore, insist on a lot of proof. But if, instead, realizing that the genuinely *definable* move is an intermediate-term leg, you focus on whatever clues can specifically point to such swings, rather than the diffuse and laggardly indications of the demise of the primary cycle, you'll catch the turn much closer to the time of reversal. You may not yet believe that the major trend has reversed, even though you know that the interme-

diate term has, but that doesn't matter: on your side is the unaltera-
ble fact that *every long-term bottom and top must also coincide with
the end of an intermediate-term move.* By playing such intermediate waves, the big swings will take care of themselves!

The indicators that warn of intermediate-term trend reversals
are almost purely technical in nature, stemming, for the most part,
from the actual behavior of the market itself (the main exception
being influences from the money market, such as treasury-bill
rates), reflecting, directly or by inference, the prevailing psychology of supply and demand. We'll discuss them in detail in subsequent chapters. Since these technical indicators are objective, in
that they are formulated from the actual announced statistics (such
as the number of advances and declines), they help expose any
emotional biases favoring a continuation of the trend. And, naturally, when such signals coincide with the rumblings suggesting a
possible change in the major trend, they add timing to that aspect
as well. Therefore, a policy of trading in and out in concert with
intermediate-term trends will help prevent you from being fooled
by a major trend reversal; you'll be out of the market well before
the long-term picture comes into focus, which most investors were
*not* as the market rolled over in early 1973. Furthermore, if you
play intermediate-term trends, you'll get some help in trying to
time the action of individual stocks as well as the averages, a
critical factor we've already shown is apt to be absent in relating
to the market's primary trend and utterly deceptive in shorter
swings. You'll be on your toes and, watching the waves and being
alert for impending changes, you're much more apt to recognize
trouble that begins to form in a stock you own.

In the years we've espoused trading intermediate-term rhythms,
we've met only one consistent objection: that the intermediate
term, lasting as it often does less than the required months, plays
havoc with being able to achieve long-term capital-gains tax status.
True enough; you might well find yourself with a serious sell signal
within hailing distance of the IRS's requirement. Note, on the Dow
chart, how both the 1971 and 1972 uptrends fell just short of this
goal; long-term capital gains are, of course, taxed at only half the
rate of short-term gains. Unfortunately, the market, with typical
disdain, doesn't give a hoot for your taxes. We're on the market's

side; the important thing is not to let something extraneous such as the calendar affect your decisions; only after you have analyzed the market itself should you factor in tax considerations.

As we get into the chapters regarding individual indicators, you'll see how consistently they've been able to give signals near the peak of an intermediate-term uptrend. Since these clues can be matched with the discernible waves of typical cycles, paying attention to these trends is the soundest way to add timing to your tactics. As you watch those signals materialize at a time when the waves have been completed, you'll know it's time to sell. Do that once and see the market tail off into an intermediate downtrend; you'll be a devotee of such swings from then on.

# 4

## *Protecting against Losses*

Bottoms are made when just about everyone who has decided to sell has done so. On the way down, prices try to lift their heads, but more sellers appear, taking advantage of rallies to unload. With virtually every single share of stock outstanding constantly available for sale, by discouraged long-term holders as well as by short-term traders, it's tough for prices to go up much when the bearish psychology holds sway. But eventually such sellers are exhausted and the bottom is reached, often followed by a sudden rush upward through a vacuum, such as the initial whoosh of about 30 Dow points the day after the May 1970 bottom, or the action after the December 1974 low, marking the end of the catastrophic 1973-4 collapse. In January 1975 the DJI gained 87.45 points, setting a record for the largest point gain in any single month. That record lasted only a year; in January 1976 the Dow shot up over 130 points, reflecting the fact that during late 1975 all those who were scared that the stock market was going to collapse again sold out. Once this selling was absorbed, buyers far outweighed sellers, and the scramble for stocks was on.

In earlier days, sold-out conditions such as these often created what was known as a "selling climax." The ticker tape would run extraordinarily late as every last share was wrung out of panicked holders. This type of bottom invariably presented less risky buying opportunities and used to be the easiest to identify, especially if you'd long since sold and were calmly watching for signs that all the remaining suckers were getting scared to death. In 1962 the ticker ran several hours behind floor transactions, and it wasn't until long after five in the afternoon that anyone knew what price he'd bought or sold at. Since then, the Exchanges have taken steps to install higher-speed tickers, as well as measures designed to reduce the number of characters needed to be printed on a late tape. As a result, the ticker no longer cries panic.

Nonetheless, intermediate-term bottoms are characterized by a concerted, and at the time seemingly endless, bout of selling, especially when they coincide with the end of a major bear trend, the outward symptoms have changed. In May 1970, for example, the clue was that, with the Dow off another 10 points to what turned out to be its low, upside and downside volume were equal when downside should have far exceeded upside on that day. Such bottoms remain fairly easy to identify and have in common the characteristic that most stocks act in unison, so that all an astute investor requires is ample buying power (from intelligent prior sales) and the ability to pick from a vast number of potential purchases.

But one factor that makes selling far more difficult than buying is that tops don't provide comparable conveniences. Owners have only a limited option of what to do with their particular stock— sell or hold. With billions of shares of common stock outstanding, all eligible to be sold, and compared to which average daily trading volume is minuscule, it takes a lot of time to form a top. The Wall Street word is "distribution": holdings need to be sold shrewdly and carefully to late and naive buyers; it can take days, weeks, sometimes months, of shares tossed into the pot before it boils over. One by one, stocks stop going up. Some stockholders may begin to worry, yet they hold on due to greed, stubbornness, inertia, or simply hope; reasons are found to explain why an individual issue is lagging, though the averages are still chugging ahead. The first round of weakness is stemmed by those who believe the lower prices compared to the previous peak constitute bargains. A new upward trend ensues, though noticeably less broad, fed by newcomers whose dream of profits has been stirred by the previous vast rally and who now look for stocks to go still higher.

Although incipient cracks can be detected in the rise, savvy professionals stay with the trend, switching from tired holdings to newly emerging favorites. They recognize that certain categories of stocks may be out of it, but others are still going up. Often such pros are so sensitive to underlying shifts in sentiment that they discern prospective trouble weeks before it actually becomes worth worrying about. Though alert to an impending reversal, they keep at the bull, bypassing those stocks which have become particularly vulnerable. Their buying power becomes concentrated in fewer issues, which, in turn, display more spectacular gains, thus buoying the general optimism. If IBM, say, is up 12, who cares that Woolworth has eased 1 1/4?

Such is the process by which intermediate-term tops gradually develop, with weakness hardly noticed at first, while many stocks still participate on the upside, the excuse being that the stock has simply paused for a well-deserved rest and will catch up to the rally later on. But fewer and fewer contribute to the rising action as the advance in the averages continues. Rarely has this divergence between individual stock action and the leading averages been so apparent as in 1972. The overall upward movement during the first six months of that year brought the Standard & Poor's 500-stock average up nearly 5 percent. Yet only 15 stocks accounted for that gain, while the remaining 485 stocks actually averaged a .5 percent *loss* during that period! An investor who was convinced on the basis of the averages that a bull market truly lived was wrong. The divergence widened in a final frenetic rally at year-end, with all the speculative money pouring into those few conspicuous stocks which dominated the DJI and the S & P averages. Meanwhile, the stage was being set for the worst plunge since 1929.

One can readily see how the public tends to lose money during such periods. Every night on the news the announcer dutifully reports the day's gain in the averages, but no one mentions that the gain was a dangerous distortion of what was really happening on the Exchange floor. At the same time, the financial press digs deep into its bag of clichés, referring to each interruption in the uptrend as a "technical adjustment while the market digests its recent gains," or "a necessary consolidation prior to a resumption of the advance." And brokers insist that "with the outlook so cloud-free, now is the time to invest in common stocks." Naturally, the amateur remains confident that it is still safe to hold, or even to buy, more; and those who were frightened by losses in a prior bear market are finally convinced that it is safe to own stocks once again.

*Someone, though, is selling.* Someone has to be distributing the shares to meet this public demand. The professional, grasping the deterioration that's been going on underneath the mask of the averages and those few eye-catching individual gainers is perfectly willing to let go of his own positions. Indeed, he needs naïve buyers to absorb all he may want to sell; for example, invariably there's a sizable increase in the number of secondary offerings in which holders of large blocks are willing to sacrifice a peak price (and to pay an extra commission) just to get the whole lot sold in a hurry.

And while this is going on, who is worrying about you? The only person looking out for your well-being is you, make no mistake about it. (Indeed, your broker is probably trying to get you to buy what the big guy is trying to unload.) Kicking yourself later for having missed a selling opportunity may be a self-satisfying punishment/pleasure, but psychic currency isn't spendable. Yet converting paper profits into cash or selling out at a loss when a deeper loss is threatened is not a difficult feat.

### "They" vs. You

If it is dog-eat-dog on the Street (and it is!), who are the big dogs? And rather than running away with our tails between our legs, can we join their pack? Indeed we can, for *one of the keys to selling success is to be able to view all developments through the eyes of professional traders,* the market's most invariably successful operators, the fabled "they" who always appear to be "doing it" to the little man.

Just as the folklore of finance has it that the "gnomes of Zurich" manipulate the foreign exchange and the gold markets, a popular belief of public investors says that "they" rig the stock market in such a manner that the public always loses. No sooner have we bought a stock than "they" take the price down and make us panic out at a big loss. If we put in an order to sell at a certain price, "they" won't let it get there; and if we do sell, "they" spring some fresh news that skyrockets the stock on up without us. Those nagging suspicions are not totally unfounded. "They" did fleece the public during the late 1800's and early 1900's, as well as via insider pools in the Roaring Twenties. The 1929 crash and various assorted and associated scandals led to the creation in the early days of the Roosevelt Administration of the Securities and Exchange Commission, which virtually put an end to blatant market rigging. Even so, despite efforts to change things, there's still "inside info"; and the intense activities of institutions have become a problem in market domination. But, by and large, "they"—the specialists on the Exchange floor, traders, and various insiders—no longer have a real monopoly of power or information. These professionals consistently make profits, not through deviousness, but through skill, constancy, and discipline, traits that any of us would do well to emulate.

Much of today's "they" is comprised of member traders who kept cashing in profits with such astounding consistency that, in the early 1960's, the SEC branded them parasites on the grounds that simply being able to make a capitalistic profit wasn't a useful function. The SEC alleged that they contributed little to the orderly functioning of the market but, rather, stood around skimming the cream off whenever and wherever they could. It was possible to clamp down because these men weren't closely connected to the Exchange's power elite (many were former clerks who'd made their way upward; others were the nouveaux riches who had bought seats after the war); there was even an element of anti-Semitism involved, against a number of floor traders called the "Catskill crew." As a result, when the SEC's new and restrictive floor-trading rules were adopted, many floor traders were driven off the Exchange floor upstairs, where, at their desks, they were able to trade aggressively, outside the strictures of the new rules.

But there are always bright young lawyers coming to work at the SEC, and in the late sixties the issue was reopened. The commission analyzed the trading activity of these off-floor traders, and the study showed that a number of them were, in fact, buying the same stock at about the same time and often selling out at about the same time as well. There were tidy profits involved: 5,000 shares bought at 15, say, and sold a few minutes later at 15 1/2, for a $2,500 gain, less only some minor bookkeeping and transfer tax costs, for a nice day's pay. The SEC noted that most of these trades took place after noon and concluded that the evidence clearly showed that "they" were getting together at lunch and plotting which stock or stocks they were going to run up that afternoon.

The SEC staff refused to believe that the explanation lay, not in a conspiracy, but simply in the way the market worked. However, a further investigation (by one of this book's authors) was carried out, and the conspiracy theory was laid to rest. This is the gist of what was unearthed: instead of catching one particularly successful off-floor trader as he returned from lunch with his cohorts, the researcher found him sitting at his desk day after day with the wrappings of a corned-beef sandwich and an empty coffee container at his elbow. "I can't afford to leave the tape while it's running," he said. "Maybe SEC lawyers can take a lunch hour, but not me." Each of these alleged conspirators was asked if he ever spoke to any of the others about what was hot. "Haven't said a word to him," one sneered, "since we were on the floor together." Another insulted trader responded, "I don't want to know what the others think. If I knew, it would affect my own judgment." Still another said, "If God himself told me what to do, I wouldn't do it until I saw that I should on the tape." None of these professionals went out to lunch with any other trader; they never even talked to each other about what they were buying or selling; and they never fixed any market sequence whatsoever.

Then how *did* they manage to buy the same stock at about the same time, and sell at a profit in similar fashion? Because, as it turned out, each acted from what he saw on the ticker tape. Everything that's done on the floor—buying or selling, 100 or 10,000 shares—is revealed on the ticker tape, yet in any given trading day there are only a handful of situations which can be translated, from tape printout to reflex action, into a quick profit. A trader would notice a certain stock, as one put it, "pecking away"—17 3/4, 7/8, 7/8, 7/8. This pecking, or "nibbling," to use another favorite word of traders, would suggest the possibility that if the price hit 18 it had a good chance of running further faster, provided, of course, that recent prior action (which he had also been attentive to) had primed the pump for such a move. One trader would snatch up his phone and ask the broker on the floor at the other end of the line to hustle over to the post where that stock was being traded and get a size on the stock; if 100,000 shares were offered at 18, it would be unlikely that demand would be great enough to eat up all those shares and take the price higher, and if it were only 100 shares, it would be impossible to purchase in sufficient quantity for the effort to be worthwhile. Another trader, spotting the same nibbling, might watch, with his hand on the phone, to see if the stock could actually get to 18 on some confirming volume. Yet another trader would simply shoot down an order to buy 5,000 at 18, make the impressive print on the tape himself, and hope that the splash on the ticker would, in turn, attract more interest. If the stock ran to 19 amid spreading board-room excitement, those traders would be selling just a few minutes later to all the buy orders generated by excited brokers reaching for their phones. The process is so quick and profitable that it's no wonder that the SEC and the public feel taken in by the "they" who gain. Yet there is nothing in any of this to prevent you from noticing the same patterns on the tape, watching the same charts, analyzing the same company's fundamentals, and darting in at 17 7/8 or 18 with equal alacrity. The chief difference, day in and day out, is that "they" act—and the public hesitates.

## How Professionals Minimize Losses

Blaming "them" is a psychologically and socially acceptable way to avoid blaming oneself. Yet professionals can, and do, make mistakes. When they buy a stock and it doesn't go up, or even if it doesn't go down, that's wrong enough for them, simply because it *did not perform as expected.* The pro reasons that the stock went against him, so he sells it. And he doesn't expect to be perfect, any more than the professional baseball player expects to bat 1,000. Knowing that losses are inevitable, *he seeks to minimize them at all times.* To be sure, his ability to take a small loss is enhanced by the benefit of not having to reckon with commission costs, but even so, if he were relatively incompetent, he wouldn't last long in the business; the loss might be less, or slower to pile up, but the return on invested capital would be dismal enough eventually to send him into another field.

Rule 1 of the professional trader is: *When a stock doesn't do what you expect it to do, sell it.* No hesitating, no questions asked or doubts raised, no conjectures of the way it should have turned out, no dreams of how it will turn out tomorrow. The pro never says, "I'll watch it one more day." He doesn't phone an analyst who's been following the company and ask, "What's happening? Is there any news?" The desire to be perfect is one of the prime emotional bugaboos of the stock market, but it's a compulsion that belongs on the psychiatrist's couch, not on the Exchange floor. And that means no berating yourself for having bought it, should it then go down, and no remorse for having sold should the stock turn around after you've gotten out and finally do what was expected. We once watched a trader jettison an entire position because it had retreated half a point. "Not acting well," he muttered at the time. But then, half an hour later, there it was, roaring not only through his sale price but also through his original purchase price, and going higher still. The trader didn't stop to berate himself; he immediately bought the stock again at the higher price. Since Wall Street is a game without end, he saw the situation for what it was: a brand-new chance.

Typically, though, the amateur confronted with the same sort of performance takes the stock's behavior as a personal affront. Instead of dealing directly with the new information the tape is providing, he will stare disconsolately at the tape, inveighing against the "they" who stole his stock from him—and then got rich while he could only watch helplessly. Obviously, this is not how it's done. An unemotional, consistent program for minimizing losses is the *sine qua non* of learning to sell efficiently. (The same, as we'll discuss in more detail later in this chapter, is equally true of selling to capture your profit before a sagging stock takes it away from you.) Unless one accepts the inevitability of some loss, one is destined to wander in the world of would be, waiting, stock in hand, for tomorrow. Whereas one of the amateur's most immediate concerns is not to look foolish, the professional's foremost interest is not to be trapped with widening losses. He sells to be safe, to be able to keep on playing. To him selling is like taking out insurance on his capital. To be sure, you cannot always be as prompt as a professional who can leap the moment he sees one tick. You have more important things to do than watch a bunch of numbers all day. You cannot react to that single tick without having seen all that came before, just as you cannot settle for a half-point profit. But adjustments *can* be made, and once you make them, you're on the way to developing your own means of reacting to the market through a trader's eyes.

Sometimes finding out that a stock hasn't done what you expected it to do requires going back to the notion you had when you bought the stock in the first place. Suppose your expectation of profit was news-oriented: the earnings were going to be much higher, or a new product was due, or a rumored merger or tender offer was going to make the stock worth more. Once the news you bought for becomes public knowledge, the test is at hand. If the stock fails by not doing what you expected it to do on the news (that is, doesn't go up), then you've been suitably, albeit subtly, warned: either no one else cares enough about the news to buy, or there are enough sellers anxious to use the news to unload. There are also times when a stock is doing so well your inner voice confidently predicts: Tomorrow morning it is going to break right out on the upside. But when the opening comes, the stock denies its promise and sags instead. Assuming your expectation made market sense, the stock's failure to follow through is a sign something may be wrong.

Market action itself can tell you that your stock isn't behaving as well as it should. For example, when the stock fails to make a new high, when renewed rallies show shrinking volume, when the market averages are spurting ahead but your stock simply isn't participating, or when, after holding well at a certain level during a correction, it finally sells at lower prices. These are all circumstances relating to failed expectations. Essentially, the stock has been unable to do what was reasonably expected of it, and that is one of the first, and often the best, clues that it is time to consider selling.

## *Using "Stop-Loss" Orders to Minimize Losses*

We are concerned here with taking our lumps—selling at a loss when the reality of the situation (failure of some sort) calls for that action. We'll try to keep the loss as small as possible, giving the stock just enough rope to hang itself, but no more. One way to cope with the amateur's handicaps of time and distance from the market (and the nagging suspicion that your broker is not paying enough attention to your account) is to commit yourself unswervingly to a predetermined selling point. Then, when the stock doesn't go up as you expected it to but goes down instead, you react to that failure by automatically selling out. Such a system can deal directly with disconcerting and destructive emotional responses (i.e., refusing to see the failure, or hoping it will go away if you ignore it) by eliminating any chance they have to get in the way.

One such arbitrary formula involves the use of a sell "stop" order, or, as it is more popularly called, a "stop-loss" order (even though it can serve to protect a profit, too). This type of order is placed beneath the current market price and is automatically set off (the term on the Exchange floor is "elected") if the stock falls to that price. Thus the stock is sold without any further decision-making; you set the price at which you want to cut your loss *at a time when you can be objective about the situation,* rather than when you are under the pressure of the stock falling. A properly placed stop-loss order can help you match the self-imposed discipline of the professional trader without having to remain riveted to the tape all day every day. It will help you sell a stock that doesn't do what you expected it to do, with no questions asked and no procrastination permitted.

A simple format is sometimes adopted for this emotion-free system, merely by putting stop-loss orders in at 10 percent below your original purchase price, on the grounds that a 10 percent loss is the most you would be willing to incur with any given purchase. If you paid 50, you would enter a stop at 45; if you paid 15, the stop-loss order would be entered at 13 1/2, and so forth. By entering the order immediately after purchasing the stock, you would *never,* despite your inner struggles to hang on grimly, take a bigger loss than that 10 percent.

Moreover, if your stock rises as expected, the same automatic formula can be continued: each time the price advances a certain amount, you cancel the old stop order and enter a new one, maintaining the 10 percent differential between the current price and the price set on the stop order; if the stock then falls 10 percent, that is indication enough that it is having difficulties and you would elect to get out. With this elementary formula, a sufficient rise after purchase will guarantee to take you out at a profit; if the stock doesn't go down 10 percent before it goes up 12 1/2 percent, you're in the game. Meanwhile, you've been protected from a loss that could get worse and worse while you're too paralyzed to sell.

Of course the above is too simple for practical use. The stock market is man's most beatable game, and putting the odds to work requires common sense, not just a formula. For example, common sense in poker (man's second most beatable game) tells you that the chance of pulling a flush with the last card in five-card stud is nearly one in five; you already have four, so there are nine others from the same suit left of the forty-eight remaining cards. Nine chances in forty-eight comes to 18.75 percent. But of course the odds don't hold if other cards in the same suit are already on the table. By the same token, relying on an automatic formula to place sell-stop orders won't produce predictable results, either, if contrary evidence is on the table in front of you.

What good is relying on a system based on stop-loss protection, for instance, if it serves to make you feel safe about buying stocks at the wrong time? "I'll take that chance," the gambler-investor tells himself, "since the most I can lose is 10 percent." But in a downtrending market, that's like placing an order for a loss on purpose. Often those who want to seek out bargains when they shoot for the bottom in stocks that have fallen already wind up getting stopped out very near the real bottom. Many of their choices, particularly in a final panicky fling, have that 10 percent more to go on the downside. This can be a very painful and unnecessary loss right at the bottom of a bear market.

Often, too, at the end of a massive bear-market decline, many stocks will appear to be starting to hold, only to undergo some last-gasp slides before immediately turning around and starting a strong advance. Chart purists have continually been baffled by this phenomenon, and call it a "false downside breakout," since what technically should have been a renewed decline inexplicably reverses into a big new bull move. (See the action of Merrill Lynch in the last half of 1975 for a flawless example.) So disturbed are they by this that they fail to see how bullish such action consistently is; there's nothing like being blinded after you're proved wrong to miss the next chance to be right. And, in such situations, you wouldn't want to have been stopped out just before the rise because of an arbitrary use of a 10 percent stop-loss point. Consider the accompanying chart of Pope & Talbot during 1973, a rather typical example. Here's a stock that looked fairly good; from November 1972 on through April 1973 POP had refused to join in the general market plunge, which made it an attractive buy candidate. But if you had bought in April at around 19 and used a formula stop point 10 percent below—at, say, 17—you'd have been stopped out on the abrupt drop to 15 5/8 in late May, just before the big upsurge began. How or why "they" did this to POP at that time is irrelevant; all we know is that any arbitrary users of formula stop orders would have been knocked out of what later turned out to be one of the market's best long-side holdings of that dire year.

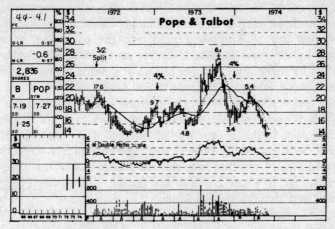

Careful observation of everything that is on the table as well as in the air, plus a sense of timing, are just as critical in the market as in poker. This being the case, it makes better sense to use *calculated* stop-loss points whenever possible, rather than purely arbitrary ones. An earlier Pope & Talbot chart would show that the entire area around 15 had provided support for the stock going as far back as the 1969–70 bear market. It would have made more market sense to have placed a stop-loss order just below that major support area, on the theory that if the stock broke *that* level, after holding so many times successfully, it would be a sign of fresh and highly significant weakness. Contrast that with an arbitrary stop at 17 based not on the stock's behavior but on the relatively accidental price the purchaser happened to have paid.

In some instances, the calculated stop-loss point could be as little as 4 or 5 percent under the purchase price; in others, as much as 20 percent. Obviously, however, such a high percentage would serve as a warning to wait for a temporary dip in the stock before buying, so that the protective stop legitimately could be placed closer and thus keep any loss limited. *The effective use of protective stop-loss orders requires a sensible purchase in the first place.* A stop-loss point that has to be placed too far below the current price often suggests the stock is too high to buy. The buyer who chases a stock that has been running wild has already lost control of his emotions and has no rational guideposts to help determine whether or when it should be sold. Such a hapless individual can be whipsawed right into the poorhouse, as is shown by the chart of Alberto-Culver on the next page. After holding throughout the summer of 1974 at 5, while the rest of the market was crashing, ACV made its first false downside breakout at the end of October, serving to frighten away premature purchasers. It then instantly doubled, from 4 1/4 to 8 7/8 in two trading days, so that anyone who chased it as it got hot and paid over 8, let's say, and protected that purchase with a stop-loss order at around 5, would have suffered a huge loss on the subsequent plunge to a new low at 4. But the stock then turned right around and straightened out again.

Indeed, there is no proper place to put a stop order in ACV during the time span of this chart. While a bottom is being formed, false moves such as the two lows are not unlikely and ultimately turn out to be all part of a base. When no sensible stop point is available, you need to track the stock more closely until the oppor-

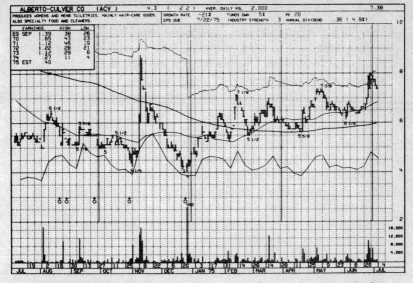

ALBERTO-CULVER CO   (ACV )        4.3   (  2 2 )   AVER. DAILY VOL   2.000                    7.38
PRODUCES WOMENS AND MENS TOILETRIES, MAINLY HAIR-CARE GOODS.   GROWTH RATE   -21%   FUNDS OWN   5%   PE 20
ALSO SPECIALTY FOOD AND CLEANERS.                             EPS DUE   7/22/75   INDUSTRY STRENGTH   3   ANNUAL DIVIDEND   .36 ( 4.9%)

tunity develops. For this, reference to a daily bar chart does the job
best, as it will pinpoint specific price levels. (Sometimes a weekly
chart will do, but often the scale of such a chart is too compact,
making it difficult to determine the exact price level permitted.) As
a rule of thumb, a sell-stop order should be placed just below the
lowest price of the stock's prior support. Generally, this can be
considered *the price at which the market is telling us something has
gone wrong.*

While a base is being formed, any stock is capable of enduring
a last gasp shake-out. Hence, if you buy while a bottom is forming,
a stop order would be premature. However, when the stock breaks
out, completing the base, you should then look for the price at
which the market would tell you the breakout was false. Using
ACV as an example, a rally across 7 1/4, exceeding the previous
high, would call for a stop under the most recent dip, at 5 7/8. Were
the stock to advance again—in particular across the 8 7/8 peak to
9 or more—we'd look for the level at which the stock had suc-
ceeded in holding on any more recent dips. Suppose the stock
rallied to 8, went back to 7 1/8, and then went to 9 1/2. The stop
could then be raised to 6 7/8, under both the prior dip low at 7 1/8
and the nearby round number as well. As proof that that particular
level attracted important buying, a meaningful support area should

be confirmed by at least three days of a subsequent rally. If the next decline were then to drop below the level at which buying had previously been found, it would be an objective indication that the stock was in trouble—enough of a clue, perhaps, to call for selling the stock out. The stop-loss order then does the deed for you immediately.

Interestingly, a tabulation of thousands of publicly-held stop orders seen by the authors shows that almost all are simplistically placed either at the whole number or, somewhat less often, at the half-point fraction. Therefore, a congestion of potential sellers is likely at those intervals, possibly leading to poor executions. The least used, and thus to be preferred, fractions when entering stop-loss orders are 3/8 and 7/8. Further validity for the use of these odd fractions is that the public also concentrates its limited-price buy orders at the round number and at the half-point level, so you want your stop order entered underneath, not wanting it to be set off while there are still potential buyers around but only after they've lost the battle to sellers. Lastly, we feel so strongly about wanting to be under a round number that if it is a "zero" round number (20, 30, 40, etc.), we would even stretch a bit to go under that level, to 29 7/8, for example, rather than a closer 30 3/8.

Another illustration of the placement of stop-loss orders comes in the chart of American Standard in 1971 on the next page. The stock had already tumbled from 40 to 20; there it began to look as if it were building a new base of support, bolstered by an intriguing sequence of rising bottoms: 19 3/4, 20 3/4, 21, and 21 5/8, indicating increasingly aggressive buyers. It seemed like a reasonable specula- tion that the decline of 50 percent was over and that a new upward trend lay ahead. Let's suppose you bought at point A on the chart, at around 23, as the stock began rising again after holding that fourth time at 21 5/8. The sense of this was bolstered by the ability to enter a protective stop-loss order quite close to the purchase price. Our choice would have been just under the most recent low; we would have entered an order: "Sell at 21 3/8 stop" (point B). True, it would have been conceivable to have aimed all the way down to the 19 3/4 bottom of the previous June, entering the stop at 19 3/8 and awaiting a violation of the entire area as a definitive sell signal. But it is usually the *first* sign of trouble in such a

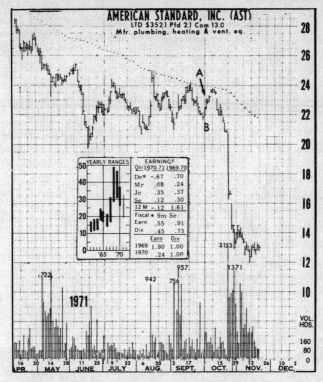

| YEARLY RANGES | EARNINGS | |
| --- | --- | --- |
| | Qtr 1970-71 | 1969-70 |
| De* | -.67 | .70 |
| Mr | .08 | .24 |
| Je | .35 | .37 |
| Se | .12 | .30 |
| 12 M | -.12 | 1.61 |
| Fiscal • 9m Se | | |
| Earn | .55 | .91 |
| Div | .45 | .75 |
| | Earn | Div |
| 1969 | 1.90 | 1.00 |
| 1970 | .24 | 1.00 |

'65   '70

1971

situation that is the tip-off to developing weakness, and in this case
the chart pattern gives the distinct impression that an initial break
would spoil everything. You can even draw in what chartists would
recognize as a "triangle" (to be discussed in more detail in a
subsequent chapter), connecting the rising bottoms and declining
tops on the theory that a breakout in either direction would be
meaningful. And, we add, even if one had opted for the 19 3/8 stop
at the outset, the failure of the rally to exceed the previous high—
halting at 23 3/4, short of the prior 24 1/4—would have been a
warning to raise the stop at once to 21 3/8 as closer protection of
your capital. At that point the triangle would have been broken on
the downside, contradicting that hitherto bullish sequence of rising
bottoms. Given the increasingly narrow limits of such a triangle,
once it is let go the move is usually sharp, just like a spring being
released. To be sure, there are always those exceptions, where the
stock manages to be saved before falling apart. But we are not here

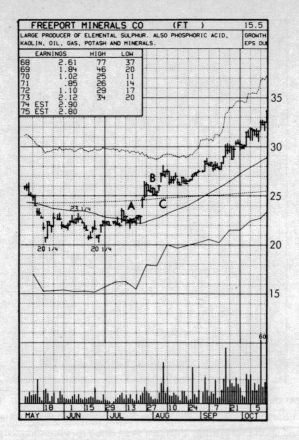

| | EARNINGS | HIGH | LOW |
|---|---|---|---|
| 68 | 2.61 | 77 | 37 |
| 69 | 1.84 | 46 | 20 |
| 70 | 1.02 | 25 | 11 |
| 71 | .85 | 26 | 14 |
| 72 | 1.10 | 29 | 17 |
| 73 | 2.12 | 34 | 20 |
| 74 EST | 2.90 | | |
| 75 EST | 2.80 | | |

to take such risks, and indeed, we've noticed that even the saved stock often gives way at a later date. For our money, we want out as soon as trouble is *first* registered, because that's the way a professional trader would act.

Let's take another illustration: Freeport Minerals, during the bear market of 1973. The market was getting progressively better that summer (it turned out to be a large-scale intermediate-term rally) and a prospective buyer of FT could have jumped in at about 23 in July. Noting the twin lows, a sensible stop-loss order could then have been placed at 19 7/8, which would have been nice and neat, not only because it was under two levels that had successfully stemmed sellers before, but because it was also just under an important round number (20). Notice, by the way, that someone who paid 23 for FT midway between those twin lows and applied an automatic 10 percent stop would have been taken out unnecessarily on the second dip to 20 1/4.

Some people are wary of placing stop orders on a specialist's book, suspecting that those market-makers on the Exchange floor deliberately drop prices just to be able to scoop stopped-out shares into their own accounts before a steep rise is to begin. This view of specialists as archconspirators is another version of the "they" syndrome, suited to the needs of amateur traders anxious to be able to blame someone else for their own losses. On the evidence, the fear is specious. The specialist could theoretically take advantage of stop-loss orders in Freeport by dropping the stock another 3/8 of a point to 19 7/8 and buying all the stock thus elected for sale. How could he engineer this? In the first place, he'd already have to own some stock in order to have some to sell to drive the price down; if he did force it under 20 by his selling, he'd be giving himself a paper loss in his remaining position, as well as passing up the chance to sell those same shares at 22, where the stock was then trading. Secondly, there would have to be some buyers down at the lower level other than himself, because he could not sell to himself; it's a violation of both Exchange rules and federal law to be on both sides of the market.

Suppose he didn't own any shares at the time, could he manipulate the price down? In the old days there was such a thing as "gunning the stops," by letting other sellers have their way until all the orders were cleaned out. But now the specialist is expected to—and the Exchange conducts surveillance to see that he does—interpose himself to prevent a disorderly market. Granted, a specialist usually likes to get rid of a pile up of stop orders on his book because they could accelerate a sell-off, but it takes *outside* sell orders coming into the market to make that action a reality. If such sellers succeed in driving the price down until it hits the level you specified, thus electing your stop, it would be because the exact circumstances you were protecting yourself against had come to pass. In effect, it would be proof that the stop was needed.

None of this should be taken to mean that the use of stop-loss orders is perfect. Rather, we believe, their application as a consistent tactic is a particularly professional way to play the game. Upon occasion, you'll get stopped out and the stock will then turn around and shoot upward without you. There's nothing you can do to avoid such situations; just chalk them up to bad luck and don't sit around moaning. Remember: it may make sense to simply buy the stock back as soon as you realize the market has tricked you. If you apply stops intelligently, following a style similar to the one outlined, their primary virtue will be that they can save you from losses that could become devastating. For our money, that insurance is well worth an occasional whipsaw. Take another look at the Freeport chart: the alert trader, admiring the breakout at A, and the way the stock held during the next few days, could reasonably buy near B, with a stop order placed at C (24 7/8) under the pullback low and also under the stock's long-term Moving Average. A break below 25 would announce that the rally had been spoiled, and you'd be out of a questionable position with a minimum of damage.

On the face of it, it may seem as if the same ends can be accomplished in your head without invoking specific stop orders (e.g., "I promise myself that if XYZ goes down another point I'll sell it and the hell with it. Nothing will change my mind then."), but you've heard that litany often enough to recognize it as an emotional dodge. All too often, the user of a mental stop point is able to tap a stream of justifications for continuing to hold on: the stock is due to bounce back; it's selling for only three times earnings; the yield is so high it's silly to sell; good news is due out next week; and so on.

For the more experienced, one compromise method is worth mentioning: the mental stop order utilized by John Magee, dean of technicians. This approach is based on the closing price only, so that brief intraday whipsaws can be avoided. If the stock *closes* below a pre-selected point (and here again this point has to make market sense), then a market order to sell the stock is entered prior to the next day's opening. In this way emotion is curbed because the order is entered while the market is closed, when you can still be objective, and there's the added advantage of selling at the opening (to be discussed later). For those confident of their ability to act decisively instead of wasting time rationalizing, this variant may be suitable.

The principal advantages of non-arbitrary formula selling are (1) it reduces the emotional turbulence of the decision, and (2) it effectively protects you against taking an unnecessarily huge loss. First of all, it is worth repeating that purchases should be made only when you know, in advance, that there is a sensible place to enter a protective stop-loss order. If the stock hasn't yet proven that it wants to go up, or if it has already leaped, any prospective point for a stop order would be a whopping distance away and you would have a wise constraint on buying at that time. Later, when the stock is ripe, if you can place a protective stop order within, say, 10 to 15 percent of the purchase price, you're in business. Having made your purchase, you are now protected against absorbing an unnecessarily gross loss if the stock doesn't perform as you expected it to.

What's more, now that you have already entered a sell order, there is no likelihood that if and when a loss must be faced you'll be unable to utter the order to sell. Nor will your broker be in a position to complicate matters. Many is the investor who resolutely has made up his mind, only to hear his broker respond, when he says sell, with a questioning sigh or a peculiarly intoned "Oh?" "Why not?" the client replies. "Don't you think I should sell?" And then, of course, the door to disaster has been opened wide.

If you place a stop-loss order whenever a sensible point becomes available, the order will be there on the floor and, if need be, it will be executed. Indeed, if such a properly placed order is entered, the stop point should never be lowered. If you can see that an expected overall market correction is likely to take you out, you've got a good signal that it would be wiser not to wait but *to sell instead at the current and higher price.* For example, if FT is at 30 when the various key indicators (as described later) tell you the bear market is about to resume, perhaps you'd wish you could change the stop order back to 19 7/8, foreseeing that FT could get walloped back down to its prior base. But is that not telling you—since you objectively can visualize the stop at 24 7/8 being "set off"—to sell at 30? And once it's sold, accept it as a fact of life, with no regrets even if the stock eventually proves you right by zooming back up. The stock didn't work out as you anticipated, so, like a successful professional, you've acted on the evidence that something has turned sour. Whatever the reason (which might not become public knowledge until after the stock has collapsed), you'll have been protected.

## Using "Stop-Loss" Orders to Lock In Gains

Once you've learned to cut losses short, you'll be ready to carry the use of stop orders into the profit side of the ledger. Let's say you got stopped out of positions in early 1969 and as the bear market comes to an end you're enviably liquid. One of your selections at the mid-1970 bottom is Champion Home Builders, which you buy at about 5 (A) adjusted for subsequent splits. CHB then rises to the upper teens for a sizable gain. If you'd used the arbitrary 10 percent formula for protecting that gain, you would have garnered the bulk when stopped out at around 14 in March 1971 (B). Indeed, having nearly tripled your investment, you might have felt the system had worked—except that there were over 100 more points to go! To follow CHB up another notch, a 10 percent formula trailing stop order entered after the next rally to 31 would have been executed at 27—and you can see how costly that would have turned out to be.

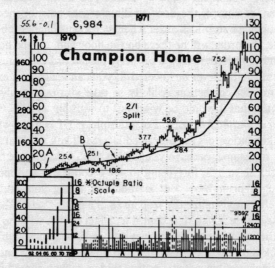

There is not always an opportunity to buy at such historic bottoms, so let's consider a more typical purchase—in this case, as the stock staged a major breakout across 19 (C). Note the black line on the chart which represents the Mansfield Chart Service's thirty-week Moving Average line, a graphic technique which smooths out the course of the primary trend by calculating its average price over the past thirty weeks. Here it can be seen that on four separate occasions the price of the stock tickled that Moving Average line, but then bounced back up away from it, showing that the M.A. was serving to define the rate of support. Obviously any stop-loss order placed just below this well-tested thirty-week M.A. line would have served as an excellent guide, keeping you in the stock until, as can be seen subsequently, the line was finally penetrated. In addition to support areas, the M.A. line can verify the stock's expected price action, and thus can be used as an intelligent guide to placing stop orders.

You might note that CHB's corrections along that upward route had a specific sequence too: there was the dip from 31 to 27, a steeper one from near 50 back into the 30's, another from 50 to 40, the sharp break from near 80 to almost 60, from 100 to 80, and, at the very top of the chart, from over 120 to nearly 100. Not one reaction went lower than the preceding one, or, to put it another way, *each reaction low was higher than the previous one.* Had a holder who wanted to stay with the stock as long as there were no danger signals simply adhered to a policy of raising his trailing stop order to just under each reaction low (and under the M.A. as well), he would have had enormous profits locked in, and he would never have been stopped out all the way to the stock's high at 130. That's perfection!

The second chart has been adjusted for a 5 for 1 split in the fall of 1971 (thus the high at 26 equals the high of 130 on the first chart). The M.A. remained unbroken during that correction to 20 (100 on the old chart) for several weeks until, at last, a sharp drop breached the pattern at point D. The investor, pegging his trailing protective stop order behind the action, would have applied a combination of being just under the M.A. and just under the prior reaction low— probably placing his stop order at 18 3/8—and sold finally, automatically, for a grand profit.

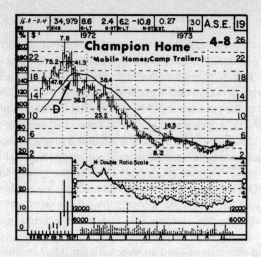

Not all stocks behave this impeccably for so long, but then, not all stocks go so far up toward that pot of gold at the end of the rainbow. No matter how far, or for how long, the stock's rise, the investor who uses this technique to make sure he harvests at least a portion of his blossoming profit is likely, over the years, to fare a lot better than the unprogrammed holder who says to himself, "That's enough. The stock is too high, I'd better sell." We want to sell, but not so emotionally and arbitrarily. Reliance on objective clues to determine when the stock has begun to lose its virtue is what we want. Stop orders aren't foolproof, but with CHB all the way back down to 3 (the equivalent of 15 on the first chart!) as the next bear market took its toll, it's clear that using a stop is a lot better than passively riding the roller coaster up and then back down again.

## Recognizing Realities

Playing the market would be wondrously simple if all stocks behaved as neatly on the way up and down as Champion Homes did in 1971. Yet it should also be noted that even CHB could have been sold out and bought back many times along the way by an aggressive trader, so long as he was alert enough to get back in. (IRS restrictions apply only to the taking of losses; if you sell at a gain, there's no restriction on buying back immediately if you want to.) For instance, Champion's penetration of the twin highs at the 50 level provided a key re-entry point for those ready to buy back in once the corrective action had run its course. If you had sold, that particular game would have been over. But the player should always remain alert in case a whole new field of play opens up. The trouble is that it is more common, having sold, to hope the stock then goes to zero; the further down it goes, the more triumphant we feel. Emotional rooting can blind you to what is actually happening; make it a point to observe your stocks as objectively as you can.

Sometimes a stock's uptrend will be so dynamic, as was Champion's, that it's hard to do the wrong thing as long as you stay with the trend. But at other times there are complications. The accompanying chart of the daily action of United Air Lines, Inc. provides a more typical challenging example of life on the Street.

Suppose you had bought UAL in February 1972 at 44 (A), and immediately thereafter, following the suggested guidelines noted above, you had placed a protective stop-loss order at 39 3/8, just below the twin lows made in January (B). UAL does what you expect it to, shooting upward, but at first there is no apparent place to raise the stop level to. Perhaps you might have considered the 47 1/8 low (C), but at the time it would have appeared too insignificant, having been established only fleetingly. In March, though, a sharp pullback was stemmed authoritatively at 45 1/2 (D), so the stop logically could have been raised to just below that support, at 45 3/8 or 44 7/8. Many investors become itchy when the stop order must be entered so far below the current price action, and they resort to a closer but dangerously arbitrary price. That's a bit like telling the market how it should behave. Such presumptuous acts have no technical significance and hence will be far less rewarding over the long run than waiting patiently for market-derived stop levels. You can see how anyone who had pressed upward impatiently by using the insignificant dip at point C would have been stopped out on the drop to point D, since it was not until that drop that a suitable price for a stop order appeared.

Does the placing of even a suitably deduced stop allow you to

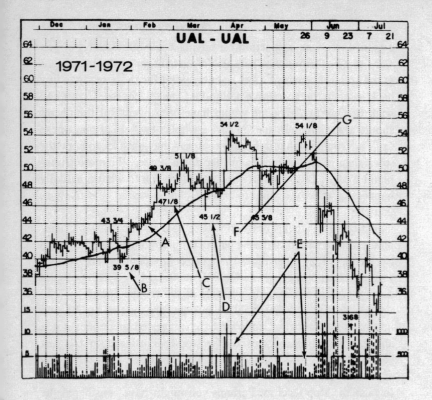

sit back and relax? It had better not! Sell-stop orders are a useful part of an overall approach to success but they are not magical, nor are they the be-all and end-all. Anyone who relies on them solely will be missing other clues of weakness. In UAL's case, in fact, that sudden plunge to 45 1/2 was the first warning that some serious sellers were on the other side of the fence. Even though it quickly straightened itself out, the stock logically shouldn't have gone down so far; even more worrisome, the same thing happened again in April following a satisfying spurt to a new high. If UAL were still healthy, buyers should have appeared on the scene at a higher price level, but they didn't. Now, although your stop order is still unexecuted, the near miss should serve to alert you to a precarious position instead of allowing you to heave a sigh of relief and go back to sleep, as so many amateurs would. The third clue then confirms your suspicions: the failure to make a new high on the next rally—54 1/8 vs. the previous 54 1/2. And there is yet a fourth clue: the greatly diminished volume during that second rally (compare the action shown by the arrows at E). At this juncture, the aggressive trader would have acted wisely if he had simply cancelled that distant stop order and sold the stock outright.

An alternative would be to scour the chart for any other clue as to where a stop-loss order could be sensibly placed closer to the current price. The Moving Average line in UAL's instance is evidently too erratic a guideline, but by drawing a line across the April and May lows, a chartist would have discerned an uptrend line (F–G) which was defining the recent rate of gain. A stop-loss order could then have been moved up to just under this line on the theory that if this short-term trend were broken it would be evidence of a weakening condition. On these grounds, a stop order could be placed at 51 7/8, but we might have respected that little area of supportive sideways action at 50 and put the stop at 49 3/8. If you cover the rest of the chart with your thumb, you can see that a break below that level makes the chart look much more negative than it had been looking. That's a tip-off to get out safely. It's much more important to *be* out than to quibble about a point or two, especially in view of the fact that the stock went down to 16 not long after.

## Using the Dow

One more exercise in the use and placement of sell-stop orders may be helpful in emphasizing the need for perspective. Let's look at the daily bar chart of the Dow industrial average for 1970, a year which included a major and complicated bottom, analyzing the DJI as if it were an individual stock.

Following a serious decline in 1969, many investors were avidly looking for the bottom. The 740 level in the DJI had considerable historic validity and seemed reasonable, which is why the decline was initially stemmed there at the end of January. Let's suppose the sideways movement throughout most of February, which suggested that the market was through declining, enticed a trader to buy. He would have placed a protective stop-loss order just under

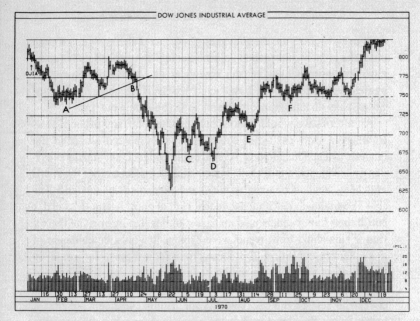

the prior lows at point A. A modest rally ensues; indeed, the correction in March seems normal and prices advance even further. But there's increasing evidence of faltering by early April; the momentum has gone out of the rally and the trader needs protection much closer. He then uses the trend line created from the sequence of rising lows. A stop placed just under that trend line gets him out at point B for a modest profit and, more importantly, before a loss-provoking smash sets in.

Indeed, as May rolls around, the situation is so steeped in gloom that every analyst, it seems, expects ruin just around the corner. Bleak financial news abounds and more is developing, exactly the kind of disheartening atmosphere typical of important bottoms. But that's a hard truism to honor when the headlines are so frightening. (No one says you are forced to buy at such a difficult juncture; our primary concern here is to make sure you've sold your holdings long before that moment arrives.) In time, a rapid rally arrives, but armed with bad economic news, the bears insist it is just a "bear-market rally" such as occurred in 1930. The Penn Central debacle unfolds on the front page along with rumors that other major companies such as Chrysler are on the verge of collapse as well. The middle section of the chart—of the DJI from the end of May to July 4—shows how the initial rally ran out of gas, corrected, tried again, failed, and broke the prior low in the next wave of selling, indicating to the bears that the decline was on the verge of being renewed.

Notice the relatively high volume at the end of May, signifying panic dumping. Months of moderate volume on the way down lulled stubborn holders into believing that there was no real selling pressure and hence no need to sell. But when the magnitude of the decline finally became scary, volume accelerated. A huge increase in the pace of trading is often a component of a bottom area; a second component is a successful test of the prior low with considerably less volume. This happened in early July, when the Dow held above its May low, even though the Penn Central mess lingered on. As the market rallied, it performed its function of discounting the bad news and anticipating the future. To grasp that this is what the market is doing is called having perspective; without it, one is left to repeat mistakes over and over again.

One mistake commonly made at such junctures is fearfully putting stops too close under the market. Having perspective—in this instance having confidence that a major trend reversal is underway —should guide you into giving stocks as much leeway as possible. Thus, by this time, a stop under C would be the wrong tack to take; not until the bottom had been successfully tested and the prices moved away from the July low was D established as a point of reference for placing a stop order. Now you'll notice, on the final segment of the chart, that the 740 level, familiar from the prior February, becomes important again, now as resistance (it's natural to expect supply to come out at that level from those who are now able to get out "even"). Then, when the next decline holds at E, above the prior low, you can move protective stops up under that level and they're in no danger of being set off when the DJI moves sideways in September, October, and on into November. Again, notice how important that 740 level is, for it is once more holding the way it did in February.

It may seem mystical, but it is empirically evident that these trading areas are meaningful to market forces. The market is, after all, a phenomenon of mass psychology, and that mass has clearly agreed on the significance of such levels. What's more, not only does 740 affect prices, but so, too, does the upper level around 790 assume increasing importance; it beat back the winter rally and now has successfully resisted this latest upside effort. A tug of war is still going on. But you may objectively back up your perception that this is a new bull market by buying and holding stocks, and not taking the unnecessary risk of buying too far away from useful stop levels. By the time October rolled around we would have thought that the ability of the market to hold at point F meant stops could be raised to that new and higher level. All those still-rabid bears simply lacked perspective at the time. It's obvious that, if the 740 level were then to break, they would have been proved right; but it never happened. In the meantime, the objective trader would have already positioned himself on the long side, with practical protection via stops just in case. Identifying that key level of 740 for his own stop-loss purposes would have made it even clearer to the investor that the successful support from above that level in October and again in November was increasingly bullish and that he was on the right track.

Knowing where you are in a market cycle is vital to any intelligent market approach. Sure, you have to weigh what the bears are worried about, but so long as you have the proper perspective on what has to happen to prove their case—and what has to happen to prove the alternative—you can proceed wisely. This is so not only at bottoms, but holds true later in the cycle as well, after an extended bull market, when optimism and blind confidence surge to the fore. As the Dow soared above 1,000 in January 1973, all you could read or hear about was how marvelous business was, how rapidly earnings were climbing, and how far up the Dow was going to go. One analyst confidently predicted that the DJI would leap to 1,500 by April. The first January issue of staid Barron's ran a now famous headline, NOT A BEAR AMONG THEM, as it interviewed a panel of experts on what 1973 was to bring. It was to bring, of course, the worst market decline in recent history—and the key to foreseeing it was perspective.

## What Doesn't Go Up Must Come Down

Given ample opportunity to rise during a bull market, the failure of a particular issue to move upward in gear with the averages can be warning enough in itself that something is wrong. To be sure, speculative flings in search of "something that hasn't moved yet" can sometimes sweep up a laggard issue or two, but by and large, the hope is that what did not happen yesterday and today will happen tomorrow, and as the bull surges on without that stock, the reality becomes progressively more urgent: *a stock does not have to go down first to show that it is becoming weak. Merely not going up is, under most bullish circumstances, a sign of trouble brewing.* Once again, it's time to flog your built-in desire to keep on hoping with that old pro's question: Is the stock doing what it was expected to do? And if some churlish voice inside responds, "No, you stubborn ninny," it had better be heeded. You can give a laggard ample chance when perspective tells you it is early in a primary uptrend, but anyone waiting for his stock to catch the last train to success has been seduced by the optimism around him. If anything, *this* is the time to bring stops up close. Indeed, it may even be sensible to sell out on the very next rally. As one professional trader remarked about instances when experience tells you the stop is inevitably going to be set off anyhow, "Why not sell *now* at a higher price?"

*Stops are valuable protection, but they should not be substitutes for making a decision.* Sociologists might call overdependence on stop orders a self-fulfilling prophecy. The order is entered as a prediction that it will eventually be executed. Given that inevitability, the emphasis (subconsciously, at least) is on the waiting, not on what the current market situation suggests should be done. In this guise a stop order can be a method of postponing the inevitable. So when you have a stock that's been acting poorly, the first question you should ask is, Would it be better to sell the stock outright? Furthermore, the situation is also altered when the overall market begins to act tired. Once you start to get negative readings in the various indicators, it is the act of selling outright which provides the protection, while holding on becomes the "just in case."

Yet there are times when that churlish inner voice is apt to argue: "Are you kidding? Sell here, when the market is still terrific?" No matter how much that dreamer tries to persuade you to keep on holding, don't listen. You've simply got to learn to set aside personal entanglements with a stock. One test is: Would you buy it when it is dawdling so drearily? No, you undoubtedly wouldn't, you admit. Would you sell it if you had a huge profit in it already, now that it looks as if a top is forming? Yes, you nod. Well then, sell it. The truth is, *the price you paid for a stock is absolutely irrelevant to where and when it should be sold.* The level you bought it at has to do with a past act only, and brooding about the price (or gloating) cannot be allowed to impinge on analyzing its current behavior. No one else—neither broker, specialist on the Exchange floor, accountant, nor the person who's about to buy the shares from you—cares what price you happened to pay.

And, of course, if the price you paid for a stock has no practical significance, then neither does the price you sold out at, except for your taxes. Grasping this point is the key to dealing with your own emotional involvement, for price is the peg that emotional hats get hung on. That being the case, we must learn to view the market as cold numbers rather than as emotional dollars, just the way the Dow averages are read as abstract points. Mistakes will still be made, but maybe there will be times when you'll be lucky too. Luck will get you the top eighth of a point once in a lifetime; a rational approach will keep you ahead of the game year after year.

No one says it's easy. But you can learn and practice how to avoid making emotionally bred mistakes by using stop orders to control the fear of taking a loss. Observe *before* you buy where the sensible price to place a stop order is so you can make sure you aren't buying after the stock has already run up too far. Then, having bought only when the stop can be placed a reasonable distance away (10 to 15 percent is desirable, using as reference not only the previous point at which the stock found support but important trend lines and the long-term Moving Average as well), and giving yourself the added advantage of the odd fraction when you enter the order, you'll have established objectively determined protection against the possibility of a big loss.

It is not enough to make sure you aren't going to get destroyed by a collapsing stock; the stop order is a strategic device that can tell you when the stock has failed to do what it was expected to do. It's supposed to go up, isn't it? Well, the stop says that if it doesn't go up, but is going down instead, you *must* be a seller. Of course, you should also be alert to raising the stop price whenever a new and sensible level materializes, and remember that it is not a crutch to be leaned on so you don't have to make a decision. You must always consider the possibility of selling out directly, at a higher price, when the stock isn't acting as expected, rather than waiting helplessly for the stock's stop to be set off.

If you can't be a professional trader all day every day, using stop orders in this manner is the practical alternative. It will keep your losses modest and make sure you get sold out of any stock as soon as it starts to turn into a losing position. You can see where this policy can lead: to a portfolio in which the losers are kissed good-bye, so that you are constantly weeding out the worst and holding only stocks that are working well for you. You will have stocks you've purchased so recently that they haven't had a chance to prove themselves yet, perhaps a stock or two that are wobbly (but you know that you'll be out promptly if the situation gets any worse), plus a whole batch of stocks showing gains. In sum, you won't have to worry about losses any more; they'll be taken in stride. Your problem, pleasurable as it is, will be learning how and when to cash in all those paper gains.

# 5

## *When to Sell (I)*

No kind of selling advice can save you from losses if you persistently buy at the top. But if you follow the prescriptions in the previous chapter you should soon have a portfolio studded with gains. That being the case, the next aspect of selling is how to tell when the market gets into trouble. Remember, the adroit use of stop orders is giving you objectively determined downside protection. With that as practical and mental support, let's develop the means to identify market tops so we can do our selling while the stocks are still up there.

The investment community is easily fooled by its slavish dependence on the Dow Jones industrial average as the signifier of what the market is doing. No matter how many other averages are more representative of the behavior of stocks as a whole (or of the stocks *you* own), it is the Dow which one's broker always cites when queried, the Dow which the news announcer reports each night. The Dow is even headlined in a newspaper that prints the chart of another average: *The New York Times* charts the NYSE composite average, while its columns invariably refer to the Dow.

Because the Dow is so widely watched and worshipped, it has its place among analytic tools. As an average, it reports on what a specific blue-chip segment of the market is doing, but beyond that it serves as a standard against which other statistics can be compared in order to determine market timing signals. First, let's examine the creaky Dow itself. It is comprised of only thirty stocks, all of them from large, well-known companies, and yet many important sectors of today's economy are unrepresented. Totally absent, for instance, are the new-era technology stocks such as Xerox and IBM, and the leisure issues like Polaroid and McDonald's. One weighty old-line growth stock has been added (Minnesota Mining), but stocks which have long since withered as bellwethers (e.g., Woolworth) are still included. Others have changed their character completely (for example, Esmark, once known as Swift, the meat packer, is now a conglomerate). Moreover, the Dow is awkwardly balanced, with four metals (now that Anaconda is gone), three chemicals, and three international oils. And that imbalance has been knocked even more awry over the years by many stock splits and other adjustments in capitalization. As a result, certain stocks have gained more weight than others. For example, if Chrysler had doubled in price in early 1975, the influence on the Dow would have been about the same as a mere 10 percent gain in Du Pont.

But for all its flaws, the Dow is representative of a certain core of the market, much the same way as Middle America is representative of "the people." The stocks included in the Dow are powerful companies and popular stocks; their market value adds up to over 20 percent of total NYSE market value. And if they can't move, or do move, it tells you something about that core. So the Dow does represent an average, often narrow, sometimes deceptive, but one that is so widely used that faith in it can be turned to our advantage.

If the Dow and the other market details we'll come to shortly are performing in gear, we know that there's nothing inaccurate about the market trend the Dow is depicting. But when something goes askew and one or more of our other indicators is no longer in phase with the Dow, we term that a divergence. Time after time, throughout market history, such divergences have represented key signals that the trend is about to change. What happens is that while the Dow makes the market look as if the trend remains intact, other forces are shifting under the surface. If you can learn to see the divergence while others are blinded by the Dow's appar-

ent health, you'll be able to take advantage of the forthcoming
change in trend, instead of having it take advantage of you.

## The High/Low Differential

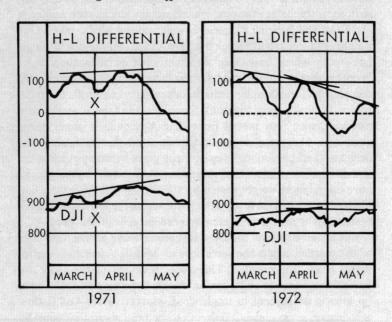

Take a look at this revealing illustration of divergence. It's the
high/low differential compared to the Dow during two three-
month periods of 1971 and 1972. In order to make the comparison
with the Dow over an extended period and to smooth out any
abnormal action on any one day, a 10–day Moving Average is
applied to the statistics. To do it yourself, simply add the number
of new highs for the latest ten trading days; add, similarly, the
number of new lows; and subtract the lows from the highs. The
difference, divided by ten, provides the current reading. The next
day, drop the first day's figures and add in the eleventh day. If you
want to plot it on a graph, it will be on either side of zero, depending on whether new highs or new lows are winning the market
battle. The key signal to watch for is divergence from the Dow, ·

showing that stocks are not behaving in confirmation of the blue-chip average. This can be read without a chart simply by noting the days when the Dow makes new highs; at first, the high/low differential will be in gear, registering new peak numbers too; later, the Dow will make a new high, but you'll notice that the differential has fallen short of its previous peak. You're on your way to spotting a divergence.

In the first chart (March through May 1971) the initial divergence appeared at points X, where the H/L differential sagged considerably more than the Dow did; and then, as illustrated by the slope of the trend lines we've drawn in, you can see that the Dow rose much more sharply. Lastly, the differential fell away much more severely than the Dow. From this chart it was apparent that the overall market was doing much more poorly than the Dow suggested. This divergence was signaling a trend reversal, and indeed, the DJI fell to 790 that autumn. The second chart, showing the same three months of the following year after a rally which had begun from that 790 level, reveals how the DJI was still going up into April while the H/L differential was already drooping badly. Three market rallies, one each month, kept the Dow going up, but there were fewer and fewer new highs, producing a divergence of considerable significance. While the Dow then fell into a prolonged stupor, hindsight shows that the high for most stocks (as measured by an all-inclusive unweighted average) occurred in April 1972.

The rule with the high/low differential (as well as with the other indicators that follow) is that *such divergences are never to be ignored.* As you can see, in both years the alert investor could have caught two successive intermediate-term tops right on the nose by following this one indicator, taking but a few seconds of calculation each day.

How does the high/low differential work? Its signal doesn't appear mysteriously from nowhere at the appropriate time; rather, it has its roots in typical stock-market behavior. During the first months of a bull move, stocks rise, and so does the high/low differential. More and more stocks join in and chalk up new highs while far fewer make new lows as the rally progresses. All is harmony. But no bull market is infinitely expansive. Eventually, purchasing power wanes and profits are sitting there like ripe plums. Now comes the first minor dip. Then latecomers, seeing that prices have backed down from their highs into a more buyable range, pitch in, and their buying sends stocks up again. The averages go to new heights, but there is usually a slackening in the number of new highs as a few stocks are bypassed; perhaps only a few, as in 1971; perhaps more, as in 1972. Along comes another normal dip. Folks are still bullish and toss their money into the pot; the Dow goes to another new high, but again profits are being taken (with fresh sellers using the stock's recent high as a guide to where to get out). More stocks look too high to attract new buying; still others are being sold by those who want to switch to enticing new items on the menu. By this time in the market rally, the ranks of exciting stocks to buy have thinned, and buying is channeled into far fewer issues. This phenomenon makes the market look very exciting, with big gains in individual stocks and new highs in the DJI, but it also leaves a whole batch of stocks sitting it out like wallflowers; suitors are after only the best-looking. What is developing is a classic case of divergence.

The same sort of pattern unfolded in the winter of 1973, when the end of the Vietnam war was thought to be highly bullish for an already rising market. When the DJI crossed 1,000 for the first time in history, the consensus was that 1,500 was not far away. Were you buying then instead of selling? Merely watching the high/low differential would have spared any optimist from the disaster that was to follow. When fewer and fewer stocks make new highs, the odds that your particular stock will make a new high have now mathematically diminished. Thus, divergence from the DJI is telling you that the chances for a further profit have shifted against you, despite the apparently lively market atmosphere. That's the sort of message we want from the indicators, because it is objective, contained in the statistics themselves, rather than emotion-laden. Something has gone wrong, and it is time to sell.

If you want to refine the high/low differential a bit, it's helpful to scan the list of new highs and lows in order to omit, as irrelevant, new listings, when-issued securities (which naturally can make new highs and/or new lows promptly—sometimes both on the same day), and preferred stocks. Remember, too, that the basis for new highs and new lows changes each year in early March; at that time, the newspaper tables drop the past fourteen months' action as a reference and a new basis begins as of January. This shift distorts the chart briefly and should be taken into account.

As an added, and often valuable, exercise, read the lists themselves when making comparisons. See if you can spot the presence of a particular industry group. It would be a sign of collective weakness, for example, if several steel companies were to pop up together on the list of new lows. By the same token, note whether the lists—on either side of the ledger—feature blue chips, or glamours, or cats and dogs, or cyclicals. That will give you a clue as to where the market's substance or softness lies. Further, look for stocks making their debuts on the lists and refer to the day's trading. Was the new high made by an eighth and did the stock then close down for the day? This would be a subtle warning that the rally may have exhausted itself, as compared to spotting that stock on the new high list for the very first time that year, shooting up a couple of points on heavy volume for a genuine upside breakout. Pay particular attention to stocks on the wrong list. If the market is in a steep uptrend, any common stock among the handful of new lows is sounding a solitary alarm which it would pay to heed.

## In Defense of Technical Analysis

The high/low differential is an example of a technical indicator, as opposed to fundamental analysis. Don't be put off by the word "technical"; it is not nearly as magical as the uninitiated seem to think. Its premise is that the market, as a game, yields to the study of risk on a game-theory basis; that is, from the market's action itself. Indeed, it has always seemed to us that fundamentalists, with their scrutiny of corporate balance sheets, cash flows, and economic conditions, have much the harder row to hoe, with far less chance of being right. One of the single most important distinctions to understand about the market is that you are never buying or selling a company; you are bidding and offering in an auction. Prices are not determined by boards of directors, by an illustrious company name, or by an exotic product line, but solely by whatever amount someone is willing to pay or accept for that stock at any given moment. Now, of course, the real person behind those orders may have based his decision on the grounds that the earnings associated with that particular ticker symbol are desirable, to his way of thinking; if so, the market action itself will tell us that someone wants to buy those shares. It's far more important for us to know *what* such buying interest is aiming for, and *how* powerful it is, than to know precisely *why* the buying is forthcoming. The market is the sum of everything that everyone knows about every company—and acts upon. So the buying and selling forces are all there, summarized by the market's own internal data.

That is not to say fundamentals don't have their place; they do, but it's a small place. Fundamentals are useful, for example, when, after already having a sense of the market's future technically, you want to decide which of two companies to buy. Basically, fundamentals are the concern of businesses themselves and economists. They relate to stock trends in the sense that so many moneyed decisions refer to them, but they have virtually no forecasting validity. Indeed, if anything, they forecast in reverse. For instance, fundamentalists revel in positive corporate results, and cannot conceive of selling during a rosy time. Yet the peak of good news is often the time to be selling, as in the winter of 1972–3, when corporations were reporting record earnings results.

If a fundamentalist approach worked on its own, an item such as the price/earnings ratio, cherished by those analysts who must justify their desk space and carpet on the floor, would be an accurate basis for buying and selling. But a glance backward shows how undependable it is: what used to be value at ten times earnings in 1973 became a huge loss in 1974, as the same stock slipped to sell at five or four or even two times earnings. At other times a stock which seems overvalued at thirty times earnings shoots up to one hundred times earnings before fading. Because so much of the market depends on mood, no fundamental analysis has predictive value.

It is, therefore, the fundamentalists who are playing the dangerous game. Their slick hundred-page institutional research report includes an analysis of the plant in Peoria but omits what is actually happening on the Exchange floor. Balance-sheet analysis can be taught, but in the end it is nothing but a game of subjectively trying to decide what price is reasonable for a stock. Is eight times earnings cheap? How about ten times rising earnings? Is twenty times too much? Or is twenty times earnings a bargain since the stock sold at forty times earnings during the last bull market? It's all a guess as to what value the market itself will place on the stock next week and next month. Technicians, on the other hand, want to know such objective data as whether there are more sellers than buyers, how strong each competing side is, and who—professional or odd-lotter—is on which side. Then we know how to play the game with the least risk.

The technical approach is based on whatever the market environment itself discloses: more sellers than buyers, optimistic odd-lotters, fewer stocks making new highs. Behind the various indicators is the consensus of those who presumably know about value, the intricacies of Federal Reserve monetary policy, the prospects of a new product, etc. Collectively they have the strength to exercise an influence on stock prices. In order to profit from their knowledge, they have to act in the marketplace by buying or selling, and whatever conclusions their opinions bring to the stock market become technical evidence. Similarly, other indicators measure the emotional responses of amateurs, who have a track record of being wrong when it counts. Thus, in a manner of speaking, the technical analyst has the benefit of Wall Street's best thinkers at his beck and call and can also determine which advice and activities to stay away from.

## A Contrary Indicator

Lacking interest in such seemingly glamorless work, the big money managers botch up selling, time and time again. The authors once visited the offices of an esteemed mutual-fund management group, a relatively successful one as such organizations go. The offices were perched in one of the city's loftiest aeries, with a stunning view of New York harbor. Dwelling within were a brood of impeccably dressed, well-spoken young men (and the obligatory woman), deciding what and when to buy, and what and when to sell. There was no desk in the chief's room; it would have been too imposing,

or, he would say, old-fashioned. Without a desk, the office meetings
tended to be more relaxed, he believed, and, therefore his subordi-
nates wouldn't be intimidated, would tell him what they really
thought about this stock or that. Such attention to detail obviously
helps a bit, since over the years this fund has performed a trifle
better than most of its counterparts, although, incredibly, not as
well as the public could do on its own.

During the market's steep intermediate-term correction of 1971
—from Dow 950 all the way down to 790—this team of money
managers sold enough stock to put their fund 15 percent in cash.
That doesn't sound like much in the face of sharply falling prices
and accompanying losses, but it was twice as good as the mutual-
fund industry's average. To be that much more alert involves some
skill, but very little of it stemmed from selling techniques. Like
virtually all big institutional investors, this fund's style is heavily
oriented toward optimism. Selling is an annoying, even alien, concept, used to take a profit and hence tolerable, or to admit that the
stock picked was a disaster and hence anathema.

Selling is a thoroughly lackluster act in contrast to the romance
of stock selection, with its exciting stories and spylike intrigue.
Very few institutional salesmen ever try to talk to mutual funds
about selling a block of stock, even though the commissions should
be roughly the same and there is a chance to earn another commission with a new buying recommendation. Indeed, so deeply in-
grained is the predilection toward buying that the manager of this
fund once remarked that, if he were assured that the market was
about to go down, the only effect it would have on his decisions
would be to cause him to buy "a little slower."

This fund's modest ability to outperform its rivals can be attributed in large part to the formal setting of upside objectives, the
price they feel each selection should achieve if it works out perfectly. So if all goes well they manage to cash in at a robust profit.
Other institutions don't indulge even in this rudimentary discipline. As a result, they can often ride stocks up, but then they ride
them all the way back down again. Funds tend to stay relatively
fully invested regardless of the market climate, usually selling out
to conceal their blunders. That is, they'll liquidate a disaster (the
Levitz they bought at 47, when it has fallen back to 9) to keep it

out of print at quarterly reporting time, so that the huge loss is buried, sometimes without any notice that they'd been in and out at all! For the most part, they rely on their belief in the inexorable upward thrust of the economy to enhance their assets.

But this upward thrust has not been inexorable over the past decade, and most funds have been unable to get ahead of the game. Their mediocre performances, for which the money managers reap huge salaries, can be attributed to the same trouble that besets the ordinary investor: being human beneath his modish suit, the big-money manager is also caught up in emotions and prejudices. He buys heavily near the top of a rally because that's when everything is stimulating and seemingly safe; at bottoms, when it seems the decline will never end and his job is in jeopardy, he finally panics and dumps blocks blindly into the market.

From the predictability of foibles such as this come valuable stock-market timing devices. The one which results from the circumstances just described is called the mutual-fund cash ratio, a measurement of the percentage of cash to total assets as announced once a month by virtually all mutual funds. Mutual-fund figures are released, usually around the twentieth of each month, and published in *The Wall Street Journal*. (Similar information from other institutions like banks and pension funds is unavailable, hence the concentration on what the mutual funds are doing.) As shown on the chart, the low points of available cash come at or very close to market tops; funds buy up, of course, just when they should be busy selling. A reading in this indicator of under 6 percent has consistently been a reliable clue to a forthcoming major market top.

Even after the market has convincingly plunged, fund managers do what seems to be an absurdly small amount of selling. Combined with the shrinkage in their assets due to a falling market, a little selling produces a relatively high reading at bottoms: ranging from 12 percent, as in 1970, to as much as nearly 16 percent in 1974. The funds will have far more than four fifths of their holdings in equities during an entire market collapse. That's not a good advertisement for professional management, but for our purposes, it's a usefully consistent timing signal based on ineptitude.

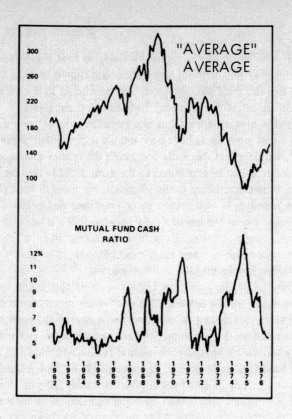

## The Advance/Decline Line

Many of our most valuable indicators are available in regular newspapers every day. In the statistical section you can find a record of highs and lows, as well as the number of stocks advancing, declining, and remaining unchanged in each day's trading. From these figures you can construct two different indicators: the advance/decline line and the advance/decline ratio. The advance/decline line is the most important of all the divergence indicators. This line is a simple running total of the net difference each day between advances and declines (ignoring the unchanged stocks). Like the high/low differential, this indicator is in gear with the averages during healthy markets, when the broad list of stocks is actually doing what the Dow claims, but will diverge when the trend is shaping up for a change. Here again, as the advance starts to falter, more and more issues will lag, fewer and fewer advancing on days when the Dow is up. Brokers around the country will hear bewildered customers complaining, "The Dow's up, so why aren't my stocks going up too?" The natural sequence of shifts from a broad, robust rally to a narrower, tired rally is available for anyone to see.

This indicator, too, will take only a few seconds of your time each day (a minute, perhaps, if you do all five days each weekend as homework). You can start at any time with any arbitrary number and then merely add or subtract the day's net difference, keeping a running total. Here's the way this indicator acted in the early seventies, as illustrated on the accompanying chart.

We've drawn a trend line for March 1971, matched against the

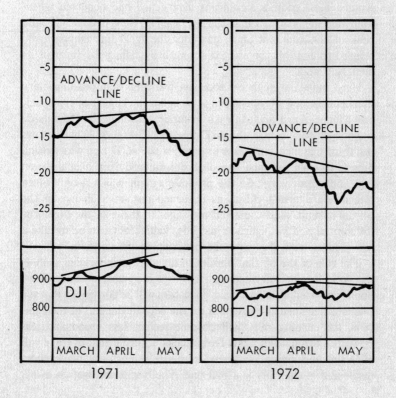

Dow's action. You can see the divergence: the Dow shot up to higher highs while the advance/decline line held fairly steady. The divergence warned of an impending change in the intermediate-term trend. The reason it was not a particularly drastic divergence was that this intermediate-term top came relatively early in a primary bull market. But now note how extreme the divergence was one year later, as another intermediate-term top rolled around. The A/D line was totally incapable of reaching its March peak even though the Dow was then busting on ahead. By the end of April 1972, the A/D line had smashed below its March reaction low and was heading down. The Dow at that time was still well above its March lows, leading those who watched only the blue-chip average to believe that just another little correction was in progress. Instead, it was the beginning of the end. A few months before, in August 1971, another significant divergence had occurred when, following the Nixon "Phase I" rally, the DJI exceeded its July rally peak of 905 and shot up to 925. But the A/D line emphatically refused to confirm the alleged strength by falling far short of its own July peak.

Here, indeed, were three successive warnings of impending sharp market declines: March–April 1971, again in August of that year, and March–April 1972. In each instance, although the Dow made the market look secure, the A/D line was diverging. What's more, the third instance came at a time when the A/D line was writing finis to its own rise, just ahead of an immense drop over the next two and a half years. So the pronouncement was not only of an intermediate-term top but, as it turned out, of a change in the primary trend. Add these sell messages to those of the high/low differential and you can see just how valuable it can be to take a few seconds each day with the newspaper and a pencil.

The rule of thumb that applies to divergence indicators such as the A/D line is: Intermediate-term tops are made on bad rallies. Sooner or later, although many investors will be convinced that it's just another normal correction on the way to the end of the rainbow, the ensuing rally will become feeble, less broad and less powerful. Strength in a few Dow stocks uplifting that average will hide the underlying weakness from the public, but divergences disclose that the rally is a bad one. The blight will not go away, will not be erased and replaced with a healthy rally again, not until the price is paid. Bear in mind that it takes time for the market to roll over. With a little experience in spotting divergences, you'll probably be early as you see the first signs of deterioration, but that can be turned to your advantage since these leading signals will give you plenty of chances to sell *into* the remaining strength of the rally (remember that the best time to sell is when others are clamoring for what you have), instead of meekly waiting until the weakness sets in. Such signals, therefore, get you out right near the top, at the best possible prices.

## The Advance/Decline Ratio

Try to convince those who rely on fundamentals that technical analysis is effective and the reply often is that it didn't work on such and such a day. Because it seems so magical to them, they expect it to be perfect, and since it is not, they reject it out of hand. And yet they use much of its lingo, particularly the terms overbought and oversold. (The word "over" implies, in both instances, that the move has gone so far so furiously that it has passed normal bounds and is due for a retrenchment to where it supposedly belongs.) These words are commonly abused by those who write about the market without knowing very much; as facile descriptions, they are used to explain any sort of unaccounted-for movement, or to justify what the writers hope to do. That is, if they've missed the rally and need to see a dip so they can buy, they'll call the market overbought to justify why they are waiting instead of buying. Thus they apply these phrases subjectively rather than objectively, often much sooner than they should. Without being perfect—for, indeed, what is overbought in one type of climate is not necessarily overbought in another—there is a way, via technical analysis, to come up with a specific measurement of these two concepts.

One can use the advance/decline ratio, otherwise known as the "Overbought-Oversold Oscillator." There are a few different ways to track this indicator. We use the identical figure already computed for the advance/decline line—the net difference between advances and declines for the day—but instead of a running total (as for the line), we want a 10-day Moving Average. Simply add up the latest ten entries and divide by ten for the ratio. An alternative method is to take a 10-day Moving Average of advances and divide it by a 10-day Moving Average of declines, plotting the result above or below the parity of 1.0. (Thus, if the Moving Average of advances were, say, 500, and of declines 250, the plot would be at 2.0. If vice versa, the plot would be at 0.5.) The chart, in either method, would come out looking approximately the same.

The advance/decline ratio is not a divergence indicator, as were the A/D line and the H/L differential. It is, however, a valuable instrument for timing more precisely the decision that the divergence indicators suggest should be taken. Suppose the alarm has been sounded. However, the day-to-day trend has been upward and you want to stick with your stocks as long as the rally can last. When, exactly, do you sell? When the market becomes overbought and is due to head downward, and that's what this ratio can measure. As soon as it reaches an objective overbought reading, you know the rally is nearing exhaustion and that a correction is forthcoming within a few days.

But nothing in the market is simple. The advance/decline ratio has certain peculiarities you should know about. First, in the early stages of a rally it can shoot up quite high. You are dropping the dreadful minus days of the last phase of the decline and substituting the plus days of a new rally. Hence, if the rally is vigorous enough to produce extra big pluses, you can quickly get a powerful reading on the ratio; it will look overbought and perhaps it is, but ignore it. The averages may dip for a few days, but so what? A whopping reading right after an intermediate-term decline (or major bear trend) is consistently a clue that the rally is just beginning and that it is going to be powerful. Hang on to your stocks; do *not* sell. This sort of action recently took place three times: first, in December 1971, second in October 1974 (which was the actual bear-market bottom), and even more powerfully in January 1975 (the start of what was then a record-breaking upswing). But then euphoria ceases; reality returns as the rally continues. In 1972, as April became May, the divergence indicators discussed earlier would have told you it had gotten late in the upswing and you should have prepared to sell. You want to catch the days when the rally has taken the ratio to just about as overbought as it is likely to get. You don't want to sell too soon, but you are on borrowed time.

Typically, each succeeding overbought peak fails to exceed that of the rally preceding it, so what you want to know is not some absolute level but rather the day—on the 10-day Moving Average —when the market is as overbought as it can get that late in the uptrend. Our personal refinement, therefore, is to evaluate the actual sequence of numbers already jotted down; by observing the magnitude of the numbers which are going to be dropped from the Moving Average, you can estimate in advance just about which day is going to roll the ratio over. Take the May 1972 overbought reading as an example, since it was an important time to get out of stocks. On May 18, a net difference of +466 replaces the eleventh prior day's −84; on May 19, +511 replaces +131; on May 22, +177 replaces −530; and on May 23, even though there are 113 more declines than advances, the number being dropped from the Moving Average that day is a whopping −1,200. The ratio has continued to advance even though the rally has been faltering. And now, counting backward, you can see in your notebook that the next figures to be dropped are +492, +412, and +573. There's no way for a faltering rally to surpass such big positive numbers and keep the oscillator moving upward. So you can quickly come to a useful conclusion: (1) the market is about as overbought as it's going to be; and (2) considering the other negative signals around, you'd better sell right then and there. In this particular instance, the DJI advanced three more days, providing ample time to sell under the guise of an advancing market, thus getting you the best possible prices left, far better than waiting to dump until the market has started down. What's more, if you happen to miss an overbought chance to get out, you at least know the next time the market has become oversold, so that you won't panic near the end of a selling wave but can wait for the next fluctuation back up.

However, do not be misled into thinking that a steeply oversold reading means that the worst is over and it is now safe to hold. Just as a huge overbought reading on an initial rally means there is much more upside action to come, a drop to an extremely oversold level, coming on an initial slide, is quite negative; you should sell without fail on the next minor rebound. An example of this behavior came in October 1976, when the Dow finally broke below its prolonged narrow trading range. The oversold reading got just about as low as it had been in over five years, signaling not that the decline was over but that it had begun in a dramatically forceful manner. Oversold readings on this indicator must literally dwindle on each succeeding move down before you can even begin to think of returning to the long side of the market.

In short, the advance/decline ratio helps determine when to act, provided you are already alert to the need. And it will let you time the lesser swings within the intermediate trend. Put more colorfully, its prime function in trading the intermediate term is to pinpoint the wave that is going to break on the shoals already detected by divergence.

## The Odd-Lot Index and Odd-Lot Short-Sales Ratio

While you are making the above quick calculations from the daily newspaper, you will find a couple of others helpful also. These are the twin indicators based on transactions involving less than 100 shares at a clip (odd lots). The odd-lotters have become a diminishing factor in the marketplace since their transactions have shrunk from nearly 20 percent of total trading in the 1930's to less than 1 percent in the 1970's. (With at least one brokerage house doing some of its own odd-lot business in-house, instead of taking it to the Exchange, reported amounts are even smaller.) But we are not interested in quantity so much as in quality. Amateur thinking is what we can track here; knowing what the odd-lotter is up to tells us about the psychology of the market. Just how does the public feel about the trend?

The two odd-lot indicators constructed from the reported daily figures are the odd-lot index and the odd-lot short-sales ratio. For the first, divide the total amount of selling (including short selling) by the amount of buying. The quotient represents the degree to which the odd-lotter is buying or selling on a given day. To smooth out any excesses, these figures are tracked as a 10-day Moving Average. Interestingly, although the small investor has often been maligned as foolish, naïve, and greedy, the odd-lotter has a much better track record at important turns than the big shots who run mutual funds. An extreme shift to heavy odd-lot buying has regularly appeared at major bottoms, while a lot of selling in recent years has often turned out to be a good idea in the long run. Contrary to what most sophisticated customer's men might preach, you should not, therefore, automatically and simplemindedly take a stance opposed to that of the odd-lotters.

Our concern, instead, is to detect when the odd-lotter's behavior changes from normal patterns or from the trend he's been following. Historically, and unfortunately, the odd-lotter also makes particular blunders, one of which is that he sells into rallies much too soon, welcoming with overeagerness the chance to get out of those stocks he's suffered with through the preceding decline. (Of course, these are collective statistics; it's not likely that the sellers on rallies are the identical ones who buy on dips.) Given this normal pattern, what we want to be alert for is any deviation.

One such deviation occurred during October and November of 1970. The market was correcting during that stretch, a phase when the normal tendency of odd-lotters is to pick up stocks as they decline, thereby creating a relatively lower odd-lot index reading. It doesn't matter what the number, so long as it can be compared to previous readings as either normal or abnormal for the circumstances. In this instance, as the Dow dipped there was an astounding increase in selling, so much so that the ratio of selling over buying reached what was then a record level of more than 2 to 1. That deviation proclaimed "Don't sell your stocks: there's a rally coming," because the emotional public refused to believe in the new bull market.

Later, in a rally, one may witness the opposite type of deviation, and as the rally takes hold, the small investor believes in it more and more: odd-lot selling, which is normal for a rally, declines, and a rise in buying appears. That is, instead of the typical action of selling into a rising market, a shift takes place; that shift reports that the odd-lotter has by that time become emotionally convinced that prices are going up, up, up. The index readings begin to drop in comparison to a still-rising Dow. They don't have to drop to any absolute level; they just have to reveal the shift in sentiment. Index readings that are low while the Dow is still going up are a clear signal of growing optimism that announces it is time to take the opposite course and do some selling.

In sum, when odd-lotters do what they normally do—buy on dips, sell into rallies—they are often right. Your concern comes when market action affects their psychology. If they begin to believe in a rally, collectively they will do less selling and more buying, and that shift is your signal to sell.

The odd-lot short-sales ratio is the other calculation done with the reported odd-lot figures. To obtain it, divide odd-lot short sales by total odd-lot sales. Here again, a 10-day Moving Average is

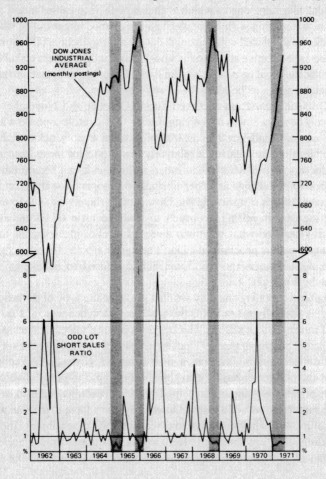

applied. This indicator became highly popular because it was so accurate in calling the major bottoms in 1962, 1966, and 1970. Those signals are apparent on the accompanying chart, with readings of over 6 percent each time indicating that right near the bottom many odd-lotters were finally convinced that selling short was the path to profits. However, the problem is that when an indicator works so well that a lot of amateur technicians start staring at it in unison, the market is apt to throw a curve. In 1974, while everyone was waiting for 6 percent again, the highest reading was only about 4 percent, certainly enough of a display of misplaced pessimism (and a considerable shift from prior sentiment), even if it wasn't the magic number.

For selling purposes, though, we are primarily concerned with the ratio's ability to signal important top areas. (Naturally, you don't want to sell when readings are uncommonly high.) As indicated on the accompanying chart (shaded areas), low readings measure non-action, the extent to which odd-lotters become so straightforwardly optimistic that they do virtually no short selling at all. Typically, a prolonged stretch of readings under 1 percent (sometimes for as much as five months), capped by even more intensive non-action of under 5 percent for several weeks (representing the shift toward even more optimism), will identify a serious warning to sell. It doesn't say when, but its caution signal is well worth heeding.

## Believing the Indicators

The foregoing are simple indicators to keep, requiring very little time each day. It is better to keep your own statistics and charts, rather than relying on outside services, because when the answer is right there at the tip of your pencil you are a lot more likely to see it and believe in it. Very few take the time. The typical shareholder is busy making excuses: the Dow is up, so his stocks will surely follow sooner or later, or, the Dow is down but it will soon rise again in some inexorable fashion. But the astute seller must learn to follow his own calculations rather than the glowing forecasts of experts or the deceptive action of the Dow. Doing your own calculations and keeping your own charts will actively provide the objective answer to "What's the market doing?" To be sure, there will still be the burden of making a decision and acting on it. Warnings are easily dismissed as being too vague, imperfect, premature, or, even, too ominous to accept. But in the stock market an indicator that cries wolf on occasion is better than a system that remains silent while the lambs are being slaughtered.

These indicators are not the concoctions of alchemists; they develop from the market's internal action and illustrate what is going on beneath the headlines. They don't tell you why, but they do demonstrate what, and that "what" is useful enough. We must also add that it is possible to extract from such a plethora of statistics umpteen different indicators, or to twist simple measurements into pretzel-like devices. We know one inventor who has decided, he tells us, that a 9-day Moving Average works better than a 10-day, and to this we respond "Rubbish." A ten-day calculation makes the arithmetic vastly easier; and nothing is so precise that the difference of a day will matter; if nine days works sometimes, so will eleven or twelve at other times. Similarly, there are those who place absolute credence in minuscule differences; if the A/D line makes a new high by +2, they are ecstatic at the signal. To us it is mathematically trivial; we want decisive readings. And then there are others who see what the indicators are saying, but when they don't want to believe the message, they rationalize, finding six other obscure indicators that say otherwise, or preferring a rumor that explains the undesired reading. It's hard work to refuse to believe simple indicators. For our money, when you see that everything is in gear, according to your statistics and charts, you can relax; as soon as divergences begin to appear, move to the edge of your chair. You are seeing the first warnings, well ahead of top time.

But don't expect them to shout off the page at an exact moment. They are guidelines, tools to help you grasp objectively what is going on in the marketplace. They may not be perfect (premature, a bit wishy-washy, even inaccurate once in a while), but that's why you want to watch all of them rather than just one. Then you can see what the weight of the evidence suggests. This is important to understand because other sources will be trying to push you in other directions. The headlines and write-ups will be surface summations of what the Dow and a few fancy stocks are doing. Your own broker will be phoning you with (what else can he say?) a mass of tales. You need protection against the onslaught of such subjective and highly emotional sources. By delineating tendencies and revealing shifts, technical indicators measure with objectivity what the market's underlying condition is; then it's up to you to decide what steps to take. When it comes to potential tops, the indicators serve to alert investors to impending trouble, like a medical exam that reveals too much cholesterol, high blood pressure, or other danger signs. Sure, the patient may survive, may just have a setback and recover, may even last longer than the prognosis suggests, but the odds are against him unless protective measures are taken promptly. So too in the market: symptoms warn, "Better safe than sorry."

The financially healthy investor, of course, doesn't wait for the indicators to jump up and grab him by the lapels, any more than the person careful about his physical well-being waits for unbearable pain to begin. There are always questions to be asked about the market—suspicious, cynical, paranoid questions, if you will—and the answers just might give you a jump on others. "Why did Westinghouse go down on a day the DJI rallied 10 points?" "Why is the list of new lows full of machine-tool stocks when everyone says cyclical situations are the place to be?" "Why did all those glamour stocks close at their lows for the day, even though they were up?" Such questions not only help keep you alert, they provide you with a sense of whether the market is all it is supposed to be. The indicators themselves, dealing with specific data and specific sectors, are ways to objectify such questions.

It's taken you far longer to read this than it will to keep up with these statistics each day. We repeat: Don't rely on someone else to do what will take you so little time. You'll find you get a much better feel for what is actually happening by keeping your own hand in. This chapter has presented two divergence indicators (the advance/decline line and the high/low differential), one timing guide (the advance/decline ratio), and two sentiment indicators (both odd-lot aspects), each based on statistics to be found in the

# 6

## *When to Sell (II)*

With indicators, as with love making, there is one essential goal;
a few interesting variations reliably achieve this goal, while a host
of others work only sporadically. Only the obsessed try them all.
At a meeting of the Wall Street Technicians Society a few years
ago, a brokerage-house analyst proudly described ninety-seven different market indicators that he maintained on a regular basis.
That gave him the appearance of being an expert's expert, but
finally someone asked: "What are those indicators telling us now?"
And the analyst was forced to admit: "I'm not sure." Some were
bullish, others were unfavorable, still others were meandering
around saying nothing. So how could he decide?

Obviously, one can overload the circuitry. There is no good
purpose served by trying to track so many indicators that the
ultimate answer is obscured. And not only can so much lead to too
little; some individual indicators yield data that is too inconsistent
to rely on; for example, we have never been able to find a consistent
pattern in what is known as "ticker-tape volume," which supposedly measures whether money is flowing into or out of a stock.
Through the years, a handful of measurements have proved themselves consistent enough and perceptive enough to be included in
any general technical approach to timing. One monthly (the mutu-

al-fund cash ratio) and five daily items (the high/low differential, the advance/decline line, the advance/decline ratio, the odd-lot index, and the odd-lot short-sales ratio) were detailed in the previous chapter. They should keep you alert to what is going on regarding the intermediate-term trend. But you should add a few other special weapons to your arsenal to further perfect your timing.

## An "Average" Average

First, you can use a good, unweighted, all-inclusive average of your own. The Dow, as we've already pointed out, represents only thirty blue-chip, old-line stocks, many out of fashion, others mummified. The DJI, like a chicken with its head cut off, can go on running wild long after the market has stopped rising, as the grand finale top of January 1973 exemplifies. The other widely used averages are the New York Stock Exchange composite and the Standard & Poor's 500. Both of these are heavily weighted in favor of capitalization, which causes its own form of distortion. Like the DJI, they have their own perspectives, and it is always useful to take a gander at how they look. But something without such distortions is also needed.

Otherwise, this is what happens: the S & P 500-stock composite and the NYSE composite (which includes all of its common-stock listings) are calculated by multiplying a stock's price by the number of shares outstanding. Thus, large capitalized companies exert an extra influence on the averages. As it happens, those are the stocks institutions favor because they can be readily bought and sold in large quantities. (Many hot-shot institutions were badly burned in 1968 because they held shares of small companies whose fancy names might have sounded impressive when they were bought, but when the institutions wanted to sell, there was no one to sell to.) Because they concentrate in such issues, their buying has a self-fulfilling prophecy about it, causing the averages to go up. In early 1973, the market looked much better than it actually was, due to strong gains in stocks favored by institutions. Previously, through the first half of 1972, when almost everyone was reaping losses in their portfolios but couldn't understand why, the S & P composite was up some 5 percent, and that gain was accounted for by a mere fifteen stocks! The other 485 stocks were actually down during that time span. The way to avoid being deceived by this sort of flimflammery is to have your own market average. Here's how.

Several brokerage offices use the Quotron desk-top interrogation machine (rather than the more frequently seen Bunker Ramo unit or the Ultronic device). The computer-fed Quotron, wired up for every issue traded on the NYSE and ASE, provides the expected data, as well as the collective percentage price change for all common stocks on each exchange at any given moment, as it relates to the previous day's close. A reading of, say, +.50 means that the average percentage change from the day before at that moment for all common stocks is a gain of one half of 1 percent. That is an average percent change for the average stock. Unlike the weighted averages or the Dow industrial, it tells you what the entire list is actually doing. As a simple illustration, if the DJI were up 10 points from the 800 level to 810, for a gain of 1.25 percent, and the Quotron reported the gain for the average stock as being +.50, you'd know the Dow had far outperformed the rest of the market. When that happens in the course of a rally, it can be a sign of serious deterioration. Divergence has reared its dangerous head again, and it is time to start selling.

Because watching an "average" average is so important, you should keep one yourself. To begin, simply start at an arbitrary base number (100 is easiest) and multiply it by the closing percentage change. A gain is then added to the base number; a loss is subtracted. Do this each day, by multiplying the preceding day's result by the new percentage change, and you've got a computer-based, totally unweighted, all-inclusive average. This "average" average is what your own portfolio should be compared to for relative performance, because it is as close to a true picture of the overall market trend as you can get.

What's more, you don't have to go combing brokerage houses in search of the suitable machine. *Barron's* conveniently carries this information each week in the statistical pages, under the headings "QCHA" for the NYSE and "QACH" for the Amex. The calculating can be done once a week in just a few minutes, giving you an average all your own. Obviously, the single closing figure will produce a simple line chart, rather than the conventional bar chart, with its high, low, and closing. Because many days will end with a small net change from the previous day's closing, we suggest using a large chart with intervals of perhaps as little as .1 percent for each line. That should make it easier to read precisely where key highs and lows occurred in the past. You can refine this even more by also posting the information on a point-and-figure chart, a technique which has no time scale. An entry is made only when a given dimension of change (we suggest .25) occurs. Whereas you post an entry each day for the line chart, the point-and-figure works this way: assume the "average" is at 100; if and when you get a reading of 100.25, you would place an X in the appropriate box; at 100.50 another X would be posted directly above, and so on, as long as the trend continued in that same direction. If and when the market declined, there would be no entry until it actually fell to the next lower level (for example, from 100.50 down to 100.25 or less), at which time you would move over one column and insert an X at the 100.25 level. This type of chart helps to depict supply-and-demand areas in clear fashion.

It is also a good idea to keep a Moving Average of your "average" average. Moving Averages, as noted previously, smooth out the distortions that can occur in a day-to-day or week-to-week chart. A 10-day M.A. is helpful for many indicators; in this instance, a much longer time span is used to smooth out the picture of the primary market trend. Traditionally, a 200-day Moving Average is used, but a 30- or 40-week, with the change made only once a week as of Friday's close, is nearly as good and need involve only one calculation, instead of five each week. Plot the Moving Average on the same chart as the "average" average to see how the trend is shaping up and to get signals. Most of us tend to be impatient and to make too much of minor jiggles; the M.A. gives us some of that ever-valuable perspective. Not until the arc of a Moving Average completely rolls over and starts down *and* is intersected by the daily average's action, can it be considered definitive that a major change in trend is underway. You shouldn't wait until this happens in the "average" average to start selling some stocks, because it is possible that certain issues should have been liquidated long before. As a buying clue, however, it is an excellent idea to refrain from buying until the bottom is established in such a manner, arcing under and heading up. But when, after a bull market has been holding strong, the Moving Average finally arcs over and is penetrated by the "average" average itself, you might as well kiss your remaining holdings goodbye. You can't argue with such a picture.

Two examples of how to apply this method to stock-market reality are shown on the following charts. In chart A, a 30-week Moving Average has been plotted along with an "average" average. Notice in the upper-left-hand corner that, at the start of 1969, both warnings happened almost simultaneously: the "average" average broke through the Moving Average and the M.A. itself arced over and headed down. This came virtually at the top of the market for all common stocks. By watching this chart develop, you might have stayed completely out of stocks until the fall of 1970, when the reverse took place.

CHART A

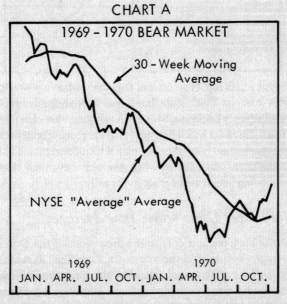

A similar top signal is shown in chart B (page 118). The breakdown through the Moving Average line occurred in January 1973, just after the Dow had made its all-time high over 1,000. With the M.A. heading downward, it was a signal to sell all your stocks at

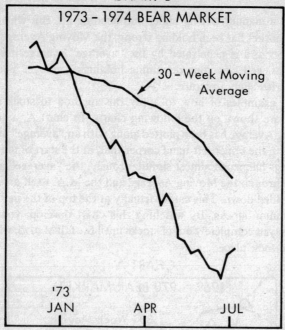

## CHART B
### 1973 – 1974 BEAR MARKET

30 – Week Moving Average

'73
JAN        APR        JUL

virtually the exact top. Now look at July 1973, when a powerful rally was about to begin. You'll note that it was then a huge distance away from a still sharply declining Moving Average, a sure clue to beware of the bear. The chart was telling you that there was room for a rally, but it was far too early to expect a major trend reversal. That came over a year later, when the Moving Average was much closer and capable of being penetrated earlier in the rally.

## Indicators Using Other Dow Averages

So now you have one antidote to the deceptions of the Dow industrial average. You should use your own "average" average for its own signals (as on the two charts), but also as a comparison to the DJI to ascertain meaningful divergences. But there is another average that also can be used effectively in this regard, the Dow utility average. Because the DJU represents a sector of the market peculiarly influenced by such factors as money rates and industrial activity, it is a technically useful barometer, even for those who are such swingers that they'd never buy a staid utility stock. Many times the DJU has led the rest of the market, topping out and heading down (or bottoming out and heading up) before the DJI. It's a simple matter to track this indicator since it and the DJI are charted one under the other in *The Wall Street Journal* every day. When this average, which usually leads the rest, refuses to participate in a rally, not just for one or two days, but for a couple of weeks or more, it is a warning of potential trouble for the rest of the list. Once again, divergence is the signifier.

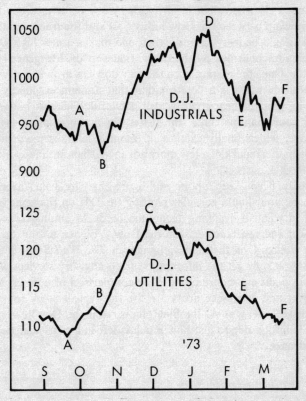

The accompanying chart shows the leading nature of the DJU at work. Note how, at the same point in 1972 (A–B), the rising DJU vs. the falling DJI forecast a big rally for the market, with the industrials then shooting up over 1,000. But, in early 1973, the DJU warned that something was seriously amiss. It kept sliding in conspicuously divergent fashion while the DJI was bouncing up (C–D), and it added its own sell signal to the many that were then forecasting disaster. As if that weren't enough, when the DJI was struggling to firm up in March 1973 and the "bargain" hunters were already at work, the DJU stubbornly refused to go along, producing a radical divergence at E–F.

One other "divergent" use of the averages is the venerable Dow theory. No need to go into detail, for the subject has been amply discussed elsewhere, but briefly, this theory revolves around the relationship between the Dow industrials and the transportations. Both should be in sync, and, when one makes a new high which remains unconfirmed by the other, that sort of divergence spells trouble. Once the market is on the way down, a drop to a new low by both averages is a confirmation that announces, loudly and clearly, that the bear trend is still powerful. The closer together such confirmations come, the better. In our opinion, a lagging average, which finally catches up months later, is much like a mathematical quirk of a few more advances than declines—indecisive, feeble, suspect.

Lastly, if you keep a point-and-figure chart for your "average" average, you should consider plotting the DJI on the same basis. This alternative graphing technique tends to emphasize where support and resistance exist in the Dow. You can do this quickly each weekend via the hourly changes in *The Wall Street Journal* or *Barron's*, or get the information from advisory services which supply point-and-figure pictures. A comparison of how far away support and resistance areas are for the typical stock (on your "average" average) vs. the blue chipper (on the Dow) can often be a helpful guide to just how much is left in a particular decline or advance.

## Volume Indicators

Along with the averages, every newspaper reports daily volume (the number of shares traded in a day). Typically, the total is printed in bar form underneath a chart of the averages. Tradition has it that increasing volume on rallies and decreasing volume on declines are signs of a healthy situation, but often that is not the case. Sluggish markets can be deadly, and the wildest volume fling of a rally may occur right at the top. Don't accept conventional wisdom unquestioningly; consider the significance behind the statistics. To be favorable, volume must continue to expand over the previous rally, and not merely in comparison with a low-keyed correction. Peak volume is usually seen around the middle of an intermediate-term upmove. Some time after that point, rallying volume will fail to exceed the pace of the previous short-term spurt, even though the Dow may have gone to a new high. This is often an early warning sign of a tiring market. If plotted against the averages on a chart, this, too, would appear as a divergence.

On the upside, beware of incredibly busy tapes. They are often a sign that the professionals are distributing shares to less savvy buyers. Heaps of 100- and 200-share transactions can cause the ticker to run quite late. When the tape reads REPEAT PRICES DELETED, it is a sign that the rally is over for the time being; then professional traders get busy taking profits. An even more extreme FLASH PRICES on the tape announces that the trend, at least for the short term, is about to reverse.

Don't be lulled by slack volume on the downside, either. That is fine to see in the early stages of a new bull market, since it indicates that there is very little pressure during a "normal" correction. But later on, the significance is different. One of the most valid of all Wall Street adages is a must for you to remember: "It takes buying to put stocks up, but they can fall of their own weight." In other words, in bullish climates, buyers have to reach up and take stock at offering prices, causing the price to rise. But in a bear market, particularly early in the trend, a 100-share order can easily knock the price down, whereas 100 shares bought may not lift it at all. Sometimes, routine and desultory selling, which is often dismissed by the optimists, can become damaging in the absence of active buyers. Those who have their eyes on the already-dead bull (whether a primary or intermediate trend), expecting it to leap up again, are deceived by such low volume, yet, as it persists, more and more buyers hold back, more and more holders turn into sellers, the prices droop, then erode, and then break. It is only at that point, in the later stages of the decline when the earlier optimists begin to panic, that heavier volume finally comes out. Once other indicators say the market is in trouble, low volume in the early stages of a dip can be far more bearish than is commonly believed.

Beyond this overall level of activity, you'll occasionally want to know what the volume was during a particular portion of the trading day. A roller-coaster game may have produced sharp intraday moves in both directions. Volume may be heavy, but from the overall published total you can't tell whether it rushed in during the rally, or if the rally was feeble and selling poured in on the retreat. For this, newspapers like *The Wall Street Journal* print a breakdown of activity by hours, which can be matched against the hourly breakdown of the averages.

Certain conscientious financial pages also separate the volume for advancing stocks and the volume for those stocks which ended the day on the minus side, and that can frequently be a helpful distinction. Indeed, it provided the best clue of all to the May 1970 bottom for traders. The DJI, continuing a collapse, closed on a Tuesday evening off 10 points to yet another new bear-market low. But a glance at this statistic showed that upside volume equaled downside, surprisingly enough, announcing that buyers were far busier than anyone suspected. While this was a spectacular "bottom" incident, the countersurge in volume appears far more frequently and usefully in top areas and provides evidence of a rotting market. The averages may be going up, but when you track volume, you'll see too much downside trading in evidence. This indication that a lot of selling is taking place under cover of the rally should not be ignored, for it is another instance where divergence tells the tale. There are those who convert such volume statistics into an indicator by setting up a ratio between upside and downside volume, or between those two factors and advances and declines. We've always felt it was sufficient merely to study the statistics quickly, checking to see if upside volume was in proportion to the number of stocks advancing, while downside related to declining stocks. It's easy to see if something is wrong or not, and if there is, with more downside activity than a "match" would suggest there should be, it is a solid sell signal.

Lastly, we want you to note the relationship each week of the

Big Board to Amex activity. This is called the speculation index. When speculation runs rampant in the late stages of a bull market, Amex volume will, in theory, shoot up disproportionately, since that Exchange contains a large number of unproven high-risk stocks. Extra-high ratios (over 45 percent of NYSE volume) have marked prior top areas—except in 1972, when there was little Amex speculation, probably because the public was already ruined from the losses they had taken after the 1968 speculative binge. Keep an eye on this relationship. It can be a useful safeguard to curb any potential enthusiasm on your part if that game starts up again. And remember that this is strictly a *top* indicator. Only amateurs try to read something into a low ratio.

## Indicators Based on the Most-Active List

Another item related to volume is the most-active list, which is also published daily. First, of course, you should scan the names, to determine the quality of those in the forefront and the degree to which they've experienced price changes. Healthy markets must be supported by companies of substance. When the most-active list becomes speculative and low-priced, watch out! Furthermore, a day that sees minimal advances—eighths and quarters—while the averages are up considerably is a sign of impending trouble. Taking this a step further, a day the Dow goes up in continuance of a rally while the most-active list shows more stocks on the downside at the close is often a sign of an exhausted upswing. Traders can expect trouble the very next day.

If you take that short-term factor into account over a longer period of time, you can create a miniature advance/decline line from the most-active list. The principle is the same. Good rallies find the stocks most in demand charging up right along. Toward the end, though, you'll find deterioration: the Dow up ten points, but the most-active list showing seven up, six down, and two unchanged. When that persists for a couple of weeks, you're getting a reliable signal of a change in trend. If the stocks showing the most market interest can't go up, failure for the whole ball game is near at hand.

Two indicators can be constructed from these statistics. The

## CHART A

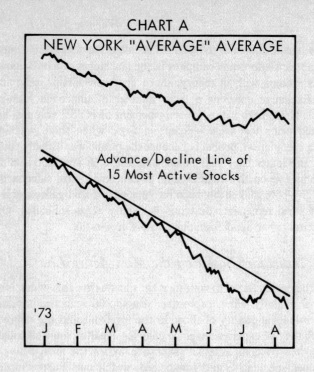

NEW YORK "AVERAGE" AVERAGE

Advance/Decline Line of
15 Most Active Stocks

'73
J F M A M J J A

## CHART B

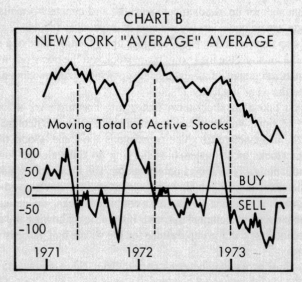

NEW YORK "AVERAGE" AVERAGE

Moving Total of Active Stocks

100
50
0
-50
-100

BUY
SELL

1971     1972     1973

first (chart A, page 124)—the A/D line of the most actives—helps spot what is happening beneath the surface, as illustrated on the chart. Note the new low this indicator registered at the end of August 1973, a low unmatched in the "average" average at that time. The A/D of the most actives was warning that the market was still seeing a drain of funds and that lower prices lay ahead for the average too.

Another indicator derived from the same statistics is the moving total of the most actives (chart B). Here we've constructed a chart to yield buy and sell signals, with a neutral band in the middle to decrease the number of whipsaws. This oscillating type of indicator is relatively short-term in orientation, usually coincident or lagging rather than leading, and will help you time a sale more precisely. It can be kept as a 30–day moving total: simply add in each day's net differential between the most-active list's advances and declines (ignoring those unchanged), dropping the thirty-first day's number. Signals generated when the neutral band has been penetrated on the downside are even better than upside signals. Note the three "sells" on the chart and how they came at important junctures, particularly the 1972 signal, which came right near the top for the "average" average. Nor does this indicator come racing back up on lesser rallies against the prevailing trend, as you can see when it stayed below signal level throughout each of the prolonged inter-mediate-term corrections on the chart.

## *Other Useful Indicators*

So much for daily exercises. The investor searching for details may be able to add to this list, as experience dictates and the stock hobby captivates, but our belief is that the best way to use indicators is to keep matters simple. Their job is to restrain emotional excesses and to provide an objective view of what the market is actually doing. They are, in many ways, a check on what is happening to individual stocks, a check that most of us need. The only aspect we might add is to make sure, when you scan the actual stock tables for the price activity of your stocks, that you don't get carried away by visions of triplings. Constantly lead with cynicism; ask yourself questions: Why didn't it close on its high? How was the volume compared to yesterday? How far is it to overhead resistance? and the like. In the end, though, the primary requisite remains the ability to act decisively, having the guts to sell in the face of whatever yearnings and opposing sentiment may abound. Toward this end, indicators can provide the objective shove to act, so here are a few other tried-and-true indicators to track. These will involve, at the most, another fifteen minutes of work on the weekend, using a financial publication such as *Barron's,* whose weekly statistical roundup provides the data.

First and foremost comes the need to find out what the professionals are doing, now that the odd-lot figures have given us a line on public sentiment. Here, too, statistics on short selling by members have proved to be the most useful as well as the most readily available. Exchange members constitute an assorted batch of sophisticated players. There are the specialists, standing on the floor and handling the auction market in stocks specifically allocated to them. Most of their shorting is a routine of the marketplace; they have no choice but to short when there are no public sell orders in the stocks they handle, or when they themselves have no more long stock to parcel out from their own account. The only leeway specialists can exercise is the degree to which they actually do go short, whether it is just enough to meet the requirements of an orderly market, or a more aggressive move. Another group of members, having complete freedom both of stock selection and trading direction, and with no responsibilities to anyone but themselves, are the on-floor traders, who roam the floor in search of quick trades. For the privilege of initiating their orders on the floor they put up a quarter of a million dollars (no pikers are allowed to play this game) and agree to abide by certain restrictive rules. Those who don't want to, or who have other things to do during the day besides trade stocks, turn to off-floor trading. Rules apply to these traders too, but not as many or as restrictive. These off-floor traders watch the same tape as the rest of us, but have the advantage, of course, of playing the game at less commission cost.

Each of these three segments of Exchange membership is required to report its trading activity to the Exchange, so that its dealings can be monitored to ensure that the rules are being respected. Weekly trading reports must be filed by the Friday of the following week. The Exchange then compiles the data and releases them to the SEC and the financial press by the next Friday. Accordingly, the statistics that appear in *Barron's* that weekend and in *The Wall Street Journal* on Monday relate to the trading activity of two weeks previous. (*Barron's,* being uppity, gives the statistics only for the NYSE; the *Journal* supplies them for the Amex too. It really doesn't matter which paper you read, though. We've never been able to find information in the ASE statistics that says anything significantly different from what you can glean from the Big Board data.) This two-week delay is not generally a problem. Indeed, when tops are forming, the end does not occur in an instant; the signal is usually given in ample time, and is often repeated for another week or more to make sure you get the message. Besides, if you do your selling in the top area, you'll be winner enough.

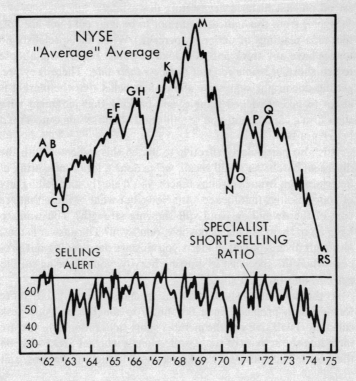

The most consistently useful of these statistics is the specialist short-sales ratio, calculated by dividing the number of shares sold short by specialists by the total number of shares sold short that week. Take a look at the accompanying chart to see how helpful this indicator can be. Over the years, readings as high as 73 percent and as low as 31 percent have unfolded. We've found that whenever readings of 64 percent or more appeared, the market was due to head south. Sometimes, as at points E–F, it was just a correction; at others, like G–H, the so-called correction was the whole bear market of 1966. Persistent high shorting during the period of the 1968 top (L–M) was a clear-cut warning; in 1971 specialist shorting warned of that extremely severe correction and then, when shorting stayed high instead of getting down into the buying area, the warning was reinforced by more high-level percentages. This was at the very time (Q) that the "average" average actually peaked and set off on that historic devastating downslide.

Signals from this indicator are not to be ignored! (Nor are bottom-area readings of under 40 percent.) When the specialists no longer have any stock left to unload to public buyers and choose to sell short, *it's time for you to be on their side.* There they are, getting downright aggressive about their belief that the market is about to take a wicked tumble, and backing that judgment with their firm's capital, and you're still timid about selling out? You'd better not be.

It is also particularly effective to match this indicator with the divergent batch. As you'll recall, we've done a lot of measuring of deterioration. In such circumstances, you'd alertly start selling any of your holdings that looked suspicious; but what of those that are part of the dwindling band still showing strength? You want to hang on to them as long as possible, don't you? The answer is that, although divergent action alerts you to start the weeding-out process, when the specialist is shorting heavily, you are being told to get out, and out you should go.

At the same time as you track the specialist's activity, one more long-division problem (or a few fingertip touches on your desk calculator) will give you the member short-sales ratio. Here you are including the activity of those professionals who act exclusively on their own. This indicator works very well in identifying tops, and when it hits an ultra-high level near 90 percent, you can kiss any rally goodbye. Yes, it does tend to simply repeat—call it, reinforce —the message from the specialists, but we sometimes get shadings that are informative. For example, if you see that the members are moving close to 90 percent while the specialist readings are still around 59 percent, you'd be alerted ahead of time that trouble is brewing, and that always helps.

Do you have another three seconds? Subtract the total of member shorting that you've just used from the total of all shorting and you've got the amount the public did during that week. Divide that by the week's volume and you get what is known as the public short-sales ratio. This indicator reveals that small round-lot traders are just as apt to be wrong at important tops as the odd-lotter; both virtually cease all short-side activity just as the market rally is coming to an end. Keep in mind, though, that this, too, is much better at calling tops than bottoms.

While you're checking the back pages of *Barron's,* there are still other indicators for those of you with extra analytical time, especially the *amount of big blocks traded* during the week. Here you'll find listed all the transactions of 10,000 shares or more, plus the price of the transaction and the price of the previous trade. If the latter is higher than the price the block traded at, the block evidently was sold by someone who wanted to get out; hence the price concession. If the block was traded on an uptick, you can assume the buyer provided the impetus; he couldn't wait.

Since this area represents those who are able to wheel and deal in such large blocks, we are learning what big money wants to do (versus what the public has told us it is doing via other statistics). There is, however, a built-in problem with the reported statistics. Many blocks appear on the tape as 9,900 shares instead of a full 10,000 and thus never make *Barron's* list. This happens because, by Exchange rule, the block seller is obliged to sell first to any prevailing bid on the floor, since that order has precedence and cannot be bypassed simply to accommodate a broker with a fat order. If there is a 100-share bid at 28 1/2, for example, the broker marching in to cross an order to buy and an order to sell 10,000 shares must first sell 100 shares to that bid (or however many shares are being bid for) and the remaining 9,900 shares at, say, 28.

Not only are a sizable number of otherwise big blocks omitted from the statistics because of 100 shares here and there, but this situation often distorts exactly what we'd like to know. In the example above, suppose the seller had 15,000 shares to unload. If the previous price was 29, if 100 shares were sold to cover a bid at 28 1/2, and if the remaining 14,900 shares were also sold at 28 1/2, then the block of 14,900 shares would appear as if it had traded at an unchanged price (when the seller had actually been the aggressor). One such block doesn't matter, but this occurs often enough to flaw the indicator. Even so, since the distortion is consistent, this indicator over time has its own consistency.

Institutions tend to dump stock in a single transaction and to buy, if possible, in smaller lots, gradually accumulating a position. Therefore, many more big blocks are traded on downticks than on upticks. So we want to know whenever the customary proportion shifts to something extraordinary. That means adding up all those stocks registered as having been sold (on a downtick) or bought (on an uptick). A ratio of about .2 is negative; when buyers come back in force and the ratio scoots up toward .5, the market is in much better shape.

A similar indicator, to which some people attach great importance, is the number of secondaries for the week. Primary stock distributions are when the company itself reaps the return; secondaries represent big boys and insiders trying to get out of a big holding promptly, selling at a peak price to a gullible public. Such blocks often aren't digestible in the regular way of trading so, to unload, these big-time sellers will pay an extra premium, not to the buyer, but to the brokerage firm that hustles up the buyer. It's called "no commission" to the public, but the broker typically earns twice as much. This is a terrific example of how stocks get distributed to weak hands from strong; and here is exactly what we should all be alert for on the tape. If you see a lot of secondaries (as listed each week in *Barron's*) up near the top, it's a good sign that those "in the know" want out. (Remember that if your broker calls up and starts a spiel about grabbing some bargain secondary offering at "no commission," you have all the indicator you need that you'd better get another broker. You can do without an agent who views the public as the duped consumer of a worn-out product and who cares more for his double commission than for your portfolio.)

Along the same lines, from time to time the new-issues market goes wild. At first you can't get any of those newly issued shares that are quickly doubling and tripling from the initial offering price. Ah, but as the speculative bubble is about to burst, guess who gets a phone call from his broker? In 1962 and again in 1968, new issues were sugar plums and the end of the rainbow wrapped in one enticing package. Two guys in a rented garage with an idea for a new product got capitalized as an avid public took down their issuing shares. So you become an indicator! When, after the good ones go right by you, brokers start calling you up to "let you in on a hot one," you know the end is near.

In situations like these, remember the IBM motto: "Think." Why, for example, does the seller of those 100,000 shares have to offer the dealer twice the normal commission to sell? Why is that supposedly hot new issue so available to you all of a sudden? A few suspicious questions on your part, plus some cynical answers (remember that no one is about to do you a favor), will keep you aware of important tops being formed.

## Indicators Based on Fundamentals

The back pages of *Barron's* also supply, for the benefit of tinkerers, data on bond/stock yields, dividend ratios, or how much of a dividend a dollar's worth of the Dow obtains. In a sense, this data comes from material cherished by fundamentalists; of course there is a relationship to stocks, but not necessarily to stock trends. Action in the market can vary wildly from what pursuers of such indicators come to decide are the norms. Fundamental indicators cannot take into account the degree to which the stock market is able to, and invariably does, go to emotional extremes. Don't hide from these statistics; understand what high or low levels mean, so that a quick glance will keep you attuned.

Lest you think economic, fiscal, and monetary matters should be dodged entirely, here's what we think you should know. First, drop a note to the Federal Reserve Bank of St. Louis and ask to be put on their mailing list. Each week they'll send a booklet free of charge that charts the important monetary statistics, giving you charts of money supply and the monetary base, which show you, instead of leaving you to rely on other people's guesses, whether the Federal Reserve Board is making money easier or tightening it. The latter, of course, is considered a negative sign for the stock market's future.

We've found, though, that while the conventional analyst waits for readings in the area of money supply (or, if slightly more aware, that of monetary base, which tends to lead money-supply trends), cannier analysts use another statistic which is actually a far better stock-market indicator. The Federal Reserve Board releases its data late Thursday each week so that it appears in Friday morning's newspapers. Among the data is that for net-free or borrowed reserves. Simply put, net-free reserves obtain when banks hold more money in reserve than they have borrowed from the Federal Reserve. When conditions get tighter, however, they are compelled to borrow more and more at the Fed window, producing a net borrowed reserves figure. On the chart, you can see the relative improvement in reserves around the 1970 market bottom and, even more important, the way the trend had already turned decidedly downward thoughout 1972, warning of deep trouble. There is no precise timing to this indicator, nor is there an absolute kind of level at which to say "Bingo." Just keep in

## Bank Net Free and Net Borrowed Reserves

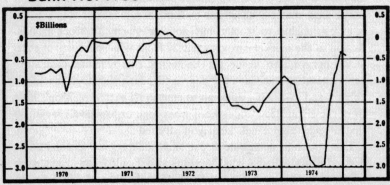

mind that net-free reserves, or trends in that direction, are basically favorable for stocks, and that net-borrowed, and getting tighter, reserves have proven to be an indicator that you should have cleared out of equities. Accordingly, any time you note that, after having been in a net-free position, these numbers slide into a borrowed trend, you're getting a serious warning to do some selling.

One other indicator in this sphere seems to work very well, and that is the ratio between the yields of corporate AAA bonds and short-term treasury bills. As the ratio narrows, the situation becomes more hostile to stocks, so that in late December 1972 the ratio had fallen for the first time below 1.4—the initial "signal" level—and by March 1973 to under 1.2—the confirming "sell everything" signal level—and the ratio stayed under that measurement for months and months, throughout the entire bear market, not to come back up again across 1.2 until the end of September 1974 (and across 1.4 for a major bull-market signal the week after). That is a great record: two near-perfect calls in a row, as well as remaining favorable (above 1.4) all during the booming rallies of 1975 and early 1976, while conventional wisdom was constantly fretting about money rates. The prior history on this is also good. You can find the statistics conveniently in the St. Louis Fed's booklet (and in *Barron's*). Here again, one long-division calculation each week can reap incalculable results.

## Three Monthly Indicators

Let's move on to three monthly statistics worth watching. We discussed the mutual-fund cash ratio in the previous chapter. Figures are released about the twentieth of each month for the levels of the preceding month, and you'll generally find the announcement buried somewhere in *The Wall Street Journal* and *The New York Times,* among others. To refresh your memory, the experts responsible for running those vast sums of money have just about spent it all when a top is arriving. Liquidity gets down under 6 percent of assets. Don't quibble about a tenth of 1 percent; the more content they are to be bought up, the warier you should be.

For another key once-a-month statistic, refer to the volume data we want you to keep each week. Volume—that is, the average daily volume—is one half of the equation in measuring the short interest ratio. This is the ratio between the announced total number of outstanding short positions and the average daily volume for the month in question. Though more exact when defining important bottoms (when the ratio should be up to 2.0), a generally toppy climate is indicated when the percentage of outstanding short positions is less than one day's worth of trading volume, i.e., the ratio is under 1.0. The raw data is released around the twentieth of each month, and is compiled as of the closing date of the fifteenth. By closing date, the Exchange means "settlement" date, so that you must count back five trading days from the fifteenth to arrive at the actual date the short position is "as of." A glance at the calendar will tell you which weeks and odd days to add up to get the average daily volume of trading activity for the period in question. Thus, you know the volume figure five trading days before the fifteenth, and knowing one of the ingredients gives you a head start on a possible signal. Heavy speculative activity, causing a sharp rise in average daily volume and coming at a time when optimism has brought the outstanding short position to a relatively low amount, can give you a negative reading, one that you can readily estimate in advance. This is not a timing indicator, but rather, it is invariably accurate and hence quite useful in lending added weight to whatever unfavorable readings you may be getting from the other indicators.

The third item worth tracking is margin debt. What we like about this indicator is that it has proven to be a genuine buffer against losing long-term perspective. It takes a lot of time to turn the margin debt's direction around; several months of rounding under and starting to increase mark major bottoms, as those who trade on margin keep stepping up the pace of tossing their money and all they can borrow into the pot. It actually tops out and begins to turn down just before, or coincident with, important tops, suggesting that traders who borrow on margin aren't so dumb and do at least some cutting back in time. A large part of this savvy probably can be attributed to the action of the Federal Reserve Board in raising margin requirements later in a bull market as part of an effort to tighten credit. Whatever the cause, if you have watched margin debt rise steeply month after month along with stock prices, you have a good warning of a primary trend reversal when the debt finally stops growing and turns down.

Lest you think that indicators always work, here's an indicator to remind you that nothing is perfect in the stock market. This chart comes from a respected and eminently worthwhile advisory service and is meant to illustrate a theory that the trend of interest rates (as represented by commercial paper) can predict the stock-market course. One can readily see how yield levels were reversing in relationship to stock-market turns. But try to forecast stock movements consistently from this chart. There was a rise in rates (A), which indeed heralded the 1966 top and the ensuing bear

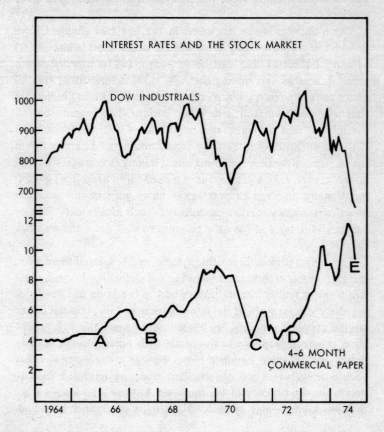

INTEREST RATES AND THE STOCK MARKET

DOW INDUSTRIALS

4–6 MONTH COMMERCIAL PAPER

market. But, if you had been scared away when a similar rise set in in 1967 (B), you'd have missed a whopping gain: the Dow went up, while the "average" average soared to its all-time peak. In 1971 (C), a rise in interest rates caught a sharp intermediate-term sell-off, while the rise at D spelled doom indeed. But look how early it was. And, talking about early, note the twin downturns in interest rates at E. The first was drastically deceptive, but even the second came a good four months and 170 Dow points too soon. Obviously, although the overall relationship is clearly there, the sharpness we need to help us make stock-market decisions is missing. Such indicators are like pats on the back: encouraging when you're already doing well; frustratingly useless when you need support.

The indicators we've discussed in the last two chapters have good track records. Using them will provide a good balance of (1) primary indicators that can be warnings; (2) intermediate-term trend indicators announcing the rally is (a) deteriorating and (b) about to reverse into a sharp correction; and (3) timing indicators that tell you to sell, sell, sell. When you get those signals, put all thought of "that last eighth of a point" out of your head; don't fret if the momentum of one of the stocks you've sold carries it still higher; ignore the people rushing about buying stocks as if they will go up forever; take a vacation if you need to, to keep from getting emotionally involved all over again; move your money into safe short-term money-market instruments (such as Treasury Bills or "money" funds); and have the patience to wait out a sliding stock market.

There is no perfect forecasting system, and besides, if there were, the grand rush to embrace it would be self-defeating. Instead, there is a form of reality: the indicators add to the body of knowledge we already possess about the stock market and its potential future course. Applied properly, with sensitivity gained through experience, they can help us win the battle with our emotions, coming down like objective hammer blows on our consciousness. They should be evaluated collectively, their evidence weighed in bulk to determine the urgency of the message. Anyone who knows what they are saying—high specialist shorting, a divergence in the advance/decline line, fewer new highs vs. a higher Dow, margin debt beginning to slacken, and so on—and yet goes blithely ahead to buy another stock in the hope of making a fast buck is hopeless. Anyone who gets those messages and doesn't sell what he already owns is a fool.

"Oh no, not me," you say. But those indicators warning you of trouble ahead—as they did in the winter of 1973—will not pick up your phone and dial your broker. That's something you have to learn to do yourself.

# 7

## The Specialists

The specialist system, the basis for the way the New York Stock Exchange functions, is, as we write this, at the root of many of the changes being suggested to improve market matters. The advent of electronic machines makes it conceivable that computers could replace the specialist who now stands on the Exchange floor all day every day. Here, at the heart of capitalism, there is scarcely any competition. Each specialist has a virtual franchise for a number of different listed stocks. The problem with competition is that either it works, and the better specialist takes more and more business away from his rival until his competitor quits or asks to merge, or it is evaded, and firms decide to do business with one competitor for six months and with the other for the next six months. What competition there was, especially during the 1930's, disappeared by the late sixties. Nor are there any isolated individual specialists any more. The need for substantial capital has led to the formation of specialist firms of several partners, and even specialist units of two or more firms working together. These units handle a number of different listed stocks at a particular trading post. Although individual partners concentrate on a few stocks, or, in the case of a particularly active stock, only one, they are always able to take over their partner's issues when he steps out to the men's room.

138

Thus, when we talk about the specialist we mean both the individual and the group. The specialist wears two hats: the staid bowler of the broker who simply functions as an agent for those orders left with him, and the jaunty derby of the dealer who gets into the fray with his own money. As a broker the specialist maintains a "book," a long, thin ledger where he records all orders in a particular stock which are not close to the current market. When orders in the book become capable of execution, whether moments or months later, the specialist simply represents them in the marketplace at the designated price. As a dealer, on the other hand, the specialist assumes the responsibility for maintaining a "fair and orderly market" in that particular stock, and does so by buying or selling for his own account whenever necessary, that is, when there are no other buyers or sellers around.

Let us suppose, for example, that various brokerage firms have received orders in XYZ from their customers and given them to the specialist for execution. The highest-priced order to buy the stock is at 50, and the lowest-priced offer to sell is at 51, with the last sale price for XYZ at 50 1/2. A Merrill Lynch broker then crosses the Exchange floor with a piece of paper in his hand, representing a customer's order which has just been entered "upstairs" and transmitted to the firm's array of clerks on the floor. Although the broker knows that the order is to buy 200 shares, he doesn't disclose this to the specialist when he approaches and asks: "How's XYZ?"

He has asked for "the market" in that stock, and the specialist would then reply: "50–51," telling the broker the bid price first and the offer second. By the customs of the Exchange, this quotation is firm, having been made publicly. The specialist can't change his mind suddenly and withdraw the quote if he doesn't like what the broker is anxious to do; at least 100 shares must trade at or within that quoted range. The specialist sometimes adds—and certainly will announce if asked—the "size" in the market for the stock; that is, how many shares are being bid for at that price and how many are offered, i.e., "one by two" (meaning 100 shares bid for at 50 and 200 shares offered for sale at 51). He cannot, however, reveal any other orders on the book. Only the best bid and the best offer are the known market.

The broker instantaneously absorbs this information and responds: "A half for two," meaning that he is making a bid to buy 200 shares at 50 1/2, the last sale price, thus trying to do better for his customer than merely taking the shares offered at 51. If he were representing a sell order, he'd say: "Two at a half," noting first the amount of shares he was willing to sell and then the price he'd accept.

Another floor broker might be at the same trading post willing to sell stock to the bid at that price, but in this example let's suppose the specialist replies: "A half to one," indicating that the quotation has now changed, the Merrill broker having produced the higher bid. That order is now the quoted bid price while the offer remains the same, making the quoted market 50 1/2 bid, offered at 51. As you can see, this terse response also tells the broker that he has failed to get an execution for the order he has in his hand. That bid constitutes an attempt to buy at a better price for his customer that turned out to be futile but was well worth trying. If the broker has been handling an order entered to buy "at the market," meaning that he immediately has to buy at whatever price is available, his next step would be to take the offered stock at 51. He cannot risk loitering at the trading post to see if a lower-priced sell order shows up because, if another broker darted in and grabbed the shares offered at 51 ahead of him, the Merrill broker would thus fail to buy "at the market" and would thereby become liable for an execution at 51. In this case, however, our broker turns over the scrap of paper in his hand to show the specialist that his buy order had, in fact, been limited to 50 1/2 and that he can bid no higher. Having business to transact elsewhere, he leaves the order with the specialist, who enters it in his book at that price. The specialist now becomes the broker representing that order in the marketplace, and he collects the floor broker's small commission for the task. Meanwhile, the specialist has announced the new quotation (50 1/2–51) to an Exchange reporter stationed nearby who feeds the information into the computer, which makes it available to brokerage offices via those desk-top interrogation devices.

Now, let's suppose the customer who had originally been offering those 200 shares at 51 decides he doesn't want to sell after all.

The order is canceled, and when the specialist glances at his book, he realizes that his next best public order to sell is for 500 shares at 51 3/4. Theoretically, that's the best offer in the market at that moment, and without the specialist system, a buyer would have to pay that much more than the last sale price at 50 1/2. But the specialist has the responsibility not to let such a wide variation in sales occur, and, clearly, trading the stock at that price would not contribute to a fair and orderly market. What he must do, therefore, whether he likes it or not, is offer shares for his own account as dealer. He has no choice since, with no other sellers around, he must be the seller, whether long (selling shares he already has in his dealer account) or short (selling shares short because his dealer account has no shares to supply). It may be that he believes the market (or that stock) is strong, and he'd rather be a buyer than a seller, but at this moment that's not an option he has. He is already acting as agent for a buy order at 50 1/2, and now the only real choice left to him is the price at which he can offer stock for sale. He could, simply, renew the offer at 51 for his own account; or he might feel that even half a point variation between sales was too much (any more certainly would be) and therefore offer stock at 50 3/4. He might, upon reflection (and sensing a changing market on the tape overhead), sell to the bid at 50 1/2, in which case, since he has been both agent and dealer on the same transaction, the Merrill broker has the right to accept or refuse the trade. Much would depend on whether his feelings about XYZ were neutral or negative, but even more would be based on what the next broker who came to the post wanted to do.

If the broker had an order to buy, say, 1,000 shares at the market, the specialist might sell him 200 shares at the 51 offer, and hike the offer again for the remaining 800 shares, on the theory that since the new buyers in the stock were strong, that strength should be reflected on the tape in terms of a rising price. If the broker had an order to buy 100 shares, the specialist might sell him those shares at 50 3/4 and still offer another 100 shares at 51, thereby keeping the variation between sales closer on low volume without too much exposure on his part. He might indeed sell those 200 shares short from his dealer account (at 50 3/4 and at 51), only to find that the subsequent broker wants 1,000 shares and so drives the price up even more, giving the specialist an instant loss on those 200 shares he's just sold short. Or the next broker might be a seller, hitting the bid at 50 1/2 and giving the specialist a fast paper gain on his shorts; he could then bid 50 1/4 for 200 shares, and if another seller came in, he'd not only garner a rapid profit but would be literally helping to keep the market fair and orderly.

Obviously, in this simple sequence, much of what happens to the specialist—his profits and/or losses, and what he is compelled to do in his dealer account—is determined, not by his own free will, but by what the next broker coming across the Exchange floor has an order to do. Trades such as these are typical of the specialist's day: no public orders around to sell, so he fills the bill, and must continue to do so even if the trickle of buyers becomes a flood. Of course, he does his best to keep his dealer position where he'd like it to be, whether short, long, or even, but sometimes the market's course of action won't give him a chance. The commission income he enjoys from agenting active stocks can be quickly wiped out by losses in his dealer account. A specialist can get trapped against the tide and lose $100,000 or even more in a matter of days, as he meets his responsibility to maintain a fair and orderly market. And yet, by doing exactly what he is supposed to—taking the place of absent public orders whenever necessary to keep price fluctuations reasonable—the specialist consistently racks up lovely profits. How? Precisely by taking the opposite stance to whatever the public orders. Even firms content to coast with the minute-to-minute fluctuations of the market, buying or selling only when they have to, without regard for where they think the Dow industrial average will be months from then, do extraordinarily well.

## Good News, Bad News

An unusually exaggerated example of how going against the crowd pays off for the specialist came on August 16, 1971, the day after President Nixon announced a drastic new game plan to cure the country's economic ills. Public and institutional orders to buy were pouring into the NYSE floor as specialists came to work that Monday morning for what turned out to be one of the most dramatic days in the history of the Exchange. It made no difference to a specialist whether he agreed with Nixon's schemes or not; he had no choice about what to do. His job is not to interpret but rather to respond to how *other* people think, and the avalanche of buy orders was already dictating his task. Each specialist, arriving at his trading post, quickly realized he was going to have to sell, and sell short, to the limits of his capital. He wouldn't be able to buy even if he thought that buying was the smart thing to do, as so many others obviously did.

In their eagerness and excitement, the morning's investors failed to play devil's advocate with themselves and ask one basic question: *Should they be selling instead?* How could anyone dream of selling in the face of this instant cure brought about by a wave of the President's magic wand? It was an extraordinarily emotional situation, yet the specialist, because he has no choice, can be far cooler than the people who have eagerly tossed their buy orders into the bubbling caldron. So the question to keep in mind is: *Should you be selling, along with the specialist, when everyone else is avid to buy?*

Let's see what would have happened by examining the action over at Post 2, where Chrysler is traded. There, the specialist firm handling the stock has had a tradition of opening Chrysler each day as soon as possible. But the challenge this day was to get the stock opened by the closing bell. The Nixon formula had provided particular aid to the then-sagging automobile industry and the Chrysler specialist was swamped under a tidal wave of buy orders.

Chrysler had closed the previous Friday at 26 3/8. Orders to buy Chrysler at the market (that is, at any price) or at a limit of 31 (that is, the buyer was willing to go that high but no higher) totaled 670,000 shares; offers to sell, however, amounted to only 269,000 shares at a price of 31 or lower. Thus, even if the specialist were to open Chrysler at 31, 17 percent higher than Friday's closing price, he would have had to be able to supply over 400,000 shares from somewhere just to match opening supply with opening demand.

Faced with such an overwhelming disparity, a simple solution would have been to raise the potential opening price higher and higher until it reached a level at which many buyers would have withdrawn and an increasing number of sellers would have come forth, so that the orders could be matched. That would have been entirely plausible within an auction market governed solely by the law of supply and demand. But the law of the Stock Exchange scowls on such drastic jumps in price, and 31 was considered huge enough. Anyone who complained about how high the actual opening price turned out to be should consider how high it might have been were supply and demand the only force in effect. Obviously, to keep within reason, the specialist would have to sell from his own account.

But 400,000 shares? Even if his firm had the capital resources needed ($12.5 million), he couldn't afford to tie it all up in one stock since he and his partners would need to meet the demands, as market makers, in more than a dozen other stocks they also had responsibility for. The specialist fortunately happened to have a few thousand shares in his dealer account, paltry compared to what was needed, but better than being caught empty-handed or short, as some specialists were in other stocks.

In extreme situations like this (of which there were a record number that Monday morning), the first step is to get formal permission from a floor official to delay the opening. Such approval is always required when, due to an imbalance of orders, a stock can't be opened within half an hour. Next, the specialist instructs the various floor brokers to notify their firms that the stock is going to open substantially higher, in the hope that more sellers might be encouraged to offer stock if they realized they could get a higher price, and that some buyers would cancel their orders when they learned they were going to be hit with a huge markup.

By the time 10:30 came, the easier-to-open stocks were already streaming across the tape at sharply higher prices. Brokers who handled orders for institutions were combing the floor in search of blocks of stock to buy; as far as they were concerned, *any* block in any stock would do. The tiny patch of floor space where the Chrysler specialist held the fort remained bedlam. Partners had to shout in each other's ear as they conferred, Exchange officials hovered nearby, and the beleaguered clerks struggled to keep the pile of orders under control. In such circumstances, once the opening picture becomes clearer, a specialist will usually announce a preliminary indication of the possible opening price range. Thus, emerging from the day's madness, the Chrysler specialist was finally able to lift his head up and declare: "It looks like around 30 to 32." It was a bold announcement, for sufficient sellers had yet to be found. Upstairs, in the block-trading departments of many member firms, salesmen were busy scouring the portfolios of mutual funds and other institutions for holders of large amounts of Chrysler stock.

Finally, late in the trading day, an institutional holder was found who was willing to sell nearly 325,000 shares at 31. Only one big-block holder had the intelligence and fortitude to disregard the torrent of unquestioning optimism and overwhelming enthusiasm pervading the Street that day! Yet here was a unique opportunity to sell a very large block of stock all at once at a price spectacularly higher than the day before. But, alas, money managers can be as emotional as the man in the street, and they are creatures of habit as well, often preferring to wait until a stock turns down and then hastening to dump the block on the market when there are few if any buyers around.

The offering of that big block reduced the disparity between buyers and sellers to about 75,000 shares, still leaving more than $2.3 million to go on the offering side. In a voice scarcely heard in the din, the specialist told anxious floor officials that he was willing to supply that amount by selling 75,000 shares short in his dealer account to get the stock open. At the same time, he was also risking another $1.3 million to sell Chrysler warrants short in conjunction with the opening of the common. Considering the unabated bullishness that still raged on the floor and in board rooms, and the fact that General Motors was nowhere near opening and so could not guide his own relative risk, this was a remarkable step. Another wave of buyers might surge in, sweeping Chrysler higher and, of course, creating a potentially catastrophic loss in the specialist's short position. The very survival of the firm was being placed on the line just to get Chrysler open by the closing bell, making it the only auto stock to print on the tape that day.

Three months later, Chrysler was selling at 25.

*As a rule of thumb, forget your own reaction to news, ignore the stampeding emotional herd, and ask yourself what the specialist's reaction is going to have to be.* If we can learn a healthy market approach from the specialist, we can also learn the penalties of obstinacy and daydreaming from the fund managers who were so busy buying they wouldn't consider selling. Within two days of that opening at 31, the total daily volume in Chrysler had dropped to less than half the shares of that one institutional block alone! Selling into lower volume was far more difficult and costly, which is exactly what happened to a large-block holder of General Motors in essentially the same circumstances. Disdaining the chance to get 85 for 395,000 shares of GM, which wasn't even able to open until Tuesday, one institutional money manager waited two months and finally settled for 82 for the same block, $12 million less than if he had seized the moment on August 16. The moral: One of the best times to sell is when buyers are pleading for your stock. And that goes for 100 shares as well as for 100,000. It is not a time to be coy.

## Using the Book

Most people suspect that the specialist has an advantage when it comes to dealing for his own account in knowing where public orders are entered on his book. The supposition goes that if he is aware of a number of limit orders to buy entered in his book at, say, 31, it makes it less risky for him to buy at 31 1/4, since the cushion of support would certainly be there. Such an advantage is trifling at best. Beyond the fact that he is standing right there, it is the specialist's knowledge, gleaned over the years and bolstered by experience, that truly counts, and what he has learned by direct observation is that being compelled to go against the crowd provides the real advantage.

In any event, specialist books have become less significant year after year for the simple reason that so little is entered on them any more. In a special study made by the SEC in the early sixties, many specialists were pointing out that their books had thinned markedly to the point where quite a few stocks had completely empty books and others only random orders far away from the current market. Since the sixties the trend toward thinner books has accelerated, caused in part by the fact that institutions now dominate trading activity and they rarely enter orders on the book.

Whether his book contains useful secrets or not, a specialist is prohibited from showing it to anyone else, except to demonstrate the Exchange auction procedures to visitors, with the proviso that "at the same time he makes the information so disclosed available to all members." One day a floor trader took advantage of this stipulation and darted over behind a Japanese trade mission to demand to see the book too. Asked later what he had learned, the trader scoffed: "Not a damn thing! There were only a few scattered orders from Merrill Lynch. I just stuck my nose in to tease the specialist."

Back in the old days, when the books contained many more orders, specialists developed a market theory suitable to their own interest in rapid fluctuations. They noticed that the price of a stock tended to move in the direction of the orders entered on the book. In effect, eager buyers at the market would reach up for shares entered at limited higher prices for sale. But, when there were few such orders entered on the book and little for them to buy, the buyers would sit back and wait, instead of reaching and thus driving the price up further. They would then enter their buy orders under the current market price as bids. In turn, anyone who came along at that point and wanted to sell would sell at the market to those bids, thus causing the stock price to retrace in the direction of the buy orders entered on the book. As you can see, this theory is connected with the ability of the specialists to profit by going against the crowd and having to take the place of absent public orders. Eager buyers drive the price up in the direction of the book, but then the orders on the book are exhausted. It is at this turning point that the specialist would be required, under the rules, to sell his own shares, or to sell short, in taking the place of absent sellers. At about the same time, other buyers are entering limited-price orders on the bid side of the book, so that the direction of the book is now toward lower prices. Obviously, that retracement gives the specialist, in a brief time span, a profit on the shares he has just sold.

Being a seller on August 16, 1971, the side of the market that public enthusiasm had forced on the specialists, proved to be the right tactic. Just one month later, 45 percent of listed NYSE stocks were substantially lower than their opening price of that morning, and the majority of these had never even traded higher than that opening price. An additional 25 percent sold at prices sharply lower than their openings within the first week, before gradually recovering the lost ground. Less than one third were higher a month later. In sum, after twenty trading days, with the DJI up 80 points in that span, buyers on that explosive opening either failed to show a profit or suffered sizable losses in about 70 percent of all NYSE stocks. Similar scrutiny of the twenty-five most widely held stocks yields much the same answer. One month later, thirteen of these were not only lower than their massive Monday opening prices but were actually selling below the preceding Friday's close before the speech! Another four were down from their opening prices. Only eight of the twenty-five went higher in the next four weeks (again less than one third) even though the averages had advanced. Thus, no matter what stock you bought, the odds of showing a profit after what was then the grandest opening fling in market history were a whopping 7 to 3 against you, and, of course, in favor of the specialist who was forced to sell. Clearly, determining which side of the market the specialist would be on would have pointed the way to the proper decision. *Selling along with the specialist is a sound policy.*

Let's return to the situation in Chrysler to carry this study further. With the specialist having bridged the gap between supply and demand, having opened the stock up 17 percent, there is a brand-new ball game, and one side or the other now has to commit itself. Will it come from the buy side? A massive number of buyers have already expressed their willingness to pay 31; that includes all those who were willing to buy at any price, so no one is left after that opening who wants to pay more, i.e., no one around is anxious to bid the stock up any further. What's more, buyers can afford to wait and see; other stocks are also providing fireworks. Thus, potential buyers are either on the sidelines or, at best, are bidding for the stock at a lower price. Indeed, the specialist actually has a pile of limited-price orders in hand, which were entered to buy at lower limits than the eventual opening at 31.

So what about the sell side? Here, too, the specialist has some leftover limited-price orders from sellers who had insisted that they get more than 31, but far fewer than those on the buy side. At first glance it would seem that just about any potential seller who was willing to take 31 would already have entered his order before the well-publicized opening. But there is one difference between buyers and sellers: sellers already own the stock. While the potential buyer is perhaps idly watching, the potential seller is frazzled, feeling the need to make a decision again and again. Thus, there is a critical distinction between sellers and buyers, which is then given an emotional goose by seeing the actual price print on the ticker tape. "If I had known the stock was going to open that high," a typical reaction goes, "I would have sold." This is even more prevalent if the stock does not immediately shoot up toward the moon.

It only takes a few, now uncomfortable, holders deciding to sell to ease Chrysler downward. The tape shows a few prints at 30 7/8, and that inspires a few holders to finally make a decision they'd been hesitant about. Seeing 30 3/4, and talking with their brokers, a few of those sellers who had greedily wanted even more than 31 now hasten to cash in too. At the same time, the specialist is now in the enviable position of profitably being able to take the place of absent buyers, covering at least a portion of his 75,000-share short position by buying stock from these latecoming sellers. In the few minutes of trading remaining on that day, about 90,000 more shares of Chrysler changed hands, much of it finding the specialist on the buy side. Naturally, because the specialist is such a big buyer, the price doesn't fall away rapidly. Many thousands off an eighth, many thousands more off another eighth, adds up to an orderly market and a nice profit for the huge risk the specialist took.

Much more often than not, the opening price following favorable news constitutes an excellent selling opportunity. This gift of hysterically anxious buyers doesn't happen often, so when it comes, oblige them. This is even more essential when the dominant trend at the time is bearish, as in mid-August 1971, when the market was in the midst of a clear-cut intermediate-term downtrend or, as in January 1973, when long-awaited news (the so-called end of the Vietnam war) arrived as the indicators were flashing the danger of a major reversal. Selling at the opening with the specialist is not only a chance to make a calmer decision but it also greatly heightens the chances that you'll get the best price too.

And if it isn't the best price, it's near enough to be satisfactory. Chrysler, for example, was to receive a new, albeit fragile, lease on life the very next day, when General Motors finally opened, up 8 1/4 points. That big jump renewed the buying spark in Chrysler and the stock shot up to 32 3/4. Sellers, reading that news in their evening paper, might have wished they'd waited. But on the very next day, Wednesday, Chrysler sold no higher than 31 5/8, and within a few more days, it had dropped under 30. It's a lot tougher to sell under those circumstances, for, even though there was a possibility of eking out a higher price, it was illusory. To repeat: It is far less nerve-racking, far easier, and far more objective to join the specialist on his side of the market.

This guideline is particularly vital when the news comes late in the cycle. With various signs among the indicators telling you the rise has gotten past middle age, headline announcements are selling opportunities. That's important to remember, because invariably the most enticing news comes right near the top, when optimism is pervasive. To keep your head under such circumstances, you don't really need to know the literal significance of the news, nor do you need the advice of an expert. All you need heed is the answer to one simple question: What is the herd doing? To find out, if you don't know, there are always reports available from the Exchange floor before the opening: "Buyers" or "Sellers." The greater the stampede, the greater the warning. The market's moments of generosity are few, but news-induced optimism rewards cynics for being cynical.

# 8

## A Basic Selling Strategy

Success in the stock market is nothing more than mastering a game of probabilities. The more efficiently you play the probable course, using the odds instead of playing a long shot, the more successful you will be year in and year out. One rule, as we've just discussed, is to react to news by being on the side the Exchange specialist is going to be on. How do you know in advance that such opportunities exist? You don't, but then neither does the specialist. What's more, while you may never know just which side of the market the specialist is going to be on during the trading day (see our discussion of the trading in XYZ in the preceding chapter), there is one time each day that you do have a chance to estimate whether the specialist is going to be forced to be a buyer or seller and that's the opening transaction. Let's probe that situation more closely to see why selling at the opening is more likely to be selling when the odds are in your favor.

In the good old days, when the prices of speculative stocks were much higher, one amateur trader bought 1,000 shares of Technicolor at 28 on a hot tip, just before going up to the country for a vacation. It took a while for TK to get rolling, but then, late one Friday afternoon, he got an excited call from his broker: Technicolor was running away on the upside, 32 1/2 . . . 32 3/4 . . . 33, all over the tape. He rushed for the newspaper the next morning and saw that the stock had closed at 33 1/2, at its high for the day. Contemplating that $5,000 was an eminently satisfactory profit, he decided to sell. But on Monday morning he decided that since it was a long-distance phone call he'd wait until after the stock had opened, to see how it was doing before placing the specific sell order. "Opened at 35," the broker told him, "but it's backing down a bit now." How much? "Oh, just normal profit-taking. It's 34 . . . no, wait, here it is on the tape at 33 3/4."

He confessed to the broker that he'd been thinking of selling, but, well, too bad, he'd missed the chance. Vacillation had set in; on Sunday he was going to sell; by Monday he was only thinking about it. Yet, you'll notice, had he simply said "sell," he could have gotten at least 33 1/2, the same price he'd been delighted with on Friday's close. But TK had been up to 35 and that changed the way it looked in his mind. Emotion had interfered twice: in wanting to see what was going to happen on Monday morning, and then in letting what actually did happen affect the decision he'd already made.

The broker, not wanting the responsibility for advice that might turn out to be wrong, was silent for a moment, and then asked, "Should I call you back if it rallies?" "No" was the response, but, with renewed resolve, he added, "I decided to sell, so I'm going to. It's bound to rally back up again. It got to 35 already, so put the order to sell in at 34 1/2."

It would be nice to report that he was saved, but then there'd be nothing more to write about. The market is not kind to the naïve. TK did bounce back, quickly correcting the initial reversal, but only to 34 3/8. And from there the path was steadily downward to an ultimately serious loss. Yet our trader had not only decided to sell but had actually put an order in. How could the situation have been botched so badly, even though the profits were there and the right decision had been made? You'll notice, for one thing, that an absurdly extraneous item was involved: the notion of a long-distance phone call. Often there is some such irrational or irrelevant impediment to be found in the history of market mistakes. But besides that, two things could have been—no, should have been—done differently. First, the order should have been entered before the market opened; and second, having made up his mind to sell, he should have used an "at the market" order rather than specifying a limit price. Let's examine these two aspects in detail, because they are basic to an intelligent approach to selling.

### The Market Order

NYSE Rule 13 defines a market order as "an order to buy or sell a stated amount of a security at the most advantageous price obtainable after the order is represented in the Trading Crowd." This means that, not only must the floor broker try to obtain the best price he can when he gets to the post where the specialist stands (the "trading crowd"), but he is also responsible for making the deal immediately (in floor language, he must not "miss the market") in order to ensure that he has, indeed, gotten the most advantageous price possible. He can't shilly-shally around too long trying to do better for you or he risks another broker coming in and doing business ahead of him. If that happens, you're entitled to an adjustment to the price you should have received.

The best reason to use a market order when selling is to be sure of getting an execution. Accordingly, certain variations have arisen for those who desperately need an execution but want to play games with the market beforehand. One variation is to enter an order which becomes a market order at a specific time, such as 12:30 P.M., a patently absurd gimmick, since the clock has no relationship to an intelligent selling decision. More frequently the game is played by overextended traders who are obliged to sell a position by the end of the business day to pay for something else they've bought. In an attempt to do better under such pressure, they enter what is known as an "at the close" order, which is defined in Rule 13 as "a market order which is to be executed at or as near to the close as practicable." In its most common guise, such an order is entered as either sell at X (a hoped-for limited price above the current price) or at the market at the close. If the upside limit is not reached, and the stock remains unsold near the close, the specialist will cancel the limited-price part and sell the stock at the market as near to the closing bell as possible, though he need not make it the very last trade of the day.

Perhaps you can see how absurd that is. Such an order entices you into holding on in the hope that maybe you'll do better. That's one of the most deceptive thoughts in the market. It violates a basic principle that, when a stock is hard to sell (i.e., it isn't going up to your limit), it should be sold promptly. If it's not rising, other sellers are in the way and buyers are scarce. Don't wait, sell! Remember that at the close the stock will be sold to the best bid in the market. Suppose the stock is 25 bid, offered at 25 1/2, last sale at 25 1/4; already you are getting a down price (at 25). What's more, the specialist knows your order is in there to sell at the close. If, due to an absence of public bids, he realizes he's the one who's going to have to buy your stock, he's less apt to take a stand. Why buy a lot at 25, and yours too, when he can ease the bid down from trade to trade? Similarly, knowing he's going to be handed your shares at the close, he can trade against them by selling short, for example, at 25 3/8 (thus keeping the stock from reaching the limit you were hoping for), and covering by buying your shares at the 25 bid at the close. It isn't so much that an order to sell at the close is wrong; it's that no one should ever put himself in a position that necessitates using it. Traders who do so are confessing to letting the market take control of their options and decisions.

But our basic guideline is to make our own decisions and to do so objectively, without the pressures of moment-to-moment occurrences. To repeat a point worth repeating, it's not serious to miss a chance on the buy side if you limit your order to a specific price, because you can always buy another stock. In a climate truly ripe for buying, professionals know there will be many stocks worth grabbing, each as promising as the other, since there's no way to know in advance which the big winner will be. But when it comes to selling, there's no such leeway. You already own the shares, and if the time has come to sell, failure to do so could be costly—fractions if you play the game of at the close, but immense if you wait for your price. It's hard enough deciding when to sell, without compounding the issue by also trying to decide at what exact price. There are exceptions, to be sure (and we'll discuss them later), but by and large, selling at the market is a sound practice. Every day profits have turned into losses because the shareholder pursued one more eighth. "I put in market orders," one off-floor member-trader said, explaining how he trades for his firm's account, "for the speed and to make sure I get an execution."

Many amateurs are reluctant to enter a market order, because they fear the specialist will somehow take advantage of it. Scalping did exist in the old days, but the consciously bad execution is now extremely rare. You may, rather, get an inadvertently delayed execution, such as can happen if the floor broker who is to handle your order happens to be far away from the booth where his clerk receives your order, has to hoof back to get it, and then has to cross the floor to reach the trading post. Another broker can reach the post just ahead of yours and hit the bid, driving the price down maybe a half point. Another problem may well be you yourself. Whereas a single tick on the tape may ring a bell in the professional trader's head, the public trader often watches an entire sequence, 1/4, 1/4, 1/4, 1/8, 1/8, 0, 0, then bingo, up he jumps, ordering his broker to sell him out, having been unable to stand the sequence of falling prices any longer. When such a market order reaches the floor and gets executed, the price may already be down near the low for the day. It is never a good idea to finally panic out in obvious company with sellers; but it is often a lovely idea to toss a sell order into the midst of a pot boiling over with buyers, on the repeatedly useful principle that when a lot of people are clamoring for your shares it is a good time to oblige them.

Specialists on both the NYSE and the Amex have confirmed our long-held suspicion that the public often has matters backward. The typical public trader fires a buy order to the floor in a volatile stock and thinks a market order is sensible in order to be sure of an execution. But after buying willy-nilly at the market, near the top of rallies, the same trader will then turn around and enter a limited-price order on the sell side, now trying to play it safe and cagey. But when it comes to getting out, especially in a volatile stock, the risk of not selling could leave you locked into a stock while it tumbles. Trying to pick the intraday price you want may seem like careful behavior, but it is really endangering your capital, waiving certainty for the sake of engaging in a battle of wits.

Do it the other way around, the specialists on the floor advise. We emphatically agree. Use limit orders when trying to pick up stocks—that is, buy carefully, and above all don't chase them—but once you've decided to get out, avoid the unnecessary risk of not selling. Use a market order.

## Limited-Price and Other Types of Orders

There is one exception to this dictum of "sell, and be out." If you have a particular upside target in mind, realistically determined well beforehand and based on objective factors (and not simply because that's a gain you'd settle for), such as an overhead supply area and technical chart measurements that confirm the target near resistance, you can enter a limited-price sell order and let it sit on the specialist's book until executed.

Such a limited-price order can be combined with an either/or order effectively. Here you aim for a higher price, say, where you can see formidable resistance overhead, while wanting to protect yourself in case the trapdoor falls open. You can then enter an order such as "Sell at 26 limit or on stop at 22 7/8." This is a sound way to sell objectively, no matter what happens.

This brings to mind the virtue of using a GTC order (good till canceled), rather than a day order, which expires if unexecuted that day. The GTC order can go along with any type of limited-price order, such as the simple limit or the more complex either/or. As you can see, the day order necessitates making a decision all over again; that psychological struggle can turn out to be a formidable stumbling block, often abetted by the notion that it didn't go off yesterday so "I'll just watch it today," instead of putting the order back in. What could happen to make the situation different? If the stock seemed a sound sale on Monday, why would it be different on Tuesday? The only thing we can think of that might have changed is your hopes, certainly not the reality.

To its practical advantage too, any GTC order retains its time priority on the specialist's book, while the day order, if re-entered, must start again at the bottom of the list of orders awaiting execution at that price. Your broker, needless to say, should remind you from time to time that you have a GTC order entered; otherwise, forgotten months later, you may get a totally unexpected execution.

What we like about the GTC order is that chance to sell into strength at an objectively determined target price. "Five minutes after buying," one professional off-floor trader remarked, "I have a GTC order in to sell at a limit price." His objective may be much narrower in scope than yours, but when you see quite clearly on a chart just about where a stock should be sold, the use of a GTC sell order can be appropriate. Just don't let the limit become a pipe dream; you must always remain willing to admit along the way that the stock isn't doing as well as you'd expected.

While on the subject of limited-price orders, it's worth noting that the public has a habit of dispensing such an order and then tacking on the phrase "an extra eighth discretion" or "or better." Such added fillips are useless. When a floor broker has received a limited-price order, he must try to get you the best price available when he reaches the trading post, whether or not you ask him to do better. If you specify an extra eighth leeway, that simply changes the limit you've established; if you say, "Sell at 12 1/2 limit, with an extra eighth discretion," the broker effectively has a sell limit of 12 3/8 to play with. And then, if he misses the market, and the stock sells down from 12 1/4, which you could have gotten, to 6, you'll feel foolish for having set any sort of limit when selling at the market would have gotten you out. That fraction of a point can look trivial compared to the ultimate loss. Put limits in on the upside if you want to establish a target; sell at the market otherwise.

Lastly, there are a variety of other limited-price orders, each with a peculiar twist. "Immediate or cancel" is a limit order which is canceled on the spot if at that time it cannot be executed at or within the limit set. It has its trading uses, but the virtues are entirely on the buy side. On the sell side, you run the grave risk of having an order canceled which ought to be executed. The same holds true for two cousins of the "immediate or cancel" order, the "fill or kill" and the "all or none." Shun them on the sell side. They introduce non-market factors to the decision-making process.

## Entering the Order before the Opening

Preceding chapters have discussed the importance of guarding against loss. It's folly to allow a losing situation of a stock not behaving as expected to become a disaster. The use of stop-loss orders is sound protection for locking in profits too. But since stops are triggered on declines, and since we now know how to identify certain signs of impending market weakness, it is preferable to take our profits by selling into strength during advances. A stop-loss order is a good defense, but as the saying goes, the best defense is a good offense. Better to let avid buyers have our shares at higher prices than to wait, perhaps paralyzed, as a subsequent decline stops us out, thereby donating back a chunk of the profit. As you can see, however, in the instance of the man holding the Technicolor shares, this requires other skills: specifically, an order entered to sell at the market, plus, we believe, a means of eliminating any potential emotion.

Easier said than done, of course. The first hurdle is in recognizing that no stock—even the one you are riding to fortune—goes up forever. Indeed, the best sell signal of all may be sounded whenever some rapturous voice inside your head exults: "Have I got a big winner!" If, somehow, science could hook up an investor's brain with electrodes which would transmit a sell order to the Exchange floor whenever this sort of self-congratulatory attitude becomes too enthusiastic, the complexities of selling would be solved.

What is more apt to happen is that we become so enamored of our beautiful choice that we don't notice wrinkles developing, the aching back, the sour moments. We're excited by news, or by the heights the stock is perched on, or by the Dow's own highs. The most dangerous reaction to owning a stock that goes up is to fall in love with it and swear that you two will never part. Not long ago we overheard one man boasting to another about an Amex stock, which had gone up from 8 to 20, and no one (yet how did it get from 8 to 20?) yet realized how huge the earnings were going to be. Without knowing anything about the stock, we muttered: "A sure sell signal," and sure enough, it was down to 15 within two weeks. The more selling becomes inconceivable, the closer to a top the stock is.

There must be a way to avoid the penchant to hang on, to see "one more tick" or "one more day." We first observed the answer long ago in the behavior of an off-floor trader. This gentleman, having retired from a prosperous business, had treated himself to his own seat on the Exchange. Not the least bit interested in sitting in front of the tape all day every day, he would invariably march into the brokerage-firm office that handled his bookkeeping about fifteen minutes before the market closed and, without taking his coat off, would study the tape for a few minutes and buy any especially active stock that was about to close on its high for the day. The name of the company didn't matter, or what business it was in, or its earnings, or its future prospects. And, having bought, he would simply leave behind an order to sell his position at the opening the next morning. No fuss, no muss; just sell at the market at the opening. His profits, as you can surmise, were relatively small, but they were amazingly consistent. Strength at the close almost always ensures a higher opening the next trading day, even though that opening turns out to be the peak for the day, or the whole move, as with Technicolor.

The rationalization may be a news item, boosting the stock when it appears on the Dow Jones news ticker during the day and then inducing added buying from those who read the news in the morning paper. Or it may be that the strong performance itself catches the attention of other investors. Perhaps salesmen are pushing a new recommendation from their firm's research department and the visible rise convinces some amateurs that it is okay to buy. And, too, there is undoubtedly some law operative in the market akin to the momentum of an object once set in motion. Whatever the reason, it is best to sell at the opening.

## How the Opening Is Arranged

While the specialist's assigned duty is to maintain a fair and orderly market throughout the trading day, it is at each morning's opening that this task receives extra emphasis. Buy and sell orders have accumulated overnight, creating a fresh battle between supply and demand. Gone is the randomness, for just this one time each day the specialist must resolve the disparity and determine a fair opening price. We've already shown how you can benefit by putting yourself in the specialist's shoes when events are about to cause an extreme opening. But the way the specialist handles routine openings can also work to your favor.

As recently as the forties, openings were incredibly hectic and not nearly as fair as they are now. The specialist then was just another face in the Exchange crowd. Each broker represented his own firm's order, and when the opening bell rang, everyone began to shout at once what he wanted to do: buy or sell, at what price, and how many shares. From the wild scene that ensued, reminiscent of the homesteading scrambles of the West, a split opening often ensued, and a stock could actually open at different prices at the same time.

Split openings have long since gone the way of downtick short selling into the land of the good old days. When volume began to perk up after World War II, brokers from larger firms found that they couldn't properly fill all their opening orders, since that would have required them to be at several different trading posts at the same time. So the rule was changed, and now the broker dashes around the floor beforehand, dropping off the pre-opening orders from his firm's customers with the various specialists involved. Because this makes his task of arranging a fair opening price more convenient, the specialist willingly waives the usual floor brokerage fee that would be charged for handling the order and lets the originating broker keep the commission (his fee is included in the commission you pay). Obviously, the broker is delighted to get the execution gratis. The result is that such opening orders have come to be known as love orders, equating the granting of monetary favors with an act of affection.

As we've said, the practical effect of permitting love orders at openings is to eliminate the random sequence and frantic scene that otherwise would take place. With virtually all orders in his hand, the specialist's task is much easier, dependent not on an unpredictable flow of orders one after the other but on the actual supply and demand. If, after the orders have been sorted, a discrepancy between buyers and sellers remains, the specialist would then meet his obligation to get the stock open by trading for his own dealer account. In so doing, he can't go against the functioning of supply and demand; if there are more buyers than sellers, the stock obviously should open higher, and specialist selling that would cause a lower price instead is not permissible.

When it comes to determining the opening price, the specialist takes all available information into consideration: the orders left with him for love's sake on both sides of the market, his own dealer position or lack of one, limited-price orders previously entered on the book away from the closing price, any additional orders brokers in the crowd may be representing themselves, and whatever a floor trader hanging around might be tempted to do. Before coming to a decision, he's likely to consider the overall market too. But, in the end, the decision must be justified on the basis of the market's law of supply and demand: how many orders to buy, how many to sell, how many are transactable at a given price. The preponderance of one side over the other determines the tilt, and then, if necessary to get the stock open, the specialist will deal for his own account. Because the specialist thus, in effect, decides on a fair price for you, and often for himself as well, our belief is that *openings generally provide the soundest selling opportunity*.

The SEC, in a special study of the securities markets, conducted in the early sixties, determined that "the opening price of an issue is probably the single most important price of the day." (Subsequently, of course, the newspaper stock tables were redesigned to eliminate this "important price" in exchange for the treacherous item of price/earnings ratios!) While other moments are random —they might prove satisfactory, but they could just as well be disadvantageous—the opening is the time when (1) there is most apt to be an excess of buyers over sellers, and (2) the specialist is able to produce the most objectively calculated (least random) price of the day. Moreover, entering your sell order before the market opens is the single best way not to be influenced by emotional factors.

## Why You Can Get a Better Price

In hindsight, it certainly would have been sensible to have entered that sell order in Technicolor before the opening. But the opening can be beneficial as well in mundane situations and in run-of-the-mill stocks. Let's say you own 100 shares of XYZ, which you thought was going to be marvelous but wasn't, so you decide to sell, figuring that it's better to set the money to work elsewhere. You phone your broker that afternoon and are told that XYZ's last sale was at 20 and, the broker adds, punching his desktop interrogation machine, the current quotation is 19 3/4 bid, while the best offer is 20 1/4. Noticing that the quote exactly straddles the last sale, you surmise that no one is particularly interested in the stock and that the specialist himself may be on one or both sides of the market just to keep things alive.

Perhaps your reaction is: "What the hell, it's going nowhere fast; let's get rid of it right now and find some action elsewhere." In this case, if your broker sends a market sell order to the floor before the close of trading, you'd wind up getting the bid price, 19 3/4. If you try to be cute about it and enter a limit order at the same price as the last sale (20), as many public players are tempted to do, you may wind up without an execution at all, unless, by chance, a buyer drifts in before the final bell rings. But you are risking, in that game, another seller hitting the bid at 19 3/4 ahead of you and thereby dropping the price even more.

But suppose you tell your broker you're going to think about it over night, and after a restless sleep, you decide that, with the market growing toppy according to the indicators and with XYZ going sideways, you are right to want to sell out. Without further hesitation, having made an objective decision based on what you actually do know (and unaffected by ticks on the tape), you phone your broker early in the morning and direct him to sell at the market, at whatever the opening price is destined to be. How simple! No worrying about what the next tick will prove, no dreams of pots of gold blinding your judgment, no prayer that it will bounce back up to where you should have sold it, no need to cling to the phone or haunt a brokerage office all day. You are going to accept whatever the specialist decides is a fair opening price, and kiss the stock goodbye.

XYZ will open either up, unchanged, or down, but it will open, because your market order must be executed. According to Rule 13, a market order has precedence over a limited-price order and must be executed even if the stock opens at exactly the price of the limit. (The limited-price order will get an execution only if there is another buyer around to match the limit order.) Thus you can go about your real business for the rest of the day, secure in the knowledge that you've made a decision as unemotionally as possible and that you're assured of an execution. The phone is not going to ring with your broker at the other end of the line hysterically crying out, "You missed it! What do you want to do now?"

Ponder for a moment how impossible it is to make a rational decision with your broker whining like that. Now, let's go back to see, in practical terms, just how that "sell at the market at the opening" would work out instead.

First, suppose someone else in this vast country has decided to buy 100 shares of XYZ at the market, and likewise, a man who lives across the street from the company's accountant wants to acquire 200 shares. When the specialist arrives at his trading post, his clerk informs him that XYZ has 300 shares at the market to buy and 100 shares (yours) at the market to sell. He ruffles through the pages of his book and notes that there are 200 shares entered to sell at 20 1/4 "good till canceled," the same shares that were being offered as part of the quotation the afternoon before. This situation is strictly procedural. He simply takes the 300 shares to buy, matches them with the 300 shares to sell, and opens the stock at the price at which he can do so as the agent, without involving his own account as dealer, specifically, at 20 1/4. Even if the limit order were not there to sell, and he had to supply stock from his own account (selling long, if he had any shares, or selling short if need be), he could still properly open the stock at 20 1/4, since a disparity between buyers and sellers (in this case, 300 to 100 shares) calls for an opening price which fairly represents the weight of supply and demand; 20 1/4 would be fair enough. Note that although the opening price was up only one quarter of a point from the previous close, you've actually gotten half a point more than you would have received had you sold the previous afternoon to the then-prevailing bid at 19 3/4. That's an extra $50 in your pocket, a reward for making your decision away from the pressures of broker and ticker tape.

But suppose the situation isn't that convenient. The specialist himself may have a long position that he wants to whittle down, and so he agrees with you that XYZ is better sold than held. With the weight of orders on the buy side and the opportunity to do some selling of his own, he could tack on his 200 shares along with yours and still legitimately open the stock higher, perhaps at 20 1/8. At worst, he could open XYZ unchanged, which is what most specialists would do if they knew they intended to continue to sell later on. In this case he'd be saying: "I'm a professional right on the floor. I own the same stock as you, and I also want to sell it now." And you'd still be doing better than you would have the previous afternoon (by $25), while guaranteeing yourself an execution by making it a market rather than a limited-price sell order. The specialist, in joining you, has not held off to see if he can do better later on, and neither should you.

This scenario is predicated on buyers having drifted in overnight, which they are wont to do—but not always. If only 100 shares to buy came in, to match yours, the stock would open at 20 (again, $25 more for you). But let's make it worse. If no buyers have come in before the opening, you'd be back to the situation that prevailed the afternoon before. Your 100 shares to sell and no buyers would probably call for an opening price of 19 3/4. The specialist couldn't permit a variation on a mere 100 shares of more than that quarter of a point from the previous closing price (remember the rules for a "fair and orderly" market). So you wouldn't have lost anything by waiting for the opening, and you still have the possibility of doing better. What's more, that possibility is nurtured in reality, rather than in sheer hope, for the odds favor getting more, even if the stock merely opens unchanged.

Finally, take the worst possible situation. Suppose orders coming in overnight turn out to be 300 more shares to sell. XYZ wouldn't open higher at all now that you've got company. Too bad, it seems, and yet there is a virtue here too. Let's say that the stock would open lower, with 400 shares to sell at the market when there is a lone 100 shares bid for at 19 3/4, which produces an opening (depending on what the specialist had to do, and wanted to do, for his own account) anywhere from 19 3/4 (if there were other bidders or he wanted to pick up shares) to 19 1/2 (anything lower would be defensible only on considerably more volume). This lower opening has cost you $25. But it has also told you that your decision to sell was sound, since other sellers have been able to shift the balance of supply and demand. And you've gained one other advantage. Instead of being on the phone with your broker a few minutes after the opening, desperately trying to decide what to do now that the stock has opened lower and the bid side of the market is even lower, you are already out on the opening. Your broker is on the phone with an investor who hesitated, who wanted to see one more tick. Now that tick spells trouble, imminent or temporary perhaps, but the startled holder confronted with a decision has to react quickly. "Any news on the broad tape?" the broker shouts across the room. An uptick, and he feels relieved; another downtick, an even lower bid—should he just settle for whatever he can get? The lull before the storm can be quiet, or a consolidation of forces. Another barrage of selling and the stock is down to 19 before he has made a decision, and then the decision too often becomes: "Oh, sell the damn thing if it rallies back to 20." And it doesn't, and he's still holding down near 10. No thanks! Not least among the virtues of selling at the market at the opening is that you relieve yourself of these enormously dangerous conversations with your broker while the tape is running.

## But Suppose There Is News

Despite the constant reiteration, and smug common knowledge, that both the market and individual stocks discount news in advance, to say nothing of the inevitable corrections that arrive after optimism has become excessive, somehow there is always a flock of sheep streaming in to buy when headlines proclaim some favorable news item. We've seen major market tops form when the whole world is bullish (i.e., January 1973), and in individual stocks, tops are constantly being made when the company announces higher earnings forecasts, or a raised dividend, or a stock split. When such events hit the headlines, the soundest reaction is to do as the specialist does, especially if the news confirms the reasons you bought into the stock in the first place. Remember the essential point: the more people are jealous of your possession, the more consistently profitable it is to accommodate their eagerness by selling to them. The ability to be perverse is a vital market skill, akin to the contrariness that keeps the Yankee farmer steps ahead of tourists.

But what should you do when abrupt bad news produces the expectation of a sharply lower opening? In the light of our guiding principle of trying, if possible, to be on the same side of the market as the specialist, and since the specialist is going to have to buy in such a situation, this is perhaps the hardest decision of all. For whatever reason—because you may have missed some nuance that would have forewarned you of trouble, or plain bad luck (a fire burns the factory down overnight)—you are trapped in a difficult situation. It can happen to anyone, even the most experienced pro. If you don't sell because everyone else is reacting emotionally and you don't want to join that mob, you risk staying with a stock that could be plunging into deep trouble; if you do sell, it could be a temporary, or even final, clean-out before a rally.

First and foremost, make your decision before the stock actually opens. Don't postpone fate by telling yourself you'll wait to see just how bad it looks after the opening. The second step, now that you've gotten yourself settled down, is to ask yourself exactly what kind of stock and situation you are dealing with. We've already touched on one question: What was the stock doing before the bad news? If the stock had already been sliding (while you've been paralyzed), the market may indeed have amply discounted the news in advance. Often the stock which has endured considerable selling will open lower, but then the pressure will lift because smart money has long since sold and only stragglers are left. If you've been trapped with a stock that seems to be getting its bad news near the end of the drop—either in its own right or as part of a bear market, as in December 1974—you must try to keep enough perspective to ignore the news itself. A rally is likely to ensue. That's a lot different from realizing you'd bought a stock that wasn't doing well, but not badly either, when all of a sudden the bombshell struck. Typically, that kind of smack can set the stock on its heels for months, or for an entire cycle. A lot more time may be needed for this kind of situation to work its way out and, rather than waiting with your money in limbo, it is usually better to sell. A third variation is when news strikes an already strong stock in which you've got a decent profit. For instance, in January 1974, rumors of an excess-profits tax for coal companies caused a sharp sell-off of about 15 percent for all the stocks in that industry group. The question to ask in such instances pertains to the stock's chart. Will the expected sell-off spoil something? That is, if the stock already shows some signs of tiredness, or if an important trend line or Moving Average line would be violated by the wave of selling, then you have a warning to get out. If the stock is still relatively early in an overall uptrend (for example, if there's been no comparable percentage drop thus far), you can expect a fair-sized rebound off the sharply lower opening, and we'd wait for that. In most instances of sharply lower openings on news, the sequence goes like this: the specialist has to be a buyer, while almost everyone who has wanted to sell on the news has done so; therefore, after the opening, there are few sellers, some bargain hunters, leaving the specialist the main seller as he feeds out the stock he has just bought. Obviously, waiting for the rebound is the way to join the specialist.

If you're alert, you shouldn't often find yourself selling into bad news. But it is such a difficult problem that it warrants more attention. To get a fuller understanding of how to act, you should know what happens on the floor when bad news strikes. A flood of orders can be expected to reach the post, as panicky sellers plunge ahead. (Make sure you've got a broker who always phones you with news on any stock you are holding, or have expressed an interest in; that's his job.) If a stock hasn't opened by 10:30 A.M., it is considered delayed; that is, a floor official steps in to formally define the difficult situation and the ticker tape will then report: OPENING DELAYED XYZ INFLUX OF ORDERS. A notice of NEWS PENDING informs you that the Exchange has been notified that something material is about to be announced and that trading should not proceed pending the announcement, so that all holders and potential holders can make a more informed decision. You should also note that a stock is considered open even if there has been no transaction, provided the specialist has established a bid and offer price. No trade, no interest in the stock on the floor. The specialist is responsible for any quotation he establishes; the next transaction must be within the limits of that quotation. Thus, if faced with a difficult situation, the specialist is not going to risk quoting the stock. Otherwise, some quick-witted money manager could take advantage of the quotation by insisting on an execution for a large block of stock which the specialist had not taken into account when framing the quotation. As a result, you'll usually find delayed openings (and re-openings) clarified not by a quotation but by an announcement on the floor and a print on the tape to the effect of: INDICATION ONLY 45–50.

In the spring of 1972, after Levitz Furniture, then trading at 59 1/2, had been delayed in opening for several days after an SEC investigation had been launched, the first clue of a potential range from the floor was an indication of 43–49. Ample time was then allotted for the public to respond to this projected possibility. The response was a large number of new buy orders, from traders anxious to cover their shorts at a hefty profit as well as those who thought they ought to buy such a glamorous stock if it were going to sell some 15 points lower. The result was that the imbalance of orders at the specialist's post shifted somewhat, and a new indication was then issued of 46–49. With the bid, or buying, side raised, while the sell side remained the same, the tape announcement was a clear word that buy orders had come in. This succeeding shift toward buying sentiment in the midst of a drastically lower potential opening was the only clue—and the only one needed—to recognize that, rather than having to be on the buy side as he would have been forced to be at the outset, the specialist now could take advantage of the rush of buyers and get away from that side of the market. That oddity might very well have told a holder to enter a sell order, that the opening was going to be the best price he could get, since the potential buyers were going to be sucked in on the opening transaction. Indeed, LEV opened at 49, went to 49 1/8 (the only tick, interestingly enough, where a short sale could be made), and eventually fell to 1 1/2.

But that's an extreme example. Let's return to a hypothetical delayed opening in old XYZ. Perhaps, without any apparent news, the specialist finds orders to buy 3,000 shares and has only your lonesome 100 shares to sell. In a relatively inactive stock such as this one, an imbalance of this magnitude can make the specialist uncomfortable. If there were no news, he'd try to find out if anything were brewing. First, he'd notify the brokers who have brought in the buy orders that the opening price "looks much higher" and, informally, ask what the hell they know about it. Perhaps, he may suspect, a tender offer or takeover attempt is in the works. Step 2 is to notify the floor official assigned to his area to get the opening delayed if necessary. Such a delay, plus a publicly announced indication, may help locate a seller or two, or to cause buy orders to be withdrawn, and the time can also be used to contact the company to find out if they know what's up. It may turn out that the orders were generated simply by a buy recommendation by a major retail brokerage firm or an influential advisory service.

One opening transaction anomaly worth citing is the clue you or your broker may catch from the tape. Watch for an opening which comes precisely just within the rule permitting the stock to open either two points (one point in stocks under 20) or 10 percent away from its last trade *without* the specialist getting floor official approval. An opening in XYZ at 21 7/8, up 1 7/8 rather abruptly, would suggest that the specialist wants to seize the chance to sell stock of his own without getting involved with officialdom (who might frown on the steep variation in price).

One of the most difficult emotional situations for a prospective seller to accept is that, when selling time arrives, the more buyers the better. If the specialist indicates a higher opening price, it doesn't matter whether the reason announced on the tape for a delayed opening is "news pending" or "influx of orders," leave in your sell order.

If, on the other hand, a delayed opening occurs because there are 3,000 shares to sell, including your 100 shares, and a mere 100 shares to buy, you've got a problem. For now you're holding a stock that shows signs of needing to be sold but, just as you've reached that decision, the stock will open sharply lower. How to sell? Most of the time, extremes like Levitz being the exception, the stock will open in the middle of its indicated price range. It will then bounce a bit as buyers are enticed, but usually not as high as the upper limit of the indicated range published beforehand on the tape, which is the specialist telling you where he thinks the upper limit is likely to be. In the Levitz situation, the bounce actually took place before the stock opened, when the "indication only" spread was lifted to 46–49, when you would have been advised to sell right then and there. Let's say XYZ has an "indication only" of last sale 20, now "17 1/2–19 1/2." Don't forget that in a more objective moment you've analyzed the situation and decided to sell.

The ensuing inevitable bounce (99 times out of 100) is for you to heed. Who is selling on the post-opening bounce? Why, the specialist, of course (and his floor-trader buddies who are in on the sharply lower opening just to snare that bounce). He was forced to the buy side at the opening and is now using the recovery to feed those shares back out.

The more meager the bounce, the faster you should sell. Beware of getting trapped all over again. There have been innumerable occasions when, as soon as the spurt of bargain hunters has subsided, trading had to be halted once more on the downside because of a fresh influx of sellers. One method of protection, once you've decided to sell, is to use an either/or order, trying to snag the bounce with a limit order on the upside just under the previously indicated offer or on stop an eighth under the opening price. Let's say that XYZ opens at 18 1/2, midway in its announced "indication only" area. You reason that the upper limit of 19 1/2 is a sensible maximum expectation under the circumstances. Being trapped, so to speak, you don't want to fuss over an eighth of a point, so you enter your order, "Sell at 19 1/4 limit or on stop at 18 3/8." In that way, if the stock resumes its weakness, you'll be sold out promptly without having to wait for that panicky phone call from your broker.

A typical example of this sort of situation developed in Campbell Soup. The stock already had been sagging when unexpected news struck: an allegation of botulism in their cans made the headlines. With Campbell trading in the mid-30's before the news, the initial indication from the floor the next morning was "31–33." It was, therefore, a situation in which an already weak stock assumed added vulnerability. There was no telling how widespread incidents of potentially deadly cans might become. Hanging on to the stock in such circumstances was too risky, thus one would try to catch the bounce after the delayed opening and get out, if only to protect capital. Sure enough, CPB opened at 32, exactly in the middle of the indicated range, rallied back to 32 3/4, and got no higher, illustrating two common happenings: it failed under the upper limit of the announced range and also under a round number. Here, too, an either/or order would have been sensible, to catch the quick rebound if possible, but with protection an eighth under the opening price, so that if the decline were to resume before the bounce got to your limit order (as it actually did in this case, down into the 20's), you'd get stopped out before it had a chance to accelerate. Don't worry about the other half of the order; if it is designated either/or, the unexecuted portion is automatically canceled.

Such selling decisions are, as we've said, among the most difficult of all, because of the added pressure of the company of other sellers. In sum, your guidelines should be: Was it beginning to look like a possible sale before the news struck? Is the potential opening price going to spoil the technical chart picture for a long time to come (break important support, plunge below a trend line or Moving Average line, etc.)? Has it already had a substantial slide discounting the impact of this news? Or is it the kind of bad news that simply has the effect of shaking out nervous traders before an already strong rise resumes? (The first such rumor can be shrugged off, but we wouldn't ignore repeated messages; consider that any "normal" rise is allowed at least one "normal" correction, even if news-induced.)

Above all, keep your wits about you. If it's time to sell, it's time to sell, whether the news is good or bad. Here's an example of the value of perspective, considering the market as a whole. President Eisenhower's heart attack came in the late stages of a prolonged intermediate-term rally, which was getting tired and beginning to emanate toppy clues. Thus, the startling and totally unexpected news struck a market which had already become vulnerable; many stocks were unable to open until that day's closing bell, when one transaction was printed on the tape. The bounce lasted the entire next day, and it paid to sell into that rebound, given the market situation, for a full-scale intermediate correction followed. On the other hand, Ike's ileitis attack came after a decline had been in effect for some time. The market trembled for about an hour, but after the news had shaken out a last bevy of nervous holders, prices began to rebound strongly and a new uptrend was actually launched on the news. Evaluate individual stock situations in the same way, always asking yourself the same critical questions: What is the overall perspective? And what is the specialist going to have to do for his own account?

## The Professional's Pet

The stock market mirrors America, and one of the peripheral images it reflects is that of the affluent society. We've been discussing the sensible time and way to sell a round lot of 100 shares, or 200 or 300 shares, but there are plenty of investors who've accumulated blocks of stock: 2,000 shares of Dow after it splits; 1,000 Merck that they've been picking up for years; 5,000 shares of Pan American Air because it always seemed like such a bargain. In the abstract, the holder can calculate the value of the block at the latest closing price; in reality, it's worth what he can get for it; and the more shares offered for sale, the more it will affect the price. In such circumstances it is wise to use the type of order professionals use to get out of big positions: the not-held order.

The not-held order provides the same sort of advantages as selling at the opening, with the added one that it can take away some of the randomness of executions during the trading day. It's not suitable for the modest 100- or 200-share transactions, but the more you have to liquidate, the better an order it can be. For one thing, the market can be tested for interest on the other side. For another, the broker on the floor can provide some experienced input, so you won't be flying blind. Hence, if you have a mini-block of 1,000 shares (less if the stock is high-priced or relatively inactive) or more, consider adding to your order the not-held (or "disregard tape" or "take time") qualification.

You'll recall that the floor broker handling a market order is responsible for not missing the market. He must get the best price available to him on reaching the trading crowd. If he tries to use his own judgment, some other broker or floor trader might nab an execution first and he could wind up having to settle for less. Since the basis of record is the ticker tape itself, the term "held" denotes that the broker is literally bound to the sequence of prints on the tape as they appear. As a result, when a broker has a market order to sell, he'll march to the post, ask for the quotation, try an offer a little better than what he could otherwise get by hitting the bid (or ask to be stopped), and in the end, if he must, will settle for selling to the best price available as promptly thereafter as possible.

In all, this sequence might take five seconds.

In contrast, by marking the order not-held, the customer is excusing the floor broker from being held to the tape sequence. In effect, he is telling the broker to use his own judgment: that he promises not to get angry if the broker misses a good price, even if it happens that the order is butchered by an incompetent or inexperienced broker, or missed by sheer bad luck. Thus a not-held sell order, which can be either at the market or with a limit prescribing the price below which the customer does not want to go, gives the floor broker discretion to handle the order as he feels best, based on his intimate vantage point. Whether or not to place a limit on the order depends on the number of shares involved and how active the stock is. Using a limit initially can be in the form of the kind of question one bridge partner asks another via the bidding: "Can I get my limit if you take your time and handle the order on a not-held basis?"

The more experienced the floor broker is, the wiser it is to give him his head. But it is always sensible to let him know in advance what it is you have in mind; the key word is "communication." In addition to specifying that the order is not-held, some of the terms institutions add to such orders are "no hurry," or "go along with the market" (meaning, ride the tides and don't buck them), or "don't initiate" (telling the broker not to make a trade at a new price but to let someone else do it first). For example, you may spot a huge head-and-shoulders top (see next chapter) forming in a stock you've nursed upward for years. You want to sell, but because the stock hasn't actually broken down as yet, you have some time to let the floor broker try to sell the block at the best prices he can get. Another example would occur after the stock has broken down and you want to sell the entire block out on the pullback rally. Since you don't know how far the rally can carry before dying, you use the not-held order to let the broker sell when he feels he should, but you make sure he knows you want out before the end of the day. At other times, the floor broker may come back to you with the information that he can get such-and-such a price for the entire block at once, then discuss with you how you want the block handled.

As might be expected, floor brokers are decidedly more edgy

when handling a sell order than a buy order, fearing that the price could tumble rapidly on them while they wait. They confess to feeling they can safely hold back with a buy order, even allowing the stock to get away, because they are confident it will fluctuate toward support again, while a sell order is handled more aggressively to be sure of an execution. Often prices can ebb on an absence of bidders, so they want to take advantage of the buyer's presence while they can. (That's a good reason to let the broker know the entire amount you want to sell; he needs to know the amount of buying he has to locate.) Oddly enough (or not so oddly, given the psychology of selling), while the floor broker instinctively wants to persist in selling instead of tinkering with the order, the institutional manager upstairs is more likely to try to mastermind the sell order by placing limits and let the buy order go to the floor at the market. Again, they've got it backward, just as the public has when trying to sell a volatile stock at a set price while buying recklessly at whatever price they can. The pain of reckoning is never in the buying.

## Back to Basics

Even now the morning of August 16, 1971—the day after Nixon announced his economic game plan—is remembered as a bullish day. After all, it was a record rise on then-record volume. Actually, it presented a clear call to sell. It was just a simple matter of being on the same side as the specialist and selling at the opening. It is obvious in retrospect, and it should have been obvious at the time, that the correct decision was to sell. But of course you have to make the decisions, and without hindsight's benefit. We hope we've convinced you that it is better, far better, to make them while the tape is still. Take a few moments to concentrate on each stock you hold. What are your feelings about the stock? Sorry you bought it? Sorry you haven't sold it already? Dreaming of riches? Fearful of disaster? Once you make up your mind to sell, stick by that decision, and simplify its execution by entering the order before the opening. You could garner a fractionally better price than if you are compelled to hit the prevailing bid the afternoon before, but if the stock is too weak, you'll at least be out before the situation deteriorates further. You certainly don't want to add to the emotional burden of selling at a loss by having to make the decision during the turmoil of the market's trading day. Any random uptick might lure you into delaying; any downtick could be a further distortion.

And don't spoil the decision at the very end by entering your sell order with a limit price attached. Knowing that the opening is the most advantageous time to sell, harness this unique market moment, which occurs but once each day, by utilizing at-the-market orders. Let the specialist himself determine a fair opening price. When he balances the overnight gathering of orders on both sides of the market, a limited-price order fights his options. If you limit your sell order to a supposedly desirable price (desired by you, for extraneous reasons, but not necessarily by anyone else), the stock might open just below your set figure, not out of any manipulation, but simply because the specialist may be able to balance the opening without you. What's more, when the specialist matches the orders in hand before the opening, a market order has precedence over a limit order. The stock actually could open at the price of your limit order without your getting an execution because the market orders balanced at that price, shutting you out. You'd feel pretty foolish, and a lot poorer, if the stock tumbled while you still owned it, even though you'd picked the exact opening price to get out at. That would be the ultimate in making sure you get punished by the market: the perfect decision, and still the loser.

# 9

## *Individual Stocks*

We've been discussing the market in general terms, setting up the background against which stocks rise and fall. Intelligent selling absolutely depends on knowing the market's overall trend. But when it comes right down to it, your selling decisions, even though influenced by those general market factors, must be made stock by stock. It's not the dignified Dow, or the high/low differential, but each independent issue that will make your fortune or break your bank. You must be able to sell an individual holding whenever it's time to sell, regardless of the rest of the market.

In this chapter we'll discuss various ways you can tell when a stock is ripe for selling. For the most part, that information is contained in the charts of a stock's action; it's not difficult, it's not exotic, but it does require that you have charts for the stocks in your portfolio. You can keep them yourself, as you should be keeping those few indicators we've already discussed, or you can purchase them from a number of sources. In our experience, the ideal compromise between the amount of time and effort needed and the wastefulness of tracking a lot of different stocks is this: keep daily charts on a handful of market leaders (GM, IBM, etc.) and the stocks you actually hold (starting charts upon any purchase) while subscribing to a weekly chart service (such as Mansfield).

That will give you the past history for stocks you are directly interested in, as well as provide the chance to study the whole market and to uncover new groups as they emerge as buying or selling candidates. As a rule, watch (or chart) only what you can watch closely; if you try to do too much, you'll find that mistakes are happening before you can catch up. And keep in mind that the charts don't reveal the future. They show exactly what has been happening up to that moment and that's all. They provide an objective picture so you won't have to make a subjective judgment. Now let's learn how to read such charts so that we can make intelligent selling decisions.

## Analyzing Rally Action

There are two ways to botch the sale of a stock that has risen: selling too early in the move, or waiting too long and selling well after the decline has set in. Let's discuss the problem of premature selling first. There are many instances where the action of a stock you hold may become disquieting. You can't put your finger on anything dangerous, but you don't like what's been happening. The chart may be saying "Not so good," yet still not be screaming "Awful." Is it temporary? Minor? The first warning clue? In such cases, you must search for other information, studying the Moving Average, the current price level in relation to the long-term picture, and upside vs. downside volume. Let's search for clues in these charts of A. E. Staley, covering most of 1974 and the start of 1975.

STA's rally at point A was a powerful move, signifying the start of an important uptrend. Note the confirming volume as the stock broke out above its prior high. If you had bought the stock around 33, in that little congestion area (point C) just before the breakout, you'd have been confident, with no thoughts of selling. But not long after A, at B, the stock inexplicably seemed to have run into trouble, like a rocket just off the pad that begins to wobble in clear view of the spectators. There was a gap on the downside as sellers poured in, and the slide carried alarmingly below the level of the previous short-term correction (which had followed A). With the Dow at this time plunging toward a new bear-market low, confidence would have given way to fear. As the stock fell under 38, you

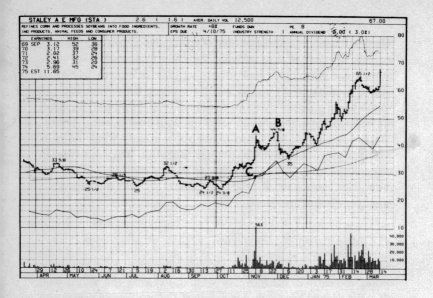

REFINES CORN AND PROCESSES SOYBEANS INTO FOOD INGREDIENTS, IND PRODUCTS, ANIMAL FEEDS AND CONSUMER PRODUCTS.

| | | | |
|---|---|---|---|
| GROWTH RATE | +8% | FUNDS OWN | PE 8 |
| EPS DUE | 4/10/75 | INDUSTRY STRENGTH | ANNUAL DIVIDEND 3.00 ( 3.0%) |

| EARNINGS | HIGH | LOW |
|---|---|---|
| 69 SEP 3.12 | 52 | 36 |
| 70 3.17 | 39 | 28 |
| 71 2.02 | 37 | 24 |
| 72 2.41 | 32 | 26 |
| 73 2.96 | 31 | 20 |
| 74 5.69 | 45 | 24 |
| 75 EST 11.65 | | |

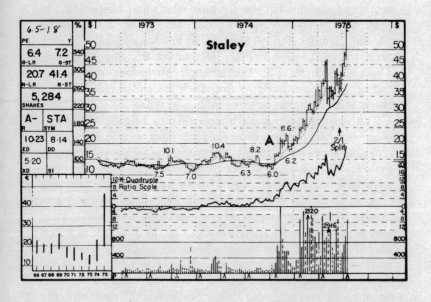

| 6.5-1.8 | % | $ | 1973 | 1974 | 1975 | $ |
|---|---|---|---|---|---|---|

Staley

| PE | | Y |
|---|---|---|
| 6.4 | | 7.2 |
| G-LR | | G-ST |
| 20.7 | | 41.4 |
| N-LR | | N-ST |
| 5,284 | | |
| SHARES | | |
| A- | | STA |
| R | | SYM |
| 10.23 | | 8.14 |
| ED | | DD |
| 5.20 | | |
| XD | | SI |

12 × Quadruple
8 Ratio Scale

66 67 68 69 70 71 72 73 74 75

might have concluded that the burst of strength had been some sort of bull trap and so rushed to grab the few dollars of profit remaining. Using hindsight, you can see that panic would have been terribly wrong, yet the short-term behavior certainly was alarming.

Hindsight isn't there to help at the moment, so let's see what the arguments against panic were. For instance, if you'd stepped back calmly, you would have taken solace in the pattern of volume. After the extraordinary burst of activity on the upside, you can see that daily volume shrank considerably during the correction, denoting only slight selling pressure, and, for added evidence, it kept on shrinking from the low level of the day of the gap to even lesser selling at the reaction low. Moreover, the unsettling decline did not take the stock down to the initial area of support between 32 and 34, and that dip to 35 stopped well above the long-term Moving Average line. (For what it's worth, it also stopped above the 10-week M.A. both then and again in January at 40. While this shorter-term M.A. is viable in this instance, we've never found it consistent enough to place great faith in.) Lastly, and perhaps most important, is perspective: (1) all that upside volume is so impressive that it argues for more than the minor rally to A and B; (2) the stock has been able to do this in the face of a bear market; and (3) recourse to an overview of STA's weekly chart shows that the entire base from the left side of the chart to the point of upside breakout (A) was so extensive that just a few days of sloppy action shouldn't have scared anyone.

It is a helpful empirical fact that the breadth of a stock's base is related to the carrying power of its rally, the reason being that the more stock which has passed into strong hands, and thus retired from an immediate return into the market, the less selling interference on the way up. Note that Staley's base, on the weekly chart (which reflects a subsequent 2-for-1 split), was forming during a disastrous bear market. Although the stock did fall, the rally in 1974, carrying above the 1973 high, followed by a decline which held above the 1973 low, was evidence of basing action. Someone wanted that stock badly enough to pay up for it even while the Dow was tumbling. This perspective should have been sufficient reassurance during that short-term period of panic, especially since the breakout level was holding and the long-term trend appeared likely to remain intact.

It is worth taking space here to note, as an aside, the nature and meaning of a base. By definition, it necessitates a prior decline of substance; the base forms as a battle commences between those who are willing to get out on any rally and those who want to buy on any further dip. The longer, and the livelier, a base develops, the better the upside potential. Staley's chart action, backed by the infusion of immense volume as the price rose out of the base (breaking out above the prior 35 high), is a near-perfect example of how winners appear right before your eyes, if you are only willing to believe them. In contrast are stocks with bases that are small, relative to overhead resistance, as in the subsequent chart of Xerox on page 181 covering much of the same time span as Staley. It is sheer folly to assume the stock will have sufficient underlying power to surpass such resistance.

We are all afraid of the unknown. The best cure for the anxiety over STA's brief misbehavior is to establish what you do know, and to assure yourself that what you don't know, while perhaps making you uneasy, can't be known, so there's no point in wasting energy about it. If your decision turns out to be wrong, so be it; at least you'll have acted as clearheadedly as you could. It is, we insist, the solid weight of the available evidence that would have kept a purchaser in Staley instead of letting him panic out too soon. And, we might add, there is nothing like a protective stop placed at a sensible level to let the holder feel he's not flying blind. In Staley's case, a stop placed: (1) under the long-term Moving Average line (heavy black line on the weekly chart); (2) under that recent congestion area of 32–34 (point C on the daily chart); and (3) under that extra-round number of 30—at, say, 29 7/8—would have kept any potential loss to 10 to 15 percent. That's a risk well worth taking in view of all the bullish action that occurred before that short-term panic set in.

But we don't have only the evidence of the past upon us; there are also certain aspects of the future that can be determined. The overall market situation should be added to the evidence of Staley's substantial base, the verification of positive volume, and the fact that the long-term Moving Average line had not been broken. To be sure, the DJI was, at that time, frightening to most observers, since it appeared to be heading south once again, but many indicators had already started to turn favorable after a prolonged bear market. By that time, for example, specialist short selling was at minimal (buy signal) levels. These indicators, plus the doctrine of contrary opinion, plus the stock itself, were all reasons to stick with the trend Staley had established on its upside breakout. Indeed, within a few months Staley rose to 120 for perhaps the best performance in the Street during the 1975 rally.

## The Second Correction

It will be recalled from our previous discussion that an intermediate-term bull move generally consists of three upwaves interrupted by two short-term corrections. The end of the first upleg and the coming of the first sell-off can be winked at as temporary misbehaviors. But the second upwave and its inevitable correction are not nearly so easily ignored as the first. It is here that some of the weaker stocks will falter and depart from the pack, never to return for the third and final rally phase. Thus, it is at this point in the market cycle that you must really pay attention to how each of your individual stocks looks. One could be so far ahead of the game that its entire intermediate-term uptrend is concluded and a top formed while the market averages are still chugging upward. At other times you may find yourself holding a stock just as it is about to resume some unfinished downside business, as with Xerox in the second quarter of 1975.

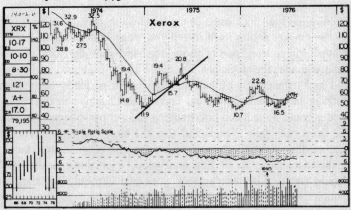

Studying this weekly chart, you can see that everything started off in reasonably good order, except for the troublesome lack of any real base for an upturn. Given a choice, you'd have bought Staley every time compared to Xerox, but the reality is that many brokers simply opt for the famous name and had never even heard of Staley in late 1974. But as the averages soared, XRX joined in, and its long-term Moving Average line turned upward and contained the first reaction. Indeed, the next rally went on to a new recovery high. Up to that point all was well.

But then something began to look wrong: the stock, instead of sustaining the upside, started sliding. The M.A. was broken, as well as the uptrend line, and then added pressure caused a break to a low beneath the previous reaction low. All of this action was solid evidence that Xerox was a sale, well before the news that the company was going out of the computer business at a huge loss. Obviously, several big holders found out in advance and, acting on that knowledge, unloaded their Xerox positions. You didn't need to know what they knew to realize you'd better be getting out too; a protective sell stop placed just below the M.A., trend line, and previous reaction low would have taken you out without any further worry. At the very least, sensible selling was called for on the next little rally to around 70 as the M.A. became an overhead resistance level.

## Using Waves

Each individual stock must be analyzed on its own. You can't rely on the market action itself to tell you what to do with all stocks. Picture for yourself one of those head-and-shoulder tops. As the head is made, the stock has just made a new high and, of course, still looks steadfastly bullish. It might seem perfectly normal for nothing more than its second correction to arrive next. Thus a holder could be seduced into hanging on, but must be alert in case the third rally fails. You'll find that the later the market is in its intermediate uptrend, the more the press and other commentators begin to enthuse about how marvelous everything is. But you should be studying every stock you own carefully for signs of trouble. Don't let the so-called experts fool you.

when many analysts were becoming euphoric—recession ended, bull market confirmed, and even a correction/consolidation already past—it was time to sell. Of course, we could pick out a handful of stocks that were still worth holding, even when the Dow plunged below its wavering M.A. and set off on an intermediate-term downtrend. These stocks are usually out of phase with the general market cycle and allowance must be made for that. Otherwise, you certainly should get in a liquid position: it is the safe tactic and gives you ample buying power for fresh stocks at the correction's end. Having flexibility as the overall market and individual stocks become suspect is always a sound policy.

As the subsequent narrower upleg, following the second market correction, comes to an end, you must be prepared to take action. You certainly don't want to overstay this one. It may be the last wave in this particular cycle, and it may even be the last for the bull market. Even though the Dow may have other intermediate-term uplegs ahead to flesh out an entire primary bull market, your particular stock may never again see the highs it has made on this one. This one may be the third and final upleg of the entire bull market, as in 1972, and you must be prepared for such a situation. Having the freedom and buying power to pick the market's potentially strongest stocks at the next bottom, instead of resigning yourself to potential survivors, is invariably the better policy. Yes, there will be stocks that will top out after the averages, just as there will be stocks that have started downward ahead of the pack. So here are a few added guidelines to remember: (1) If a stock has reached its major overhead resistance area, sell without waiting any longer. After having already had a rise, the stock is highly unlikely to have the strength left to plow through an extensive area; rather, it is apt to be tired and in need of a more substantial correction. Such a resistance area may appear as a prior cyclical top (such as the 880–900 range on the DJI chart), a heavy gathering of activity, best seen as a heap of Xs on a point-and-figure chart (such as the DJI's 840–880 area as formed in early 1974), or a combination of the two; (2) sell if and when the stock starts failing after a period of success, and then rounds over toward its Moving Average, intensifying the need to sell if the M.A. ceases to rise and starts to roll over; (3) sell as soon as the stock starts showing a pattern of lower lows on what might otherwise look like innocuous minor declines. And lastly, (4) sell, even if no other signal is evident but if the indicators have turned negative, the Dow and other averages are toppy, and the stock itself, having fulfilled a five-wave move, is clearly vulnerable. In sum, if market action and indicators tell you it's time, let someone else gamble that there's more left.

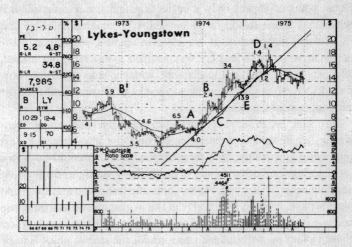

Lykes-Youngstown is a stock that became busy when it defied the great bear of 1974. At point A, the stock actually completed a good-looking base and was officially in an uptrend while the rest of the market was still plunging. It then stalled for many weeks (B), when it ran up against the resistance from the prior 1973 rally peak B'). A nervous trader might well have been tempted to take his profit and run at this time, and considering the state of the rest of the market, it would have been hard to advise him to hang on. But selling would have been a mistake. Stocks do act independently, though, and we think an investor should have noticed the reduced volume during the sideways action and the fact that the stock never came close to breaking its long-term Moving Average. Rather, a protective stop placed just under this long-term M.A. line (around C) would have made sense. Such an investor would still have been holding when the stock staged another upside breakout across 12; the initial purchaser at A would have doubled his money at D, when the Dow first started rolling.

That's an excellent illustration of using the upward direction of the Moving Average to keep you from panicking out of a stock that is acting well. The key, as we've said before, is perspective. As a practical matter, when the M.A. is relatively far away, any stock will be tired by the time it gets down that far. Hence it can reasonably be assumed that the M.A. will hold, and in such juxtapositions, you can expect only a correction and not a reversal. But while that is one lesson to be learned, LY contains another: that is, you can never relax. It would have seemed, according to the action up to point D, that LY was destined to be a truly big winner, as a new bull market got under way, with the stop protection now raised to E, thus guaranteeing at least a 50 percent profit on the original purchase price.

But look at what happened subsequently. Something went wrong, as if sand had been tossed into the gas tank. LY lost momentum, broke the long-term uptrend line that could be drawn (connecting four points made it particularly valid), and the M.A. actually began to arc over. When both the trend line and the M.A. were broken, trouble was clearly in the works, and an alarming top became increasingly visible. The stock should have been sold on those violations, without even waiting for the stop at point E to be set off. You don't need to wait until the boat actually sinks to know that when it springs a leak it's time to get off.

## A Few Rules

A few guidelines can be culled from these examples:

1. Smart selling has its roots in smart buying. Getting in on a stock as it breaks out of a substantial base is the path to gaining latitude: if you've bought too high, even a normal correction can give you a heavy loss. Remember that one of the best means to avoid this beforehand is to examine where you can place an intelligent stop. If you can put it within 10 to 15 percent of your purchase price, okay, but if the stop would be much further away, that should act as a brake on your buying. By the same token, make sure that the base is substantial enough to exceed overhead resistance and that the supply is sufficiently far away so that the stock has room to move.

2. Now that you've set yourself up for a potential gain, let the stock have every chance. So long as its longer-term Moving Average has turned upward and is trailing along underneath the current price, the stock should be held at least through its first short-term correction. Try not to let the price decline frighten you out.

3. Become very careful as the stock approaches the time for its second correction; you may be nearing the true high. If, at this time, the stock has come up to an important resistance level, it is folly to try to milk it for any more. Take your gain.

4. Ditto if the market itself is giving off some warning signs; don't hope that your stock will bloom for one more rally if the market itself seems unlikely to.

5. Try not to be so nervous that you sell too soon, as long as the stock doesn't do anything wrong (violate a previous low, fail to make another high, etc.).

6. A stock which fails to participate in a rally along with the rest of the market is announcing that something is amiss; holders should switch out of it and into something more in tune with the trend.

7. If you do have a stock that's moving, the best way to take a trading profit is to sell into strength at the resistance level (two examples on the Xerox chart on page 184 are: the heavy resistance formed in 1975 between 70 and 80 called for a sale in the first quarter of 1976 on the rally to 70; this rally, in turn, left resistance in the low 60's, where a sale would have been called for on the mid-1976 rally).

8. If these factors are not present, it is preferable to wait patiently until an actual top forms.

## *Analyzing Tops*

In the preceding section we've shown you ways to avoid selling before the end of the rally. But it is equally important to avoid selling too late, after a stock's decline is well underway. This requires an understanding of how to spot a top as it is forming, of what to look for on the charts, and of how to react to what you see. Let's start with the ideal, the stock which has risen nicely and then started forming an important top. Such a top may be defined as a trading range in which, as an intermediate- or long-term upmove comes to an end, supply begins to meet demand and eventually overwhelms it. Sounds simple enough, and indeed it is, occasionally.

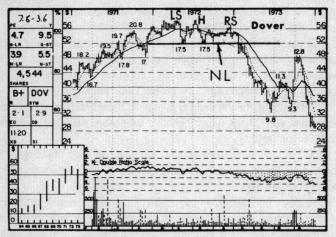

Here's an example of what we mean. After a major uptrend that began in 1970, Dover, at the outset of 1972, spent an entire year carving out a near-perfect, highly visible top, and then neatly gave up the ghost early in 1973. The chart shows what technical analysts call a "head-and-shoulders top" (about which more in a moment), but even without making that sort of technical identification, you can see evidence of a top in the making. By the middle of 1972, certain details argued against harboring hopes that the stock would continue to rise. For one thing, the long-term Moving Average line had ceased to go up and was already moving sideways at best, even though the stock popped up to a new high on the tape. Second, volume had begun to trail off despite the higher prices. And then, even if you had held despite these delicate warning signs, later in the year, when the Dow was heading for record high ground, DOV failed to make a new high. There were, thus, three clear signs of trouble. Moreover, the market in general was giving off unfavorable clues. It was time to sell.

An aggressive investor would have sold Dover well before the year ended and the stock broke down, most probably in the summer, when the M.A. was delineating the end of the uptrend in no uncertain terms. But even a passive investor, were he reasonably alert, would have gotten out in plenty of time. He would merely have had to notice the head-and-shoulders top forming and to have drawn in the corresponding neckline, connecting the two dips. In its simplest form, what happens is that the stock, in an uptrend, experiences a normal correction and then proceeds to another new high. But the next correction carries a bit further than it should, and then comes a rally which fails. In its failure it manages to approximate the first rally peak, thus creating a matching shoulder, while the twin correction lows can be connected in a trend line as the neckline. We've marked these features on the Dover chart; a protective sell-stop order could have been, and should have been, entered at 51 7/8, just below the neckline, so that, even if the holder did nothing else, he would have been stopped out nicely when the stock broke down.

By virtue of its roots in reality, the head-and-shoulders formation gives the lie to those who conceive of technical analysis as something conjured up by mystics. The right shoulder is formed by a failure of demand; the stock might still be saved even then, but a breach of the neckline indicates that sellers now outnumber buyers. The fact that you will typically see more volume on the left-shoulder rally than on the move that produces the head, and, in turn, more volume while the head is being formed than while the right shoulder is experiencing its rally reflects the gradual overcoming of demand by supply. By placing a protective stop just below the neckline, you can be confident that you'll still be on board should the rise resume, but you'll also be sure that you won't be caught holding a stock that starts to head down with dispatch.

Here's another example of a head-and-shoulders formation, a terrific one involving General Medical Corporation. The top began to form while the Dow was still bullish, although the overall market indicators were becoming more and more bearish. Here, again, the head-and-shoulders pattern was readily discernible as it formed over an entire year. Both DOV and GMD took that long, and when you see that extensive a top forming, watch out: the bigger the top, the bigger the subsequent fall is apt to be. We've labeled the various components of the General Medical top on the chart. In this instance there was almost as much volume at the head, and far less on the right shoulder, and when the neckline was broken at 40, the price fell 10 percent rapidly. The traditional rally back to the neckline was so brief that it can only be seen on a chart of the daily action rather than here. (Dover's chart shows a more extensive pullback rally to the neckline after the official breakdown, thereby providing another good chance to sell.) The eventual bottom was under 14.

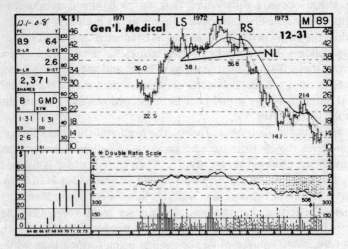

But look carefully at the prior action, and you can see that an important sell signal had been given earlier. While the price flirted with the Moving Average throughout the summer of 1972, the M.A. was decisively broken later that year, at about 44. Thus, the alert holder had all the signal necessary to sell into the strength of the right-shoulder rally, rather than wait for the definitive neckline break. The more negative the overall climate, the more quickly one should act on any such signal. At the very least, however, a stop-loss order placed just below the neckline (at, say, 39 7/8) would have been obligatory.

The head-and-shoulders formation is so reliable a technical pattern, it occurs with such frequency at important market turns, and it is so highly pertinent to low-risk, short-selling techniques (see next chapter) that it would be well to review a third example, this one a definitive textbook case.

The unfolding of the major head-and-shoulders top in the weekly chart of Teleprompter took place during the same pre-bear-market climate as General Medical's. These are the salient features: the left shoulder forms on sharply rising volume (1), as the fresh rally stems from impressive bullishness. The rally ends, and a normal correction sets in, which normally holds at just about the still-rising Moving Average. An intermediate-term market rally is still in progress, helping to boost TP to a new high on its next upleg. But the volume, on this apparently bullish move, is lower than before (2), and diminished volume diverging from a higher price is never a favorable sign. Then comes a confluence of warning signals: the uptrend line connecting several bottoms (the more, the more valid the line) is decisively broken (A–B); next the long-term Moving Average line is broken and starts to roll over, signifying that a change in trend is already underway; the correction goes too far down, past all those prior lows, and forms an apparent neckline when the next rally ensues. And that rally, forming the right shoulder, comes on even less volume (3). How many signs that it is now desperately dangerous to continue holding TP does an investor need?

At the outset of 1973, even as the Dow industrial average is making its new all-time record high, TP plunges below the neckline (at about 30), thus conclusively completing the huge top.

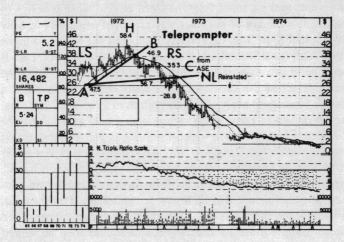

After a few weeks of trading around 26, there comes a pullback rally, which stops, conveniently, right at the neckline (C). No one conversant with our theses should still be holding such a stock, but that pullback rally does provide an ideal time to sell the stock short, as we'll discuss in greater detail subsequently. To review the sell signal sequence: we believe anyone holding such a stock long should sell as soon as those twin warnings of the breaking of an uptrend line and the Moving Average line takes place. If that initial chance is missed, then by all means don't miss the right-shoulder rally. And if you've just returned from the wilds of Borneo to see such a chart, by all means sell on the pullback rally. Since TP ultimately went down below 5, it is clear that feeling locked-in, or that it was too late to sell because the stock was already down from 42, is an absurd idea.

The kind of increasing failure that produces a head-and-shoulders top is not the only type. The chart of Eastman Kodak on page 196 illustrates one aspect of the selling problem.

While the DJI was still racing ahead in a powerful upsurge, one of its key components was evidently bogging down. But it would have taken diligence to spot the trouble under the euphoric head-lines. Nothing was wrong with Eastman Kodak as it registered successive new highs and higher lows on dips, except that an important trend line (A) which touched at three points (although two points make a trend line, the third is vital since it serves to confirm the validity of the line) was breached negatively in May 1975. Still, EK held up deceptively well until the failure to make a new high (at RS) established some unfavorable aspects. Line B could be drawn in across the lower tops, while line C could be drawn in across the two lows. This established what is called a triangle formation. More of this formation in a moment. For now, the key aspect to know is that when such a configuration can be identified, the direction in which the stock is going to move next is as yet unknown. The stock can, theoretically, break out either on the upside across line B, or on the downside through line C. However, you can also view this formation as a small head-and-shoulders top (identified as LS for the left shoulder, H for the head, and RS for the right shoulder, with line C serving as the neckline). Often, triangles form by themselves and should then be viewed

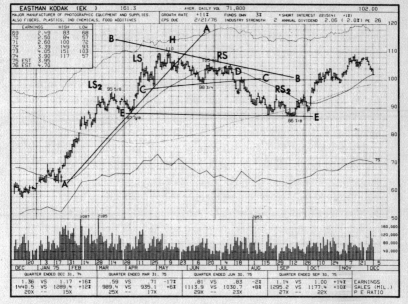

neutrally. Let the breakout itself tell you the next direction instead of trying to outguess an often malicious market. But when a head-and-shoulders top can also be identified, it adds weight to the evidence that the breakout will be down, as it was in this case. Anyone holding this blue chip, and wanting to give it as much rope as possible to hang itself (due to the extremely bullish climate), should have been protected by a sell-stop order placed just under line C. Failing that, the typical pullback which ensued (D) also provided a chance to get out virtually whole. The stock abruptly plunged, as you can see, another 12 points.

Now reflect on how much better such a seller would have felt a few weeks later, with EK down under 90. By that time (August 1975) the overall market was in the midst of a correction instead of a rally. The stock had held just about exactly where it should have, at its long-term Moving Average (the dotted line), and also where the March-April action had found support. This action made it possible to draw in a left shoulder (LS₂) and, on the rebound, a potential right shoulder (RS₂), plus potential neckline E, that etched out a much larger head-and-shoulders top pattern. The holder at this moment must now be intensely anxious. Does he sell on this rally in case it turns out to be a big top? Or should he take the chance that it may survive? Of course, he would have to place a stop under neckline E for protection, and were that to happen he'd have gotten 12 points less than an alert seller would have gotten at D, not to mention the wear and tear on his mind. Once again, it would have been better to be safe than sorry.

One further point is worth making. As it happened, EK was saved, and it did not break line E. Instead, the rally continued, as did the bull market. But, and it is a big but, who would have wanted to hold EK for about a 15 to 20 percent rise (the typical gain when a stock survives its H & S) when many other stocks were zooming 100 to 200 percent in early 1976? What's more, by late 1976 Kodak was finally under line E. Anyone who held because it was a blue-chip company would have been better off fleeing when that first, relatively small triangular top appeared and was broken on the downside.

## The Triangle

Let's take a moment to discuss what the triangle is, other than an identifiable pattern carried over from mathematics. It is, as is the head-and-shoulders formation, derived from the realities of stock action. As we've said, not all stocks make their highs together. Hence, while the highs for certain stocks may straddle two rallies, in the case of a triangle the sharpest point comes first, and the failures or rallies follow in succession. Yet there is success on dips, as each meets support at a successively higher level. The net result is that you can draw a down-slanting trend line across two or more peaks and an up-slanting trend line across two or more bottoms. Since you have rising lows, implying continued demand, and falling tops, implying continued supply, you really don't know in which direction the stock is apt to break out. But you can make reasonable deductions based on the rest of the market.

In 1970 a large number of triangles appeared, along with many head-and-shoulders bottoms, so that, since the stocks had endured a prolonged bear market, it was reasonable to assume that the breakouts would be on the upside. Similarly, triangles appearing in late 1972 and early 1973 were entitled to more than mere suspicion that they'd break down rather than up. And, of course, when that triangle line is broken on the downside, it is a sign that the forces of supply and demand, which hitherto had been battling to a standoff, have come to the end of the fight, with sellers finally winning. Since triangles often appear as consolidation patterns in the midst of a major trend, unless you have considerable confirming data as to potential direction, it is wise to wait for the actual breakout. Here are two examples of triangles forming (in mid-1976) that we would wait for. (Examples of triangles at tops that could have been anticipated by aggressive investors will appear later. See Telephone and Monroe Auto, pp. 203 and 207.) These triangles, in both Ford and Data General, have incipient aspects of tops: the

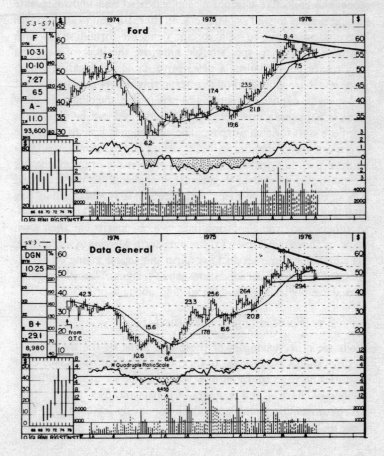

stocks have already risen a distance and the Moving Averages are starting to fade. The potential is certainly there, but at the moment of these charts there are few other toppy signals (neutral indicators, a prolonged sideways market). The stocks could emerge on the upside, and if so, such consolidations could produce good subsequent gains. You wouldn't want to be out. But if the stocks were to break down, you can imagine how ghastly the charts would look. The answer is, be ready, via protective stops, to sell if and when the break is on the downside.

There you have the essence of charting. It is not esoteric; it is, literally, the picture of what everyone is doing in that particular stock, the collective wisdom of sophisticated and knowledgeable market players as well as of dunces, all there for you to see and tap. There doesn't have to be a specific definable formation, as with Eastman Kodak, to spot trouble brewing; the item of practical importance is not hailing a descriptive name but locating which price levels are vital. Although interpreting charts may be difficult and inexact, requiring practice and experience, the charts do show what is happening in an objective fashion and can be used right from the start for that purpose. The challenge is how to recognize important trend changes without getting bogged down in a labyrinth of pseudo-scientific refinements, or a maze of guesstimating alternative courses. Over the years technical analysis has fashioned a host of ingenious systems, but actually it is sufficient to pay attention to these objective factors: (1) trend lines; (2) head-and-shoulders and triangle formations, which consist, in their own ways, of those trend lines; (3) the long-term Moving Average line; (4) whether volume serves to confirm the action: rising on breakouts, fading during consolidations; and (5) signs of failure: inability to make a higher high and/or to hold above a prior low.

## The Point & Figure Method

We'll see other examples of these and some of the many other pictures stocks are thought to form in subsequent pages (see Case Histories on page 202). But now let's examine an entirely different method of charting and compare its merits and uses, under identical circumstances, with those of the previously featured high-low-close daily and weekly bar charts.

To many, a point & figure chart, with its vertical columns of X's, is about as lucid as a bucket of tar. But the element that gives these charts their odd character is also what leads to their usefulness: P & F charts have no time axis. Whereas bar charts get an entry for the range of each trading day (or week) regardless of what the stock did, P & F entries are made only according to price intervals, regardless of how long it takes to achieve that interval. If, for example, the price interval is to be one point, an X would be entered whenever the price moved to the next whole dollar level from the previous X; that is, a rise from 19 to 19 7/8 would be meaningless, while to 20 would call for an entry directly above the previous X, in the same column. Were the stock then to continue advancing to 21, another X would be inserted above. However, a subsequent drop back to 20 would require shifting to the next column and down one space for the entry of the new X. Thus both ticks at 20, on the way up and on the way down, would be side by side. Meanwhile, you could actually have a fluctuation as great as 1 3/4 points. For instance, if the last entry were made at 19, and over a period of several days, or even weeks, the price eased to 18 1/8 and then edged up to 19 7/8, and back and forth within that range, no X would be drawn. The overall result is a compression of movement, which can be even more compact if you use an interval, say, of a minimum of three points rather than one for each X entry. Two results flow from using such charts: (1) Many years of history are compressed in a relatively small space; and (2) activity within particular price ranges is more clearly delineated, that is, if the stock were to move between 19 and 21, you'd have several entries in that area; if the stock were next to move above the 19–21 range, it could then be said to represent an area of support. If the stock were to break down below 19–21, the area would represent overhead resistance.

One further note: the dependence of P & F on jogging up and down to create its formations leads to a problem. Where bar charts can be plotted on semi-logarithmic scales, so that the proportions of moves are equivalent on a percentage basis no matter where they occur, P & F does not have such charting flexibility. Every X has equal value, whether entered at 80 or at 8. This means that as a stock price drops, P & F chart activity diminishes, since the same two X entries would represent 25 percent moves at 8 but only 2.5 percent at 80. The result is that low-priced stocks have less lively and extensive charts. The problem is mitigated, but not solved, by opening up the scale in the lower price ranges. In the Teleprompter chart, the price axis below 20 has been expanded to half-point intervals.

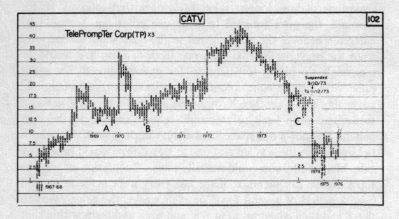

One outstanding feature of "timeless" and "volumeless" point & figure charts is how clearly they pinpoint areas of supply and demand ("resistance" and "support"). Here's a P & F chart for Teleprompter showing the same action as that revealed in the prior bar chart. You can see the support area created in 1969 between 12 1/2 and 15 (A). Compact and clear-cut, it served as the base for a powerful rally in 1970, and proved itself as support later that year on the subsequent sell-off (B). Even far to the chart's right, the action in 1973 found that same area serving as support (C) for quite a while on the way down, that is, before all hell broke loose. Thereafter, with the price below it, what was formerly a support area now became a resistance zone, inasmuch as prior buyers in that 12 1/2–15 range now had losses and would emerge as likely sellers when and if the chance came to get out even. Indeed, TP rallied to about 11 in 1976, where it ran into a huge roadblock. Once you identify key support and resistance areas, respect them.

## Choosing Charts

Our own experience has been that a weekly bar chart is akin to the point & figure variety in that it presents more history at a single glance and clarifies resistance and support areas, but it also adds the sense of time, which is very important when trying to catch breakouts. And it gives you some valuable perspective over a whole trend. A weekly bar chart, with volume, is our choice for anyone who wants to keep (or purchase) only one style of chart, with the added benefit that only one entry per week is required if you are maintaining your own.

The P & F chart is handy for checking on important support and resistance areas, so we always like to have a copy around for reference, but we don't believe it is a primary method. Extra-long-range bar charts, such as those published by M. C. Horsey, also serve as valuable references. On the other hand, the daily bar chart has the disadvantage of presenting only a limited point of view due to the way the action spreads out over the page, as an illustration of the old cliché of seeing the trees and not the forest. Daily bar charts have the virtue, however, of helping you to be more precise in timing action. Breakout points are clear and, with experience, you can often get a good sixth sense of exactly when important action is about to occur. Although it may take some guts to act on what you are seeing on the charts, especially when it conflicts with what the crowd is saying, you'll be amazed at the practical advice a chart can give you on what to do, even if it doesn't answer the question why. Here are a couple of examples:

At first glance, General Motors seems to be moving so erratically that there is little pattern. Let's take the GM chart and break it down, not into what looks indecipherable, but into those elements we can see. First, for example, you can see that, at point A, the stock broke sharply below its long-term Moving Average. You can also see, if you peer a bit closer, that the break completed a head-and-shoulders top. Since this was a time when our indicators had already warned of an intermediate-term decline developing, no one, according to our prescriptions for selling, should have held

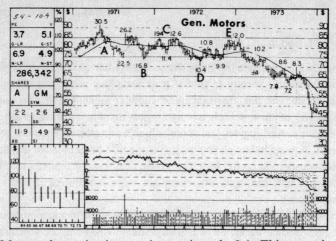

GM past that point in 1971 (approximately 82). This was given
further emphasis when GM's actual breakdown occurred on a
downside gap (that is, one day's opening was lower than the previous day's lowest price), and the stock never closed that gap all day.
Such gaps across a specific breakdown point are superb confirmation of the legitimacy of the break. Thereafter, GM's price kept
slipping. But nothing on Wall Street is so simple. Nixon's August
economic game plan gave such a boost to the auto industry that
GM opened on a huge upside gap, which, as we've already discussed, was an excellent chance to sell if you hadn't done so previously. Even lazy institutions with huge positions in this issue were
granted the chance to sell—and missed. What this chart history of
General Motors teaches is: Never rationalize that you've been
saved.

Let's follow what the subsequent sequences say. Just look at B:
GM was setting a lower low, while the succeeding rallies (C) were
intimidated successfully by the resistance established during the
August surge, a clue that a lot of sucked-in investors who had
bought then were now trying to get out near the break-even point.
Thus we already have a pattern of lower highs and a lower low and,
when the second of those rallies came as the overall market was
again emitting intermediate-term sell signals, it was trouble time
again. The subsequent decline took GM to another lower low (D).
Clearly, General Motors had become a stock to avoid. Even though
a small base formed in the latter part of 1972, it was certainly not

viable enough to overcome the substantial overhead resistance. While the Dow was rallying to its all-time high, this blue chip was still stuck below its previous highs (E), as formidable resistance was in evidence between 82 and 86. The original intelligent sale price of about 82 held up throughout that entire period and GM was still a good sale despite a big new bull-market rally.

This recent history of General Motors provides a case in point as to how resistance comes into being, and how it affects a stock's subsequent behavior. Obviously, the many buyers of the stock in August 1971 had no chance to sell at a profit, nor did those who'd bought at the prior head-and-shoulders top, so whenever the price came back to that area, these purchasers were all too willing to get out near even. Additional sellers came from among those who had bought at B and D, saw the stock struggling, and realized the indicators were then turning sour. Resistance levels are born and grow this way, constituting an area where a sizable amount of potential selling can be expected to follow. By the time the year-end rally arrived, the prior failures had served to establish that area as resistance, which, in turn, generated even more selling on the way to point E.

Often, by examining areas of upside resistance, you can get a good idea of just how high a rally will take a stock. Black & Decker's action in 1975 is an example of a stock that suddenly ran out of gas at the end of its second upleg. Actually, the troubles could have been anticipated. Although the base is clearly a double bottom with a valid upside breakout across the M.A., it isn't a very big base compared with the overhead resistance running through 1973 and the first half of 1974, centered in the 36–40 area. A stock fresh out of a substantial base area might have been able to assault this supply while it still had youthful vigor, but by the time the second upleg came along, with the market late in an intermediate uptrend, BDK had lost momentum and there were too many willing sellers on hand around 36 for BDK to climb any further. Thus, way back at the outset, a sensible upside target of 36 could have been established for this stock and would have been right on the button. To us, a chart like this literally tells you in advance where you must sell.

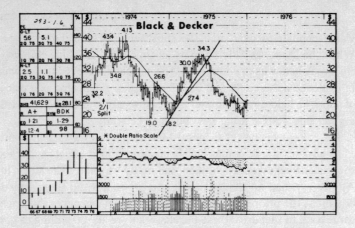

Even optimists who believed BDK could bull its way through the resistance would have had a second chance to sell at the next signal, when the major uptrend line we've drawn in was broken. Yet another signal was given as the stock broke its M.A., and the M.A., in turn, slipped downward. Now the picture is one of a stock which has failed at resistance and is in a downtrend. That would have taken you out near 32, four points worse than if you had paid attention to the heavy resistance area, but 12 points better than the next important low.

## Case Histories

To show how this selling approach can be applied in actual situations, let's review what happened to a number of stocks during the 1972–3 top period. Bear in mind that, while we have selected pictures of situations that worked, the system we have presented is not perfect; indeed, it is not a system at all but rather an approach to the stock market which is helpful in minimizing errors and maximizing profits. Many people were trapped at that top, and the cry of the so-called experts was, "How did we know it was coming?" Yet you'll see how readily apparent the warnings to sell were, even as the Dow was going to its record high at 1,050. And keep in mind that the prevalence of such warnings in so many stocks was, in itself, a valuable indicator that the whole market was in trouble at that time. When stocks are already breaking down, not up, it is folly to be bullish about the Dow.

Let's start with that *grande dame* of Wall Street, American Telephone and Telegraph.

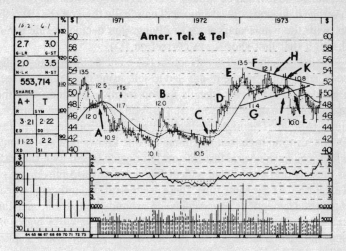

Let's assume you've been a buyer of Telephone at the end of 1971 as it breaks out across the Moving Average line. It rallies swiftly to 48 (B), where it runs headlong into the resistance formed earlier that year (A). Telephone happens to be a relatively slow-moving "widows and orphans" stock, but its chart patterns merit the same consideration as if it were a rank speculation: a fast rise to resistance calls for taking the profit, especially when there is no evident base to justify expecting more (and when you can see on a longer-term chart, or even from the insert, that there is plenty of supply over 50). The argument that the stock has been bought for safety or for its dependable dividend is naïve, as you can see. There's nothing safe about a stock capable of sliding from 48 to 42, as Telephone did. Surely, selling at the higher price and buying back at the lower, which would have been a gain of $600, is a lot better than the stock's dividend yield.

Having sold alertly, let's suppose you get back in on the next upside breakout (C). You'd encounter the same sort of resistance at 48 as before, but this time there are two fresh factors to take into account: first, the entire 42–44 area has now assumed the appearance of a base, thus holding out more upside potential than before, and second, the prior drive at 48 has already absorbed some of the resistance, so less can be expected on this trip. Besides, the Moving Average has swung upward more dynamically than on the (B) rally so, with the whole market also rallying, you decide to ride it out through that first short-term correction (D).

The second short-term correction (E) coincides with a 1971 rally peak, so it would not be ill-advised to sell, using the strength to get a good price. However, there's no top forming yet and, with the market still looking euphoric at year-end, let's suppose you continue to hold. The high, in January 1973 (F), coincides with the Dow's all-time high, but of course no one knows that yet. Meanwhile, you have several factors now telling you to sell. Not the least of these is that you've had a clear five-wave upward movement in Telephone. At the same time, there are the various indicator warnings, the tremendous overconfidence around the market, and the extraordinary volume accompanying that last rise. Ultra-high volume so late in a move is often the "blow-off" variety, when a spurt of latecomers, anxious to get in on the action, leaves a vacuum underneath, through which the stock can fall precipitously. Given the way other stocks were failing and then breaking down, we believe the aggressively alert holder would have sold Telephone at this time. But since there is still no top in evidence, some investors might want to stay around to see if higher prices might be forthcoming. (Remember to be consistent: if your style is to insist that a genuine top form before you sell, that's fine, so long as you maintain that approach in each instance.) Thereafter, we have a dip to G, a rally to H, a dip to J, a rally to K. By connecting the three tops and the two bottoms with trend lines, we have etched a triangle formation, while the volume shows gradually diminishing activity of the degree typical of triangles. Supply is battling demand, with each side coming closer and closer, so that the fight must be resolved shortly. Were Telephone to break out on the upside, it would be hailed as a consolidation; with so many other stocks already breaking down and with the indicators in distress, this triangle could be presumed to be a top. It becomes academic when Telephone smashes through the lower trend line at L, and by then the Moving Average is turning down.

Sell Telephone? Sure! The lowest a seller would get in this instance is 49 7/8, based on a stop-loss order entered just under the lower triangle trend line, and taking the round number 50 into account. At that point, a rough calculation, based on the width of the triangle at its widest of about 6 points (F–G), subtracted from the point of breakdown at L (50), suggests a drop to 44. Since the chart shows base support in the 42–44 area, you have a logical downside target, long before anyone knows just how bad the bear market is going to be. Since that sum represents nearly three years' dividends, selling is certainly sensible, and would have seemed even more so when Telephone hit bottom at 40.

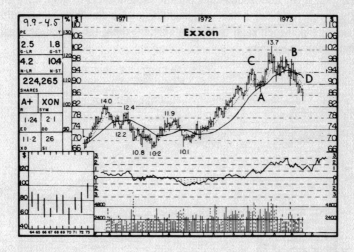

Exxon was a solid winner in 1972 as it broke out of a good base formed while the stock was ignoring the prior intermediate-term upleg. The extent of the base, plus the room to move (see the absence of much resistance in the insert), made XON look like a viable longer-term holding. The dip to A was alarming because by then the Dow industrial average had already topped. But Exxon managed to hold above its prior low point and its long-term M.A. was still rising, so there wasn't enough of an individual top to warrant selling—yet. The warning didn't come until (B), when there were several successive failures to push upward, each halting lower than the try before. By then the M.A. had clearly reversed as well. It became more a question of time than direction, more a question of extent than whether. After all, compared to other stocks at that time, the top was modest; a chart reader, in fact, might have considered the possibility of a rally, from 90 back up to 95–96 or so (D), to match a prospective left shoulder (C).

This is a crucial moment, however, and just because that scenario is a possible future course doesn't mean it should be counted on. Here's why. A right shoulder provides time for holders to sell out at relatively good prices, not far under the top. It is part of the distribution process, with strong sellers feeding stock to weak buyers. So, if the action does not permit such holders to get out, with the stock tumbling before any right shoulder can form, it usually means a pell-mell rush to the exit. Often, then, the first slide is an extremely steep one.

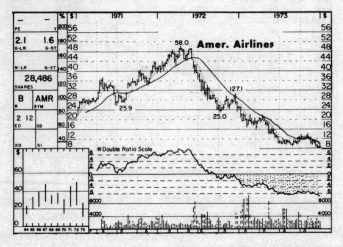

Although you can see the top on the American Airlines chart, and the sensible time to sell, at a glance, we've included this situation to illustrate a comment made by an NYSE specialist who, when asked how he'd survived the terrifying bear-market onslaught of 1973–4, replied, "You had to believe in selling the stock all the way down." He went on to explain that, as a specialist, forced during the slide to buy for his own account when no one else wanted to buy, he couldn't afford to be mesmerized by the notion that, because the stock was already down by half, or more, it had become a bargain worth holding. During that entire decline, it was never too late for the specialist to sell (for AMR went even lower in 1974).

The same thesis holds true for a public owner of this stock. Notice that in late 1972 a chance arose for a sensible sale to be made, when AMR rallied from 24 to about 30 and came smack up against its Moving Average line. The important point here is that you could not afford to rationalize, "Oh, well, I missed selling at 44, so now I might as well hold." The sale could actually have been made about four times above AMR's 1974 low, after all those "could have" and "should have" excuses were erased.

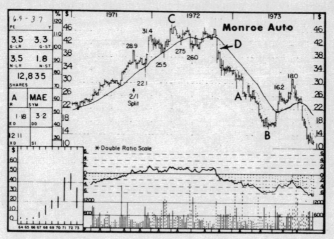

Here's a neat and tidy, five-phase, intermediate-term rise with an equally tidy top. Monroe Auto progressed sideways through most of 1972, well before the Dow was finished. Where would you have sold? If not after the third upleg (fifth wave) at around 47 (C), which would have been a perfect sale, then certainly somewhere in the later stages of that prolonged horizontal spell. There you would have been convinced that you didn't need a cyclical stock selling at 30 times earnings when it couldn't go up after three tries at its early spring high. And there was a last-resort chance to sell at D on the downside break, when a new low beneath that entire sideways movement, with its head-and-shoulders elements plus a now down-pointing M.A., made it emphatically clear that the major trend had changed direction. This chart proves that you had better sell when you realize you ought to sell, no matter what tantalizingly higher price you may have missed. Many investors say that they'll sell on the next rally, which sounds nice, but the next rally may not carry back up as far as the current price level. Don't play the future when the present is what is known.

Later, if you'd bought back around 18 (B), you could calculate your target as the resistance in the 25–27 area (A). Since the tiny base didn't justify a vaster move back toward the old top, here was a chance to know where you should sell, so you could have the order ready. You would have been fortunate too, for MAE subsequently went down well below 10.

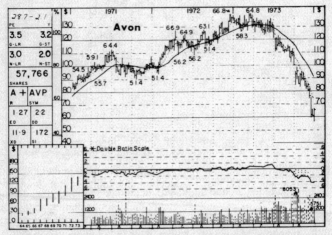

Avon was a glamour stock that bit the dust along with the other high-fliers. But notice how long AVP's uptrend persisted before it finally got clawed by the bear. Indeed, the authors were premature in selling Avon, since a top appeared to be forming around 100 in the second half of 1971. The M.A. was beginning to arc over, and if you place your thumb over 1972, you can see how toppy the stock looked. But the stock reversed when the market rose in early 1972. It wasn't a stock to buy, because of its lack of impressive volume, but AVP managed to keep rising.

In 1973, however, clues to an even larger top became evident:

upside failures; lower lows on dips; the M.A. rolling over dramatically this time; an increase in volume on the downside. The stock staged an initial downside break at approximately 123, and completed an even bigger top, breaking 110. When AVP hit 20 later, it didn't matter much whether you'd gotten out prematurely in the 90's on the 1971 false top, or as it broke down successively in 1973. With a top so big and so ominous, there is room for miscalculation as to when to sell, but absolutely none as to whether.

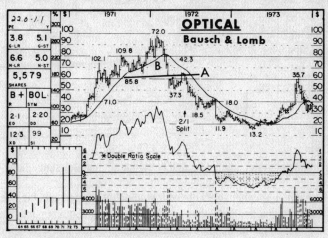

The time: February 1972. Bausch & Lomb had been one of the market's most popular glamours, shooting up fivefold. The Dow was still rising, and the various technical indicators had not yet signaled that intermediate-term trouble was coming. So there were plenty of excuses for being overly relaxed about holding BOL. The plunge, when it came, arrived with devastating abruptness. When that sort of rout occurs, you can't just sit back and say, "Oh, well, it was just some overdue profit-taking."

There really was no clue and no good time to sell before that break. You might have lifted your stop-loss order to just under the latest reaction low at the onset of 1972 (under 78 at B), but if you didn't, the plunge would have been a shocker. A chartist might have anticipated some right-shoulder work to match the 60–80 range action of 1971, but it never came. And yet there was, finally, an intelligent chance to sell, as BOL rallied back up to resistance at point A. The holder who hoped for more, who dreamed of getting the old highs back, was doomed; the stock market does not offer so many chances that any one can be ignored.

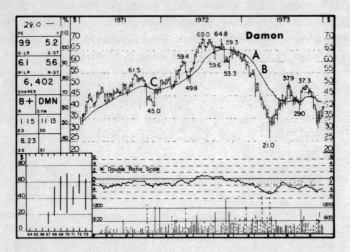

Damon is another example of a stock that topped out far ahead of the averages. It, and other stocks like it that did not participate in the late 1972 third upwave, helped to produce the divergences between the advance/decline line and the Dow industrials (and also between the high/low differential and the Dow). The deterioration in the indicators was a reflection of what happened to many individual stocks, beneath the surface of what the newspapers were extolling as a strong market.

While the Dow was rising to 1,050 in January 1973, Damon was already establishing a pattern of lower highs and lower lows. Volume had expanded on the downside, and its long-term Moving Average had rounded over decisively. This rotten action called for a sale as soon as 60 was broken (A) or, at the latest, at the break below 55 (B). But you would have had no disagreement if you'd wanted to sell at year-end, when the top was forming. Why cling to last-ditch hopes when a stock is acting this way? It's not as if you can't buy it back if the climate changes. While some might prefer to wait for a top to be completed, others opt for "one failure and then goodbye."

Studying this chart, you might wonder if circumstances wouldn't have called for a sale at point C in late 1971, when there was a disruptive break, a rally to resistance, and an M.A. turning down. Yes, you could have sold, and switched into something else at that time (for the bull market was still chugging along). If so, you would have gotten about 48, which, in the long run, wouldn't have been so very different from getting out on the top's completion at 60 (A) or 55 (B) a year later, especially considering that the stock went down to 5 before the tide was stemmed in 1974.

It is also worth noting a rather typical bear-market performance along the way: the rally that doubles a stock's price but is just part of the major downtrend. What is sticky about DMN's move from 25 to 50 is that it is abrupt, having had no base formation before-hand. Unsupported rallies like this are the way bear-market bounces look. They may be profitable, but they require nimbleness and a willingness to admit that the bear market still prevails. As long as you relate your action to intermediate-term moves (and not the primary or short-term), you'll find yourself capable of taking advantage of these rallies and still getting out in time. As it turned out, the area around point C supplied the resistance that halted this rally, but the break in the uptrend line would have also been a good clue as to when to sell.

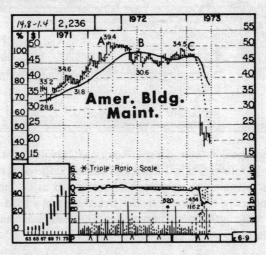

When a stock like American Building Maintenance has had an uninterrupted upward run, as defined by both a trend line and the long-term Moving Average, you know that the odds for a correction have increased: the risk begins to outweigh any further potential reward. Simple common sense, therefore, would have dictated that at point B enough was enough. Why not get out as soon as rallies begin to fail? Or would you be deceived into hoping that the rally at point C is going to carry ABM further toward the moon? We trust not, because the stock stopped at the resistance area previously formed at point A. If you hadn't gotten out by then, you literally didn't get another chance for 20 points!

This is as good an example as any to argue against the technique of selling out only part of a position in case your original decision is wrong. There's merit to selling into strength (as in giving your broker a "not held" order), but when the signs point to selling because of evident weakness, as at point B, sell everything.

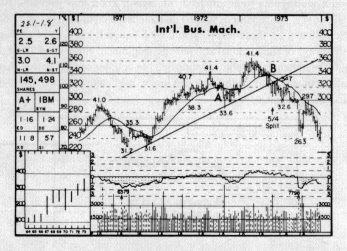

Because there is considerable emotional involvement with a company like International Business Machines, the personality of these stocks makes them perennially tough to call. Analysis of what is actually happening to the ticker symbol—IBM—rather than the company becomes paramount. Let's examine what IBM's chart tells us.

First, the Moving Average meanders through the pattern, making it difficult to get a long-term fix on the trend. Yet, if you peer more closely, the M.A. has validity for intermediate-term moves. There's an upside breakout at the end of 1971, and another at the end of 1972. Two downside breaks (A and B) signal the end of those particular upswings. Selling at the time of either downside break seems valid; it is only hindsight that says B would have been better. In either case, we're not talking about a big percentage difference, and both are a lot higher than the bear-market low near 150.

But here's a further test. What would you have advised your mother-in-law if she'd come to you at the time this chart was printed and asked what she should do with her IBM? That's the kind of advice that carries a big risk. But the chart certainly looks like a huge top on the verge of breaking down. It's IBM. But it can still fall—by half, as it later did. It's IBM. Can't it be held until it comes back? Three years later, it still hadn't! And in the meantime, the intelligent seller would have experienced a unique feeling, that of having his profits and his capital tucked away as the market careened downhill and everyone else was in hysteria.

# 10

## Selling Short

"Don't Sell America Short" is a slogan we've all grown up with. There is an enormous emotional resistance to selling short in the market; that is, to selling stock not yet owned by borrowing the certificates to deliver to the buyer and hoping to return those borrowed certificates later with shares purchased at a lower price. The short sale is a bet on trouble. The act seems to be expressing a lack of faith in the future, in the economy, in the country. The psychological discomfort is made worse by one's guilty glee if trouble does indeed arise. Further, there is a sense that "it's not nice" to sell something one doesn't own and a suspicion that short-sellers are at the mercy of stock-market manipulators. None of these is true.

Unfortunately, emotional distortions are more prevalent in short selling than in any other market transaction. The fear typically occurs just as a market is experiencing its last gasp of strength before topping out and heading into a substantial decline, and is least apparent at the bottom, just when the notion of selling short should be dismissed. During any market cycle, the concept of selling stocks short is wholly legal and aboveboard, is a necessary element of the auction market (adding liquidity), has been scoured of any taint of manipulation, and, most important of all, can be a conservative approach to capital management during declines.

## Some Elementary Notions of Short Selling

Specialists sell short as part of their obligation to help maintain an orderly market. Their shorting, as we noted earlier, is usually done out of necessity, when they are the only sellers available to supply stock to an eager buyer. Without such shorting, price increments in market rallies would be abnormal and unmanageable. Similarly, the need to cover, or buy back, the shares that have been sold short, thus closing out the position, adds buyers to the marketplace, a particularly helpful factor during a retreat, since it supports stocks which otherwise might find no buyers.

To enable their public customers to sell short, stock brokers arrange for the needed stock certificates to be borrowed, so as to be delivered to the buyer, who, of course, is entitled to receive bona fide shares. This borrowed stock comes mainly from shares held by the brokerage firms for margin accounts, and left with the firm as collateral for the loan. The stock remains borrowed until such time as the transaction is completed by purchasing the equivalent number of shares in the marketplace. That may be days or years later. It doesn't matter, for the Internal Revenue Service treats all short-sale transactions as short-term gains or losses. The system works easily for active and popular stocks, but from time to time a thinly capitalized and/or closely held issue may prove difficult to unearth in margin accounts. This is how the "short squeeze" can develop: many overanxious short-sellers in a stock with few if any certificates around to be borrowed to deliver to the buyers. Naturally, if he is unable to make delivery to the buyer, the short-seller is obliged to rush back into the market to cover the sale himself; he has been, in effect, "squeezed." Accordingly, one blanket rule in selling short is not to get yourself in instant trouble by dealing in obscure issues where it may become impossible to borrow stock. Stick with broadly held issues, with relatively large floating supplies; and, if there is any doubt, ask first. If your broker comes back with word that it will be difficult to borrow, but he'll find certificates somewhere, tell him to forget it; you don't want to be anywhere near such a situation.

### Not So Speculative

In order to help dispel any of the emotional trepidations you may feel about going short, let's deal with some of those fears directly. It is important to recognize that short selling is not a radical act or a highly speculative deed, as it is often said to be, but is actually a sound tactic in its time. The stock market goes down as well as up, as you may have noticed, and not taking full advantage of both those phases is poor capital management. Selling short is, simply, the most sensible way to protect your money during a major bear market. What's more, even though the market goes up some two thirds of the time and down only one third (which may make it seem feasible to wait out the declining period), those down periods can be explosive. Consider one recent cycle: it took eighteen months through 1969–70 for the market to tumble from 1,000 on the Dow to 630; thirty months, nearly twice as long, to struggle back up a trifle higher, to 1,067; and then, in less than twenty-two months, it was all wiped out on the plunge to 570. Since a lot more money can be made in brief stretches of time on the short side rather than on the long, it would be foolish to ignore this tool when playing the market.

In sum, you are protecting your capital when you use the short side during downward cycles, plus giving yourself a chance to actually make your capital grow while your neighbors are bemoaning their losses. But if shorting is so rewarding, and there are billions of shares available to sell short, why is it that the maximum number of shares held in short positions is so small? During the 1969–70 crash, for instance, a mere 20 million or so; in 1976 a record level was set, but it was still less than 30 million shares. For most people it is evidently unthinkable to sell short; even institutions (the so-called professionals) are adverse to the idea. As a matter of fact, most mutual funds have bylaws prohibiting such a tactic, at least in part to pacify fearful customers. Thus, during a bear market, those traders can do no more than hope that their holdings will decline less than the averages, for there is no way they can profit.

The vaguest but perhaps the most pervasive emotional barrier is that a short position is unorthodox in the expected scheme of things. It is done backward—selling first and buying later—and that's hard to grasp. In addition, the seller has invested capital (he must put up the required sum according to the margin rate then in effect, and is subject to margin calls should the trade go against him), but he owns nothing. He is also accustomed to the notion that, even if he is wrong on the long side, at least he has those certificates to live with until the stock comes back. Owning nothing but having the potential to lose a great deal is scary.

Theoretically, there is no limit to the amount of money you can lose if a short sale goes against you as the stock rises in price. Conversely, the most you can make is 100 percent if the shorted issue goes to zero, whereas you might double or triple your money on the upside if you hold the stock. True enough, in the old days there was the outside chance of being caught in a corner, such as the infamous Northern Pacific corner of 1901 or the Piggly Wiggly maneuvers of 1922, but such a disastrous bear trap hasn't been sprung on Wall Street in over fifty years. Bringing off a corner (in which the perpetrators buy up all the available stock so that short-sellers must come to them to buy back at astronomical prices) requires such immense sums these days that it is unlikely ever to be seen again. Whatever losses may be involved in selling stock short can certainly be avoided by ordinary defenses.

## The Practical Side

Before getting into tactics, let's review the processes involved in short selling, since they differ from an ordinary long-side sale. When you order a stock sold short, your broker, adhering to the rules, must so specify on the sell order sent to the floor. The floor broker must execute the order on an uptick, a price higher than the last different price. Since the coming of the SEC and reform legislation after the 1929 crash, a stock can no longer be forced down directly by orders to sell it short. Everyone—specialists, professional traders, and public alike—must sell short only on a rising price; someone else has to take the initiative to purchase the stock. Very rarely will there be a bid on the Exchange floor entered at a higher price than the previous sale price, so usually the short sale is made by a buyer's stepping forward to take your offer. This can be nerve-racking. The stock, since it is still in demand, is likely to go still higher, however briefly, against your short sale. This is a fact of market life that must be endured. Proper timing will keep it to a minimum.

Let's follow an example to see how it works. Suppose you spot a stock you think is likely to go down and you enter an order to sell short; the last sale price was 70 and you put that as a limit on your short order. Since it has previously sold at 69 7/8, a sale at 70 will be on a zero-plus tick and would be legitimate, so your shares are offered at 70. If the stock were next to sell at 69 3/4 instead, your order, being limited, would still require a buyer at 70; had it been a market order to sell short, the specialist would reduce the offer to 69 7/8, since this would be the best price at which it could be sold on an uptick following the trade down to 69 3/4. But imagine that it is sold at 70. The buyer must then pay $7,000 to your brokerage firm, for which he is entitled to a stock certificate signifying ownership. Your firm delivers such a certificate from among those it is holding "in street name" for its own margin customers.

The firm gets the $7,000 from the buyer, and it also gets money from you, at least enough to meet the margin requirements, to secure the trade from your side. Even if you put up the full amount of the transaction, it still goes into the margin-account ledger. Now the brokerage firm has extra money, yours plus the buyer's, from this trade and thus should not charge you interest in your margin account. Indeed, the extra money, instead of being borrowed from the bank to loan to the firm's margin accounts, can be rented directly, so that the firm gains the full profit of the interest charged, an immensely profitable arrangement that has often made the difference between a firm's surviving or not. Then, when you decide to close out your short position, you simply buy the stock as you would any purchase, except that the order is designated "to cover short," and the certificates received by this purchase are used, via the brokerage firm's back office, to replace the previously borrowed certificates in a bookkeeping transaction.

This simple sequence can serve to assuage the fears created by one of the oldest bugaboos against short selling: that there is a potentially limitless loss. Obviously, in this manner, you can lose no more than the margin clerk, doing his duty, will permit you to lose. A margin call is a severe but practical limit on short-side losses, particularly since one of our inviolable rules of emotional restraint is: Never put up more money when you get a margin call. (Of course, you should never let yourself get even close to a situation where a margin call is imminent.) Thus the concern that possible short-side losses could be limitless is really just one more psychological hurdle, designed to keep you from enjoying this capital-protecting and enhancing tactic.

To be sure, if one could choose which side of the market to play, almost everyone would pick the bull side, except for those who recognize that their own psychology functions best when selling short. But the market rarely offers such a simple choice, and even when it does, it's not for long. Let's suppose you realize the market, as measured by the averages at least, is heading south. What can you do about it? Sell, to be sure, as already advised, but with your now idle capital, would you shift to supposedly defensive issues? Not when you realize those stocks can get enmeshed in a bear slide too. Buy golds? They don't perform against the trend with consistency. Buy paintings for protection? Real estate? How would you get your money out when the time came to get back into stocks? What about bonds? Typically, interest rates rise with tighter money during bear slides, and that means bond prices decline too. About the only alternative is a simple savings account, unless you recognize that the market is in trouble and that the best thing to do with your capital is to sell short. If you'd been short from 1929 to 1932, or during the 1973-4 crash, you'd have emerged with a lot more capital, and been able to buy a lot more shares, than just about anyone else around. What's more, you'd be continuing to track stocks, using the same indicators and other tools as before, and you'd be much more alert to spotting the bottom than that neighbor of yours who sold at the top, put his money in the bank, and stopped looking at the stock pages for months.

In brief, pick the stocks with the most potential to move the greatest distance, be it up or down. And when there are times you don't like the market generally, but do want to hold on to certain stocks that are still healthy and that you expect to continue to do well, selling weak stocks short can be a vital hedge against the market's onslaughts.

## Timing the Short Sale

If selling short is essentially the antithesis of buying long, does it follow that your tactics can be the reverse of the way you buy? No, the market does not make things that easy. There are several important differences in viewing the indicators and in actual tactics.

We've already examined a number of useful indicators based on short-selling statistics that tell us a lot about the market climate by revealing the emotional states of mind of various segments of the marketplace—odd-lotters, specialists, Exchange members, and the public itself. Based on their activities, we can establish guidelines —no, absolute rules—as to when to act on the short side with relatively little risk. These are tight restrictions, but why play a difficult game by giving away odds? Instead, adhere to these simple rules and you'll short near intermediate-term top areas and cover as the next bottom approaches.

1. Rule 1 is that you should sell short when the odd-lot short-selling indicator has been under 1.0 for several months as calculated by dividing total odd-lot sales into odd-lot short sales, and maintaining a 10-day Moving Average of the result. You may short with even more assurance when the 10-day M.A. gets down below the .50 level.

2. As a corollary, never sell short when this indicator has risen from under 1.0 to over that mark. Start covering already established positions on a rise across 2.0. Make sure all short positions are covered (closed out) when this indicator produces one-day readings above 3.0; that may be a trifle soon, but better safe than sorry. If the market has been tumbling and you are tempted to go for a quick trade on the short side, check the odd-lot shorting figures first. High one-day readings tell you to curb your emotions.

3. As you can see on the chart on page 221, it is okay to short when Exchange members are also acting on that side of the market. At point A on this chart (April 1972), member shorting hit a peak, as the DJI reached a top and shortly thereafter began to decline. (This top, you'll recall, was the peak for most stocks, as measured by the advance/decline line, even though the Dow industrials even-

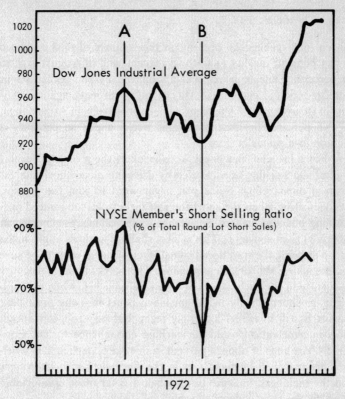

1020
1000
980 — Dow Jones Industrial Average
960
940
920
900
880

NYSE Member's Short Selling Ratio
(% of Total Round Lot Short Sales)

90% —

70% —

50% —

1972

tually had one final fling at year-end.) You will want to see member shorting readings over 85 percent (such as occurred two weeks in a row in January 1973, as the Dow topped out over 1,000) and preferably near 90 percent; then you can get to work selecting shorts, knowing that the risk is minimal.

4. The chart also demonstrates that member shorting ebbs considerably near important bottoms, as in July 1972 (B). When member shorting drops to under 60 percent, it's time to start covering, particularly when you see the public becoming pessimistic enough to dare to sell short.

5. Exchange member activity includes the deeds of the specialists themselves, but we also need to keep a separate calculation for this. Join the specialists as short-sellers when their percentages get up near 64—the more persistent, the better the signal—and start covering your shorts under the 40 percent level. Specialist shorting in

March 1966 reached 69 percent; in the summer of 1968 it got up to 71.5 percent; in May 1969, to 68 percent; and in August 1971, to 67 percent. Time to cover was announced by the specialists in October 1966 (38 percent) in May 1970 (35 percent), again in August of that year, at 32.5 percent, and, impressively, in August 1974, at 37.6 percent, the first of several weeks under 40 percent—a prelude to a major bottom.

6. For a broader viewpoint, keep track of the monthly amount of total short selling as measured by the announced short-interest position outstanding. Since you never want to join the masses, avoid shorting when the short-interest ratio (total announced outstanding position divided by average daily volume, as reported in *Barron's*) rises above 1.6. This is a bit shallow—others might insist on 2.0 as being the traditional signal level—but we want to be sure you are taking as little risk as possible. This sort of high level occurs frequently in the early stages of a new bull market, when the mob begins to short heavily in the mistaken belief that the prior bear market is still in effect. You may react that way too, but a high short-interest ratio should be warning enough not to act. Conversely, readings of under 1 percent in this ratio, particularly when they are matched by signals from the specialists and odd-lotters and the members, indicate times when it is far more comfortable to be on the short side of the market.

## Additional Precautions

As these indicators begin to be favorable to short selling, it becomes time to select individual stocks. It is interesting to note that there is information available on short-sale candidates that is not available when buying long. The Exchange not only announces the total outstanding short position once a month, it also breaks the list down into the amounts shorted in individual stocks, publishing those with the highest amounts or the sharpest increases over the past month. A large short position suggests that many people believe the stock will fall. Although that may seem like added confirmation, don't join them. Every one of those short shares will sooner or later have to be bought back in, thus giving stocks with substantial short positions an extra source of support.

As always, there will be exceptions to the rule, but there's no need to defy the odds. Even in the devastating bear market of 1973–4, heavily shorted items like International Flavors, while falling, never came near fulfilling their apparent downside potential; the crowd was too great. As a rule, steer clear of issues with large short positions (relative to their capitalization and floating supply), because the least bit of a rally can send some timid bears scurrying to cover, and the resulting demand can feed on itself emotionally, causing the stock to bounce in a highly uncomfortable manner. What's more, professional traders both on and off the floor concentrate their buying in stocks with large short positions, figuring that the rush to cover will add extra points to their trade on the long side. It's simple: don't be part of a high short position in any stock. By the same token, don't dig out a stock so thinly capitalized, so infrequently traded, that when you go to cover your own short, you have to reach up a few points for available shares. It is worth repeating: before shorting, make sure there are ample shares around for you to borrow.

Next to shorting too late (like the odd-lotters) and getting trapped with the crowd in a too-popular short, the most frequent mistake amateurs make is firing both barrels at a stock that has been soaring upward so frenetically that it seems obvious that it must soon get socked. As tempting as such a target may be—after all, the amateur reasons, what goes up must come down and this baby has already gone up too much—there are several arguments against shooting at it too quickly. First, of course, is that the unusual strength itself is a warning to stay away. The market always goes to an excess. Second, this strength is apt to keep the initial dips in the stock's move relatively minor and to make it among the first to rally when the market turns back up. Third, those amateurs who haven't heard our warnings and have sold short too soon get forced into covering, giving the stock renewed upward thrust. Fourth, the good reason for the stock's having raced up so high usually comes out in headlines around this time, causing the short-seller who has exclaimed "Too high" at one point to finally decide that it belongs way up there, now that he knows the news. Many short sales get covered near the top at substantial losses in just this way. Fifth, as you've seen in the charts, and will see over and over again, it takes many weeks for a top to form, sometimes even a full year, so what's the hurry? Why try to aim for the top eighth? That's the fastest way to be wrong. When it comes to owning a runaway stock, you may become such a nervous holder that you start to cash in a long-side profit by selling some of your shares along the way, as in a "scale up" order. But it is never a viable idea to sell short just because the stock has already been run up so much that it appears due for a correction, or because it has begun to look overpriced. It is one thing to protect an already-established position by locking in some profits, but entirely another to commit fresh capital to a new position via a downside bet.

Selling long closes out a position; your choice is not one of selection but of timing. But selling short requires the same sort of careful scrutiny that you must use when buying. Just as it is sheer luck to buy close to the ultimate bottom when bargain hunting, it is also mere accident if you happen to get off a short sale close to the all-time peak of a high-flying stock. Philosophically speaking, we believe in waiting until the stock has proven itself: by being strong enough to go up; by turning weak enough to have completed a sizable top. Tops, remember, take time to form, and the conservative short-seller avoids the still-rising target and waits until there is decisive evidence that his candidate has become tired, has established some resistance overhead, and clearly has reversed direction. Even then, there'll be some mistakes (that's the challenge of the marketplace), but usually the stock can be caught near the best price available, as it is about to fall apart, after the top has formed and immediately upon the downside breakout. Patience is rewarded as the risk is reduced.

### The Inevitability of Being Early

The problem of patience becomes complicated by the requirement that short sales be executed only on upticks. Many people understandably fear that if they wait for the stock to start sliding, their short sales may never be executed at all. Accordingly, they toss in "at the market" short-sale orders as the stock starts to tumble, with this result: on each sale at a lower price, their offer to sell short

becomes the best offer in the marketplace, one eighth above the last
sale price in order to be an uptick; after the price falls a whopping
degree, the market's customary fluctuation comes into play, buyers
arrive, the short is executed at the first uptick, several points lower
than when the order was entered, and the short-seller is bagged at
the outset of a rally, often causing him to panic to cover the short
during the bounce. This, naturally, can be abetted by floor traders
who know that orders to sell short at the market have piled up in
a specialist's hand, since they can see the loose orders tucked into
his book, where they are unable to be recorded since they keep
changing price as the stock falls. If you see on the tape a sudden
string of sales up one eighth of a point, you'll know that professional traders are grabbing all those "at the market" short-sale
orders as they try to "give the stock a goose."

To avoid the frustration of watching the stock you want to short
tumble steadily, while your short order remains unexecuted (until
it gets that execution at a dangerous price), the discreet short-seller
will place limit orders at sensible prices and then wait. The price
may have to be adjusted subsequently, due to later action, but by
being patient, or switching to another stock, you can reduce the
risk of this sort of trading trap. (Note that we are talking specifically about making short sales. It must be repeated that when
selling out a long position, where no uptick restriction is involved,
a market sell order does the job promptly and properly.)

In addition to the inevitability of being early to avoid the tribula-
tions of chasing a stock down, the nature of the market creates its
own problem. Even after a top has developed over an extensive
period of time and it appears that enough is enough, there may be
more. Consider 1972 and the tops which formed along with the
advance/decline peak and subsequent negative market action from
April onward. Along came that last upward dash over 1,000, starting in November. Many stocks which had already clearly formed
tops had rallies which ultimately could be seen as part of the entire
top formation, but which at that time could have been nerve-
shattering for the investor. Often, such a kick can carry a popular
stock to a new high, and while, in the ultimate pattern, that action
turns out to have built the head of an even huger head-and-shoulders top, at the time it sure looks as though you'd better run for

cover. And even if a new high doesn't arrive, the rally may carry above what looked like the first line of resistance, so a close stop used as protection gets set off.

This is the nature of the stock market. If you have sold out a long position, the temptation will be great to start buying again, and many investors have given back their bull-market profits in just this sort of suckering. If you're short, life is even more difficult; you haven't had the bear market yet to prove you're on the right track, all the optimistic news is against you, and then there's the rally. There isn't much you can do about it: (1) Review your protective stops to make sure they're sensibly placed, and if they are, leave them alone. If you get stopped out, that means the stock did something it wasn't supposed to do from your point of view, so you've been protected and can come back to fight again another day. And (2) review the indicators, and if you are reconvinced that trouble lurks, you've simply got to be patient, knowing you were early and now have to suffer through a rally until it dies. The year-end rally in 1972, which took the Dow across 1,000 in early January 1973, wasn't all that uncomfortable. Shorts in many stocks had only modest rallies; others simply got back to major resistance in understandable, albeit irritating, fashion. It can be endured, if you see from the overall indicators that the market really is topping out. And remember, just because you may have been early is no reason to be averted from renewed shorting. It certainly wasn't "too late" in February 1973!

Here's what to look for if you might have been wrong:

1. Is the Moving Average still rising? It should already be arcing over. If it is still heading upward, you really were premature.

2. Can you make a sensible case for the market drop having been just an orderly correction within an on-going bull market? Have the key indicators actually reached signal levels or were you trying to anticipate them? Has anything in the market's action heralded a violation of the uptrend? Has there been a lower low in the Dow on a dip, a divergence in the high/low differential, an important trend line broken?

3. Is the individual top you spotted still there, or have higher highs and higher lows started to appear?

4. How does the volume stack up in that stock? Does it rise on

substantial volume or on far less than seen earlier? Are there any signs of churning: heavy volume and little price change? That helps.

5. What are other stocks in the same industry doing?

If you've made a mistake, or so it seems, by all means get your house in order. It's best to have already established a sensible place for a protective buy-stop order, since you can see the emotional pressure you'd come under at this point. Let the stop take you out of the position, proving that you were wrong at least for that particular period.

6. But don't be faked out by good news. Remember that bullish news items are the fool's gold of market tops.

Eventually you'll learn to accept being early when selling short, simply because it is as built into the system as taxes. The distinction you'll have to make is when. You may notice, upon reviewing such checkpoints, that you were premature. In that kind of situation a close stop may be best, taking you out quickly at a minimal loss if the stock still has more to it. However, as the top gets bigger, as the Moving Average rounds over more and more, as the indicators flash signal after signal, give the stock more leeway. You may be early, but you are unlikely to be wrong, so if the stock has more rallying within the overall top area, let it wear itself out by placing your protective stop sufficiently above the pattern so that it will be set off only if you are proved emphatically wrong.

## Shorting at Primary Tops

Given these parameters, let's take a look at some actual examples where selling short is applied. Obviously, some of the disasters discussed previously would have been profitable shorts as well, but the point of view is different, so let's begin fresh with one of the stocks already discussed, Teleprompter. You'll recall that in the winter of 1973 the DJI had just reached an all-time peak, accompanied by a batch of negative signals which the eternal and preponderant optimists were blind to. There was no way to tell in advance how extensive and precipitous the drop would be; all one could do at the time was determine which stocks should be sold, and of those, which looked like the best shorts for an intermediate-term downleg. With hindsight, of course, one can see many more stocks that could have been shorted with impunity, but when you are right in the middle of the fluctuations, trying to minimize risk, it's a lot tougher to plunge ahead.

Now let's take another look at that Teleprompter chart:

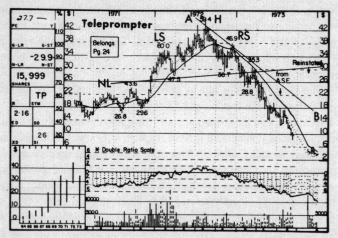

Here you can see the major head-and-shoulders top as it formed in late 1972. We asked, in Chapter 9, how many signals a holder needed to become convinced TP had to be sold. There was the lower volume as the head and then the right shoulder formed, the break of the uptrend line off those successively higher bottoms during the rally, the long-term Moving Average rolling over and turning downward, and the warning formation of the right shoulder itself. In our opinion, a reasonably alert sale of a long position would have been around 34 in the week or two *after* that right shoulder had clearly formed. That's not top dollar—the high being well over 40—but it is a sound sale price and not far off the 38 or so that an aggressive seller would have gotten by selling the moment the Moving Average and the uptrend line were broken.

So much for reviewing the long sale. What about shorting this baby? With a price/earnings ratio of 35–45, it certainly was an attractive candidate as the top was formed. The lack of quality, the observation that other CATV stocks were also struggling and lending group confirmation, and the satisfactory pattern of trading all added to the appeal. But singling out TP as a short-sale candidate is one thing; the stock still has to provide a low-risk entry point. At the time the right shoulder formed, the DJI was still going up, and that might well have been too uncomfortable a situation to try to buck on the short side. You are now interested in initiating a position, and that's different from having to close a dangerous one out.

The key point to remember here is that you are looking for a low-risk place to put your capital in the hope that you can make it grow. Forget anything else, particularly that the stock has already dropped from the low 40's. TP becomes confirmed when the head-and-shoulders top is completed, breaking the neckline. The interested short-seller should have, so to speak, a shopping list, and could then spot TP on this list as being worth watching closely. The stock has plunged to the 26 area, so the thing to watch for is a chance to short the stock on any pullback rally. Such moves are a normal expectation and typically retrace to the area of the neckline. Here the potential short-seller cannot be intimidated by the fact that the stock is now rallying, and he can't be frightened away by all those upticks, because he needs one to get his short off. But where? Note that there is now heavy resistance in the low to mid-30's, plus the neckline, plus the now established long-term downtrend line (A–B), plus the now descending Moving Average line. (All of that gives a chance to place a protective stop overhead; in this instance a likely level would be 35 1/8.) Given these facts, we'd have entered an order to sell short at 29 7/8, feeling that the round number at 30 might be the maximum extent of the pullback. As it happened, TP managed to edge a mite higher than that, but such a price, however momentarily early, would have proved terrific in the end. And, as the stock began to decline in earnest, the holder of that short position could feel more comfortable knowing that TP, a popular speculative favorite, was now scaring out holders as it fell. Because the stock was actively traded, the pressure remained high. (One might also suggest that a short-seller could even add to positions such as this as they prove themselves; for example, shorting more the next time a downside break was made, in the 25–26 area. As a general rule, why look for a different situation when you already know one that is working out?)

Such a seller might have wondered where to cover the by-now successful short, especially when noting the degree of support evident on the left side of the chart picture in the 18–22 range. However, a measurement of the head-and-shoulders top (from about 44 to the point the neckline was broken near 30) comes to 14 points downward, or 30 minus 14, for a target in the neighborhood of 16. With the overall market decidedly bearish, our tactic would have been to place the buy stop, now protecting a profit, just above the Moving Average line, at, say, 20 1/8 at first and then lowering it to 18 1/8 after those two little attempts to get across 18 failed. Now, if you'll take a quick look back at the P & F chart of Teleprompter (see Chapter 9), you'll see that substantial support exists starting at 15. Given that prior support, an entirely acceptable alternative to the use of a stop order would be to cash in the profit in that neighborhood. Perhaps, having seen the stock bounce off 14, one would then seek to cover on the next dip. However, hindsight says it would have been better to use the stop method, since it would never have been set off and you could have stayed short all the way to under 5. When you have a remarkably clear point at which to place the stop (18 1/8 being just above two rally peaks as well as a Moving Average line that has flawlessly marked the downtrend thus far), it makes sense to stick with those aspects.

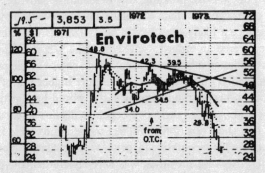

We've drawn in on this chart the obvious triangle formation which developed in Envirotech. A triangle, second in reliability to the head-and-shoulders formation, requires at least two points of lower highs and two of lower lows for a symmetrical formation. A

descending triangle would have a flat bottom line of two or more
dips managing to hold at about the same level. In theory, triangles
can produce breakouts in either direction; while there are times
when you must wait to see which it will be, when there has been
a prolonged run up, and when head-and-shoulders tops abound
elsewhere, it can be reasonably expected that the breakout will be
on the downside, as it turned out to be here.

EVT didn't give much time to get a short off once the breakout
took place. When you see such a formation, you can alert yourself
to the price at which the downside break would be an accomplished
fact, in the hope of catching a quick intraday pullback to the trend
line. Thereafter, you can mark the stock down as a genuinely
bearish situation, with plenty of resistance overhead, plus a weak
industry group popular enough to bring out a ton of stock once the
slide begins in earnest. Some patience, therefore, would have spotted that subsequent pullback to near 48, where the long-term Moving Average line also served as resistance, not a bad price to get
a short off at, in view of the ultimate drop to 15.

While we're picking your shorts from visible and traditional
charting formations, let's take a look at another of those major
head-and-shoulders tops that marked the big 1972–3 top, this one
in Coleco. Here was one of those little-known institutional pets of
that era, with an absurd price/earnings ratio of over 50. Note that
it wasn't necessary to catch the top eighth in order to turn a hefty

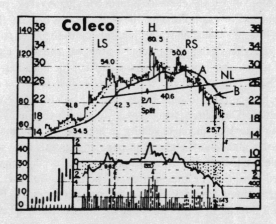

profit in this stock on the short side. Indeed, Coleco eventually fell to around $2 per share.

But while there was no rush, we'll wager that at about point A, that sideways movement for several weeks was a pretty good tip-off that the neckline was inevitably going to break. So here you might have ventured a trifle more daringly by going short, with, of course, a protective buy stop placed above the right shoulder's rally peak. Be careful when placing your initial stop; you want the protection, but you also don't want to be so close that a last-gasp rally attempt takes you out just before the stock becomes a big winner on the downside.

Often, when a stock hangs just above the breakdown point, as Coleco did just above the neckline for several weeks, it is building up for a more rapid plunge once the dam lets loose. In this case, the stock fell apart so rapidly that the typical pullback rally was not even in sight, although during the trading day after the break there was a brief return for the alert to benefit from. We want to warn you, in such cases, not to toss that order to sell short in at the market. To avoid being crucified, always place a downside limit on the order on the next lower round number, and no lower.

Once you have your short order executed, and the stock starts behaving badly (meaning profits for you), be alert for the chance to lower your protective stop so that a move which reverses the trend will take you out of your position but minor bounces will not. In the Coleco chart, the clear long-term Moving Average provides a good guide. For example, once the neckline was broken, the stop could be lowered to just above both point A and the M.A., to about 28 1/8, and then, after the plunge below 22, the stop could be lowered to just above point B and the M.A., which is about 23 5/8 on the chart. That would put the stop order just above an area of some resistance that no minor rally should be able to penetrate.

Automatic Data Processing was also among the many stocks that had no sensible business selling so high (about 90 times earnings). Just a glance at the chart on page 233 reveals how sound a short sale AUD was, but when should you have taken that step? It looked tempting in the vicinity of point A, but the needed components for a low-risk short were not yet in place. For one thing, you'll recall that this was near the start of the market's final

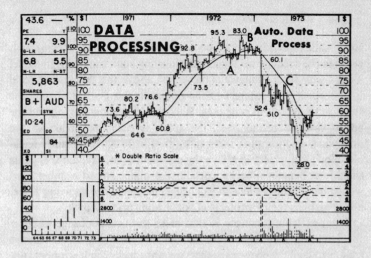

| 43.6 | — | % | $ |
| --- | --- | --- | --- |
| PE | Y | 110 | 100 |
| 7.4 | 9.9 | 100 | 95 |
| G-LR | G-ST | | 90 |
| 6.8 | 5.5 | 90 | 85 |
| N-LR | N-ST | | 80 |

**DATA PROCESSING**　　　　**Auto. Data Process**

95.3　83.0　B

92.8

A

73.5

80.2　76.6

73.6

64.6　60.8

60.1

C

52.4　51.0

28.0

* Double Ratio Scale

5,863 SHARES

B + AUD R SYM

10·24 ED DD 84 XD SI

64 65 66 67 68 69 70 71 72 73

rally, so that the overall market indicators were not then so one-
sidedly bearish. There were shortable stocks developing, but AUD
was less ripe than they were. For example, it was more important
to note at the time that, although the long-term Moving Average
was fading, it had not yet definitively rolled over. If you'll put your
thumb over the right-hand half of the chart, leaving only point A
visible, you should get a gut-level sense of an incomplete picture,
one that is arcing over but has more work to do. Although in the
long run you'd have been right to go short at that lovely price,
when the rally arrived you'd have had some sleepless nights unnecessarily. Patience would have been preferable. And, as you can
see, a close protective stop order, telling you that you were early,
would have taken you out on the rally back up toward 100, where
the double top finally formed. Of course, if you had gone short
prematurely, you could readily have started over again when further evidence developed.

It is not unusual for the evidence of a stock breaking down to
finally become clear when the overall market indicators are also
clearer. The savvy market observer could well say, "I know AUD
is a great short up here at 90" and "I know this rally is no good
and I want to sell short into it." But that will make him early every
time, and if he waits, little will be lost as long as the trader is alert.
By point B a "double top" had been etched out, and we see a
sideways movement similar to that noted in Coleco p-231. If a

stock slides quickly, it can be oversold (for the short term) as it reaches the breakdown level, and thus any such move might fizzle. That's why such a sideways move just above the breakdown level is of considerable interest to the potential short-seller: it puts the stock in shape for his purposes. With the M.A. now having had the added time to round over, the stock is ready to break on the downside, and jumping the gun by that little bit is certainly feasible. Now, a stop placed above the double top, at, say, 100 1/8, gains the added benefit of being just above a major round number, and would have been a mere 10 to 12 percent above the shorting price, not a bad degree of protection for a high-priced stock.

The next thing to note is that after the initial plunge another short-selling situation developed. As yet, you see, there'd be no reason to cover a proven success; we want to let such winners run. You would, of course, have lowered your protective stop to 80 1/8, just above the initial bounce and above the M.A. It wouldn't have been touched off, and by point C on the chart, you'd already have seen three successively lower rally highs, plus a matching set of lower lows. All that adds up to a picture of continuing weakness within the context of a major bear market. The investor who saw this, but was inhibited from acting because "it should have been shorted at 90," simply deprived himself of a good profit.

Having added to that initial short position, or taken a new one at that juncture, the stop could now be dropped to just above point C, at 75 1/8, to relish the next decline. But now what? The stock is collapsing, but you know that no stock goes straight down forever. Rallies always intervene. Do you cover? In the summer of 1973, a number of indicators began to improve and to give some favorable signals. You may not have believed the bear market was over, but as the stock fell, the wise course was to at least review where the next important level of support could be expected. Reference to a point & figure chart book, which would have had much of the past history compressed, or, alternatively, Horsey's *The Stock Picture* chart book, which goes back more years than the Mansfield charts, is needed. Here you would have seen that AUD developed considerable support around 35 even as it made its 1970 bottom. Furthermore, note the useful application of a simple measuring tactic: from 90 to 65, the initial plunge dimension amounted to 25 points. Subtract this from the 65 level, where AUD broke down again after its period of consolidation, and you get a downside target of approximately 40. In combination, therefore, you had the basis for targeting the downside at 35–40, at a time when the overall market was shifting to at least a bear-market, intermediate-term, rally climate. The truth is, it takes a strong will to cover a successful short, the same kind of decision-making we want you to get in the habit of doing when selling a successful long. But, given that the market is imprecise, you can't ask for better objective reasons to cover at a huge profit than two different approaches producing the same target area. If a third reason is needed, note the powerful reversal week: the stock is down, but it reverses to close the week sharply higher. That action says you're in for more than just a brief bounce. For our money, therefore, we'd have covered that short near 40 on the decline, or around 45 on the rebound. However, if we had not, and were still short as the rally continued, there is a point at which we'd have stuck it out. With heavy resistance overhead, starting around 65, plus the fact that no base of any sort had formed, indicating at the least that a test of the low was required, it would have been wise not to cover late in the rally. Why, then, would it not have been better to simply stick with the short all the way? The answer is that there would be no way to know whether the subsequent test of the low would be successful or not, putting pressure on you down around the 45 level as to whether to cover or not. By covering, and garnering your profit promptly when the target area is reached the first time, you free your money and avoid that potentially difficult decision.

## On the Way Down

The market is an ever-changing phenomenon, and you can never recapture the brilliant trades of yesteryear. So when the bear market takes hold, it is no use crying over lost profits and all those "I could have shorted XYZ at the top" excuses. Today's picture is all that counts. Fluctuations, rally attempts, oversold bounces, always come along to change the picture. We are back to the importance of perspective once again, with the added note of emphasis that what you see right now is the reality, not the vision of what might someday be down the road.

Because there are such pullbacks, as well as, according to Elliott's wave theory, a genuine intervening intermediate-term uptrend, because in a bear market an enormous amount of premature bargain-hunting causes frequent rallies, and because the IRS deems shorting a short-term capital gain no matter how long the position is kept open, trading the short side as opposed to investing in it is not such a bad idea. To be sure, sticking steadfastly to a successful short like Teleprompter or Coleco can ultimately prove triumphant, but it isn't easy to stay around that long and it takes a substantial bear market to wreak such damage. Since we know that stocks fall rapidly in short bursts, with ensuing rallies often giving you a chance to get back in, thinking of yourself as a trader during such periods will produce the properly aggressive approach.

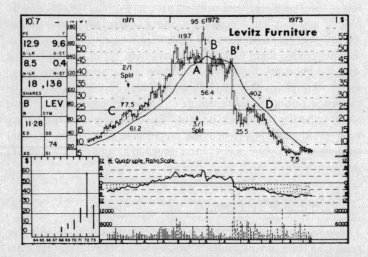

Here's another example of what we mean. Levitz sprinted from 10 to 50 in a year, and then started to move sideways as 1972 arrived, well ahead of the coming bear market. At point A it looked as if a downside break were imminent, and many seasoned pros went short at this point, figuring that LEV was unthinkably overpriced and about to get its comeuppance. But Levitz, like many bull-market runaways, was not so cooperative. The stock shot up in a burst of frighteningly fresh energy; the shorts felt squeezed, and their covering added buying impetus to the fling. As you can see, the stock actually went to a new high.

To be sure, an apparent top had formed, but the stock had not broken 45 and the Moving Average line was still rising. If you were long, the rarefied air, in conjunction with the apparently imminent downside crossing of 45, might very well have led you to sell out, or, at the least, raise your protective stop to 44 7/8. But it was still too early to sell short. In this case, it wasn't even possible to get off a perfect short at 60, except with sheer luck, for, although the chart doesn't show it, that was when the SEC suspended trading for a while. But by our line of reasoning, the perfect time to sell short is the least risky time, and that came later, when the 45 level was finally breached and the Moving Average had rolled over and headed downward. There was a pullback rally to the M.A. (B), and that bounce failed when it met resistance in that range of the upper 40's; a second similar opportunity came a few weeks later at point B¹, when the weakness was even more evident. (Note how the volume had dried up by then. Even if you felt uncomfortable in such a swinging stock, a stop just above point B would have afforded close protection and never been touched off.)

A rip-roaring slide ensued and the short-seller, thinking like a trader, could well have reasoned that a fall of 20 points, virtually in a straight line, meant LEV was getting due for a technical rebound. Over to the left, at point C, you can see a small area of support. A reasonable target might be assumed, therefore, in the 20–25 range, but the subsequent action, smashing deep into that support area, was a solid clue that the stock was still extraordinarily weak. There would be nothing to prevent you, as a trader, from adding to or establishing a new short position when, at point D, LEV was failing below its long-term Moving Average line at a time the overall market was shouting warning cries that it was about to begin its major plunge. A short sale anywhere down to the 20 level would not have been amiss, even without the benefit of hindsight.

## The Jones Boys' Philosophy

Many years ago we learned a valuable lesson from contact with a hedge fund (a fund, not offered to the public, which is set up so that its managers can both buy and sell short) then being managed by the Jones boys, the nickname for a group of money managers led by Mr. A. W. Jones, who was considered the father of the hedge concept. Late in the 1962 decline, we met someone who had access to their portfolio activities, and we asked what the Jones boys were presently selling short. The answer was surprising: Brunswick Corporation. The stock was already down from 77 to 14, which seemed sufficient, so why were they selling it short at this low level?

The answer is twofold: first, on a simple mathematical basis, if the stock were to drop from 14 to 7, as indeed it soon did in the last stage of that bear market, wasn't that a sizable profit in and of itself, regardless of the larger decline that had already taken place? You can't go back and play that game at your convenience, but you can analyze the current situation and determine that BC at 14 looks like a good short. Second, since the stock had already fallen in that manner, it had already proven itself to be weak. Instead of trying to catch a stronger stock just as it was breaking down, this hedge fund's tactic was to take less risk by shorting an obviously already-ravished stock. Perhaps in part this extreme attitude reflects some nervousness when dealing on the short side, and was more defensive than aggressive, but regardless of motivation, it works. Stunned issues such as this are capable of producing abundant and relatively safe profits, even if close to the so-called bottom. Indeed, weak stocks become even weaker with far more consistency than they reverse and rally. Let's go back and take another look at Levitz with this in mind.

It would have been easy to apply the Jones boys' philosophy to LEV at point D, for the stock had already proven weak, was still overpriced fundamentally, had trapped a lot of now-frightened institutions at twice the price, had a still steeply descending long-term Moving Average line, had formed a small head-and-shoulders consolidation pattern above 20, and was in this precarious position at the outset of 1973, just when the bear signals were being given for the entire market. Whether you had previously covered or not, this was an entirely new situation, and one well worth taking advantage of.

The chart below shows you what rewards would have been reaped had you followed that attitude in 1973 without regard for prior events. A new consolidation area emerged as a triangle between 6 and 9; you can see how, if you applied this "short the dead and dying stocks" attitude, a short sale made when the stock broke out on the downside, for a price of about 6, would have reaped 2 points on a relatively fast drop to 4 (not a bad percentage play) and ultimately, if no sensible stop-loss order was touched off, to 2. By that time, the rest of the market was perking up and there were plenty of indicators that shorting was no longer suitable.

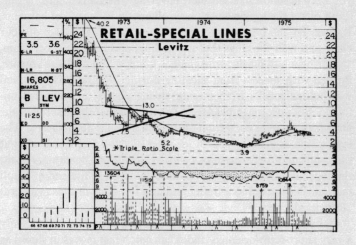

When assaying short sales during a bear decline, and looking for already weak stocks, again it is important to check the monthly reports of outstanding short positions. Although there are inevitable exceptions, we feel much more comfortable not being short those stocks in which large positions have already been taken. Don't go too far afield, but avoid the obvious situations. Stick with actively traded stocks with ample floating supply. And, since you are dealing with stocks that have been severely eroded already, the primary emotional aspect to be wary of is the reaction—both yours and the stock's—to bad news. Being short, you may cheer at news of another earnings deficit or a huge write-off, but if the stock fails to react to the news by falling further (it may even hold absolutely steady or rise instead), you are being told that the bottom has been reached and you should close out your short position.

## Another Warning

Do not confuse what we have just described with a situation similar on the surface but entirely different in reality. We've been taking you through a bear market, a genuine primary downtrend, when you want to be short, not long (recall 1973–4). Accordingly, while you may function like a trader, covering when a rebound is due, don't chase the long side the way others do in search of bargains. Rather, let the bear-market rally come. Sit on the edge of your chair and wait for clues that it is fading, and then go short again.

During a bull market, the game is much different. Here you are, flushed with success from shorting during the previous bear, and with added profits from buying stocks as the turn upward unfolded. But now the indicators have told you that the first full-scale, intermediate-term correction of the bull phase is due to arrive. The temptation is great to sell short; after all, you feel like a whiz at the game, and there are stocks with evident tops appearing. Albeit, the tops aren't nearly as big as they would be at the end of a bull market. Do you act as a trader and aim for a few of those vulnerable stocks?

Our vote is no, not during the bull market's first correction. Only a very short-term-oriented trader can catch fast moves in stocks as they tumble and be quick enough to cover before the whole profit vanishes on the next rebound. For the rest of us, it is simply not sensible to trade against the primary trend (and that goes, of course, for buying stocks during a primary bear market). The chart of Tandy on page 241 is an example of what we mean.

If you stick your thumb over the rally, you'll see that Tandy had formed what looks like a nearly perfect head-and-shoulders top, with the neckline at 35. Indeed, the right shoulder seemed to be unable to rally any higher, because the Moving Average line was resisting and beginning to level off. Wouldn't you be able to make

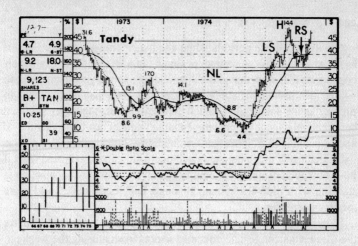

a huge profit by shorting TAN, especially since (1) the market was flashing correction signals, and (2) the stock, being up fivefold, looked particularly vulnerable? Any fool can see, in hindsight, that such short-selling ideas ought to have waited for definitive proof via breaking the neckline at 35; people who tried to anticipate this break got badly burned. With TAN an ideal-looking situation at a correction time, you can see why it simply isn't safe to sell short against the major trend, especially so early in the bull market.

### Yes, but . . .

There is, however, one powerful argument against this point of view. Let us suppose you see a possible correction coming but you are holding certain stocks long that you believe will be relatively untouched by it. They are still strong and could well be big winners some day down the road. What's more, there may not even be a correction, so you don't want to sell them, even though you realize you may be hurt if you're wrong. What's the solution?

The answer harks back to Mr. Jones: a hedge fund of your own. By going short to balance off the long positions you want to keep, you are in some degree protecting yourself in the event the decline turns into something more than you expected. This notion of turning your own portfolio into a mini hedge fund is even more useful the further into an uptrend you are (as in the fall of 1972). It is also viable during those periods when the major trend is blurred and it looks as if a sideways course, perhaps via a wildly swinging roller-coaster ride, is in order. You'll have some longs you want to keep —after all, individual stocks tell the tale—but you'll also want to protect those positions. In such circumstances, the short side can be effectively used to provide balance, safety, and the chance of added profits. If an investor uses hedging, holding both longs and shorts, a much more conservative portfolio can be attained than if he foolishly assumes he is being conservative simply because he is sticking with blue-chip issues through hell, high water, and mere market corrections.

In hedging's simplest style, you'll have picked longs from among the market's strongest sectors and shorts from among the weakest. In theory, if the market does rally, your longs should rise much more than your shorts go against you. And if the market slides, the shorts would come to the fore profitably, while the longs rested. With a little practice, you ought to be able to pick and choose accurately enough so that even when longs go up, shorts will be going down. With a little luck and a vacillating market, it is feasible to have longs on the list of new highs, while on the same day your shorts are among the stocks setting new lows.

Because you are using the short side as a hedge, or the long side, for that matter, if the weight of the evidence (but not the full measure) is negative, we've found that selling short those stocks that are already under duress is the ideal approach. Save shorting those stocks which are completing vast new tops for that time when a new bear market is coming into being, as in January 1973, when you no longer want to own any shares. A substantial number of stocks topping out is the time when your hedge fund should be 100 percent short, but, at other times, aim for a balance which reflects the possibilities of the overall market itself. If, for example, it seems to be about 70 percent bullish, you could fashion a portfolio of seven stocks long and three short. Or, converting this to money exposure, how about 40 percent long, 20 percent short, and 40 percent in cash reserves such as treasury bills, since the market game isn't all that decisive at the time. The deceptive sideways action from March 1976 on into September of that year is a prime example.

How would you calculate this proportionate representation? One way is to estimate the degree of bullishness or bearishness in the market as a whole via the important indicators, factoring in the extent to which prices have moved already. Or total up the number of individual stocks that look like potential buys or are already strong, versus the number that are toppy or already in downtrends. Remember: what you are basically in search of, whether long or short, is to have your money in the best possible stocks. That means those with the least risk and the most profit potential, regardless of direction. "Best" has nothing to do with "proper" or "dignified"; it has to do only with their potential to move up or down.

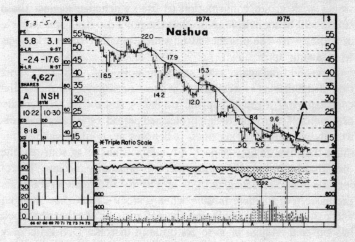

The Nashua chart is an example from the same period as the previously shown Tandy chart. The market was ensnared in correction time, but because it seemed to be still early in an ongoing upward primary trend, there were bullish stocks worth holding. Indeed, after the correction had lasted several weeks, some stocks actually looked buyable while others still looked dangerous. But, rather than shorting Tandy, note how much safer it would have been to short Nashua at point A. While the basic thesis is not to sell short during a primary bull market, and particularly to ignore the first intervening correction, as a hedged approach to portfolio management, this sort of stock would have been both safe and, as it turned out, satisfactory. The downside profit potential is nowhere near as great as an apparent top such as Tandy's would have been had TAN broken down, but the percentage play was certainly fine, from 15 down to under 11 with little risk.

The primary uptrend did indeed resume with a bang in January 1976. That was a time to be 100 percent long, but subsequently the market became very tricky, with the averages whipsawing back and forth. There were a number of stocks well worth continuing to hold long, but at the same time sound analysis said that the bull market was a year older and a lot more tired. This produced some noticeable negative group action, and it was possible to uncover shortable stocks with group confirmation to use as a hedge against those stocks still being held long, so that the portfolio itself was capable of rolling with the punches at all times, whether the market was whipsawing up or down.

Time and time again, as we see it, the notion of playing the short side of the market is weakness. On some occasions that means the completion of a major top; on others, a stock that has already proven itself in trouble over a prolonged period, especially as it fails to rally when the market does. It denotes, it should be added, far more than the obvious aspect of fundamentals going sour. By the time that becomes public knowledge, it is usually too late. Therefore, technical evidence, with its objectivity and ready visibility, is the basic tool for determining when a stock's trend has changed and can continue to guide you thereafter as to whether the stock has suffered enough or is to continue in distress. Dividends may seem invitingly high, or price/earnings ratios may appear remarkably low, but the market knows.

In 1974, Bowmar Instruments, a major entity in the then red-hot pocket-calculator field, fell to 1 times earnings. That's right: one! The price of a share was equal to its year's per-share earnings. How much lower could Bowmar possibly drop? Those who bought the issue on this premise got the answer a few weeks later when Bowmar went into bankruptcy and was delisted. Rather than being the upside speculation it seemed to be, it was the perfect short. Weakness is as weakness does, technically; believe what the market is telling you above all else.

## A Brief Summary

Let's review the salient considerations in selling short:

1. Be patient. Wait for the top to be completed before taking action. Better to go short at a lower price, and know that the stock has already broken down, than to try to anticipate that it is sure to fall. Try to avoid being caught in a last-gasp, nerve-shattering rally.

2. The least risky time to sell short is on a pullback rally following the breakdown. Be alert for such a pullback both immediately thereafter and a few weeks later, looking for a chance to get your short off just under a rounding-over Moving Average as well as just under a resistance area.

3. Assume, because you need to sell short on an uptick, that the stock will probably go against you a bit after your order is executed.

4. Never use an "at the market" order to sell short when the stock is declining on the tape.

5. Make sure that there is a sensible place overhead to enter a protective stop order.

6. Avoid strong stocks that look as if they're too high or ought to come back down. Instead, search out proven weak stocks, those whose strength is in the past, based on a clear-cut trend reversal and a downside break of an important level. We repeat: some patience until the long-term Moving Average rolls over and starts downward is vital.

7. Do not ignore stocks that have fallen considerably already. There are times—corrections, hedging needs—when stocks that are very weak are the safest shorts. They do not readily rally and still may produce sizable percentage gains on the downside.

8. Pay attention to volume on rallies. Heavy volume on the upside is a warning that the stock may be reviving in strength. Also, heavy trading on the downside, followed by an abrupt reversal upward, is often a sign that the decline is over (although time is then needed for a base to form).

9. When it comes to covering your short position:
   a. Always start with a protective buy stop, so that you can

be taken out objectively if the market tells you you are wrong.

b. Be alert for bad news; it frequently comes near a bottom. If the bad news comes and the stock shrugs, it is telling you that all the sellers are gone and it is time for you, too, to depart.

c. Cover shorts if the market indicators reach favorable levels. No need to milk the last eighth from the short any more than to hang on to a stock for the last upside eighth. A bird in the hand . . .

d. If a rally catches you, as it well might, and reveals signs of more power than you expected, do not panic. Instead, remember that there will customarily be a test of the low. Such tests are necessary to help form a new base, and they provide you with a quieter chance to cover your short. Best to assume that the test of the low will be successful.

e. Cover if there is a trading delay with more sellers than buyers. That can be a climactic occurrence.

f. Remember that you can always cover and live to go short again on the next rally. It is just as destructive to be a stubborn short as a hopeful long.

Shorting is a more difficult activity than buying stocks because, especially for the novice, the subconscious desire to be punished, to lose, to be wrong, has added to it the implication that the negative side of the market is not nice. But once your head is clear, you'll find that selling short has a nifty bonus to it: your ability to sell long is greatly enhanced. Erased will be the perennial optimism, the culturally demanded unrealistic notion of up, up, up. You'll be more on your toes. Looking for a profitable position in either direction, without prejudice, will help you spot tops in time. You'll be far more willing to step forward and sell out your long positions, and you'll constantly track the indicator clues so that your timing will be sharpened as well. And, as you take profits down near bottoms, you'll have a lot more capital to buy stock with for the next rise.

ager to charge fees pegged to a percentage of generated market profits (this is not true, by the way, for managers of commodity portfolios), and no firm pays a regular salary to its salesmen unless it is commensurate with the degree of commission business being written. A broker may have it in his heart to do right, but he has to do business first. The broker swears he'll be forthright with his customers, but when a man calls up and wants to buy General Motors, can he tell him it's not the right time when, in a tricky game like Wall Street, the customer might be correct? How can he afford to tell his clients, "This market is weak, sell everything," when, first, they'll be taking losses in stocks he put them in (which may cost him some customers) and, second, if they sit on the sidelines, perhaps for months, there won't be any income, no matter how right he may be, and they might then leave him to go with a broker who promises more action. Even the best of brokers tend to be affected by a need to find the exceptions to buy, to hold, while the great mass of customer's men can become stubborn, panicked, prayerful, overexuberant, and biased, all with your money.

And his employers back him up. A brokerage firm that issues genuine selling advice is as rare as a penguin in Palm Beach. That is, unless, of course, it comes after the market has already tumbled so badly even they have become frightened. There are even times when a firm knows a stock should be sold but will not say so, perhaps because such a recommendation would jeopardize its other, more profitable relationship with the company as its investment banker. Brokers' consciences are soothed by semantic salves. If you learn to read between the lines, you'll realize that the words "fully valued" really mean the firm thinks the stock should be sold. Another camouflage is the phrase that it is "removing XYZ from its buy list, but the stock is still a long-term hold," meaning that it's been going down so badly no one should go near it, but if you're already stuck, hold on, because it should recover within your lifetime. Or, "The quality of XYZ is such that it will inevitably go back up after the current sinking spell." Such language means they're selling their own shares out but don't dare announce it. A similar absurdity that arises from the merchandising nature of the brokerage business is when they write in their newsletter that the stock is expected to go down over the short term but is a great buy for the long pull. Even though he admits that there will be a built-in loss at first, the broker wants you to buy now, instead of advising you to wait for the bottom, because he needs that commission now, before you take your money to another firm.

We could carry on at great length about the tragicomic aspects of expert advice from the brokerage community, but no doubt you've experienced just about all of it at one time or another. There is no simple solution, no broker with a Midas touch. The customer's man you must find, and settle in with, is not a genius, who will be dead wrong during the next market cycle, or a hot shot who will blow sky high as soon as the market turns, but a broker who fully understands your particular investment philosophy. Let him know you, what you want to do, how you want to exist, and the kinds of moments when your own instincts are apt to be right (or wrong). He need be no better than your next-door neighbor in analyzing the market, but if he understands you as a customer, he can look out for your interests while he sits there watching the tape. He should, furthermore, be constantly alert, so he can provide you with pertinent up-to-the-minute information (if need be via an immediate phone call); he should enter and have executed with dispatch any orders you send in; and he should work for a firm that handles your clerical needs efficiently. How do you then profit in the stock market? Well, the rest is up to you.

This book was designed to help you with your problems, so that you can learn a more objective way to do your selling. The preceding chapters—on indicators, on reading charts, on entering your sell order itself—are all aimed at achieving independence from emotional confusion so that you can make objective decisions. Once the basics have been absorbed and mastered via experience, all other, more sophisticated devices will come easily. But before we leave you out on a limb, let's run through an overall philosophy.

## Patience, Perspective, Failure

The more we learn, and live through, in the stock market, the more we are convinced that success can be summed up in three words: patience, perspective, and, unfortunately for alliteration, failure.

First, patience. The market, it can be said, acts more slowly than any person believes it will. How many times do we wake up thinking, Today's the day, when hope alone is involved? Cycles last longer, trends last longer, even short-term rallies and sell-offs last longer than expected because we are so impatient. Our impatience is tied to our dreams and our fears. The net result is that investors tend to think a rise is over much before it really is, and they sell too soon. This is especially true when recent performances have made the investor impatient for what he has become familiar with; a bear market gets him in tune with selling and selling short, so when the bull comes along he is still thinking bearishly and is anxious to jump on the sell side—much too soon.

Later, of course, lethargy sets in. The past is forgotten. Everything has turned out okay. Patience evolves into paralysis. One becomes akin to a bureaucrat: when first taking the job, the civil servant is eager to get things done and acts too quickly. Learning that lesson, he determines to wait patiently, trying to fulfill his job slowly but surely, until finally, with little to show for the years put in, the bureaucrat decides that perhaps it is better to do nothing at all. The proper moment has already gone by.

Can these twin foes of impatience and paralysis be combated? In our opinion, no one (except the professional trader) should be playing an in-and-out game. It is easy to be right for eighths and quarters, but impossible to profit thereby over any stretch of time. Any reader of this book should be aiming for the bigger swings of intermediate-term trends. That, of course, requires the patience to sit through intervening shorter-term fluctuations. The only way to do that is to make sure you accept in advance that you are going to have to endure days when your stock will go down, and that once in a while you'll wind up with a loss that wasn't a loss earlier in the move. Such mistakes will, we believe, be offset considerably by the much greater profits made by letting other stocks run their course. Then, when you finally do begin to actually see, and not merely anticipate seeing, tops form and trend lines break, you must act so that paralysis doesn't take over.

Two tools will help: first, give priority to weekly charts rather than to daily ones (which should be used more for timing exactly when to act), and second, apply Moving Averages. We've found no use for 10-week M.A.'s, which tend to feed impatience, but there are considerable virtues to the 30-week, or 200-day, Moving Average lines, especially in keeping you from moving too soon but forcing you to move before it is too late. These two tools, as you have probably already noticed, lead right into our second key word: perspective.

Obviously, longer-term charts and longer-term Moving Averages can provide visual pictures of great help in terms of perspective. You'll see, for example, how far a stock has fallen if it has held in that area before, how big a base it has built, how much it has already bounced, how long that rise has gone without a correction, and if the move has had the scope to pull the Moving Average along with it or has been against the M.A.'s trend. A glance at such a chart, therefore, can answer the simplest and most important question of all: Where, in its cycle, is the stock at that very moment?

You also need to gain the perspective that the various indicators provide. Sure, the stocks tell it all, but it is too easy to look at them through subjective eyes; indicators have unassailable statistics that will provide a check. As we've tried to show, you don't need a million different indicators. You do need to spend a little time every week and follow those that have good historical track records, because they will show you what is reasonable to expect and what is not. If several important indicators have readings in their warning zones, you have the perspective to combat what will then be widespread optimism. Conversely, there will be times when a ton of bearish sentiment isn't matched by the readings of the indicators (the last few months of 1975 being a classic example), so you'll grasp that it is not a good time to sell. And that, after all, can be as important as knowing when to sell.

In addition to charts and indicators, there is a third aspect to perspective. It is vital to remember that selling is not the reverse of buying. That is the basic error fundamentalists make. They often reason that, having analyzed a company and ascertained that there are satisfactory fundamental reasons for owning that stock, they will also be able to apply the same approach to spotting when to sell. But stocks are often—quite often, indeed—screaming buys based on fundamentals, such as near the bottom of a bear market when price/earnings ratios are low and dividend yields extraordinarily high (see the bottom in May 1970, for example), but few dare buy because the hysteria of the bear is so strong. This relative undervaluation—in hindsight, of course—can last for weeks and even months, while the stock is still buyable. Only the technician, seeing the indicators begin to turn and the individual stock charts begin to improve, can overcome emotion and buy. Thereafter, the fundamentalist, even though he feared to put his money on the line, realizes that he was on the right track and believes that he will also see when to sell.

But such is not the case. The time to sell may come for reasons that have little to do with corporate fundamentals, such as, simply, when everyone who wants to buy has already bought; or when the industry fades from fashion; or when the rest of the market becomes toppy and pulls even good stocks down with it. More frequently, the time to sell comes in advance of knowledge that the fundamentals are shifting. That doesn't mean they become bad, but only that, perhaps, the rate of growth has ebbed for simple mathematical reasons, or there is a strike or something else interfering with progress for a quarter or two. A few insiders may know, but the brokerage firm's fundamental analyst may not spot the shift quickly or may dismiss it as merely temporary; the insider selling, though, affects the charts, and the charts, in turn, pronounce that the stock has had it. Time and time again, the stock sells off severely before the Street becomes aware that the company's fundamentals have shifted. In many other instances, the stock has formed a top and then smashes down when the news strikes. You can base your buying on a combination of fundamentals and technicals, but *you must sell when the technicals say so, despite the fundamentals.* That's where perspective comes in.

But what are we talking about when we say you must sell? Our third key word is, you'll recall, failure. The more we work in the marketplace, the more convinced we are that, of all systems, the only guide that works consistently is the notion of failure. It won't, obviously, catch the top eighth, but it will be close enough and it is clear enough so as never to be missed.

You may recall that, in *The Hound of the Baskervilles,* Sherlock Holmes was given a valuable clue because a dog didn't bark when he might reasonably have been expected to. Wall Street's equivalent is the stock that fails to make a new high, or to rally, when it ought to have done so. Is that all? Is life so simple? Of course not. You have no perspective, in terms of time, when a stock fails to make a new high in the course of its uptrend. After all, suppose it is merely resting. Suppose it makes a new high next week? Myriads of investors cling to stocks long after they should be sold precisely because of such supposes. The failure doesn't come from that aspect alone: also required is an actual failure on the downside; that is, the stock must first be unable to continue its advance (failing to make a higher high) and that must be followed by a drop below the level which had previously held (making a lower low). That is failure.

The longer a trend has been in existence, the more significant any failure is. All stock tops are a collection of failures within a particular area. By having a clear sense of where you are in a cycle (perspective), you will be able to judge failure better. Thus: believing that a stock has been forming a base, you buy. Failure then comes if it sells at a price below the range of the base. Or, knowing that the stock has been rising for a prolonged period, you recognize failure when the uptrend has been ended via lower highs and lower lows. In sum, you must know how to take a loss and how to take a profit, both difficult, by recognizing when the stock has ceased to do what was expected of it.

## A Last Word

The one thing we can guarantee is that none of it is easy. Just try to walk that fine line between not selling too soon and not procrastinating one day too long! Any time any one of us, from professional trader to odd-lotter, can boast of taking a profit, we have done something right. Luck is a mere bonus. What was right, simply put, was that a stock was bought cheap and sold dear. But don't let anyone claim that the two halves of the act are equally easy. Only someone who has never played the market game would believe that.

We've maintained throughout that it is only after a stock is bought that the hard-core intrigue, subtlety, and treachery of the market come into play. All you have to do is take a loss once in a stock that otherwise looked flawless, made perfect sense, and perhaps even went shooting up after you bought it, to know how infinitely difficult the market can be. As in any challenging game, the contestant has to be prepared to answer both to the mood of the market and to his own personal capabilities.

More than anything else, it is this inner struggle that distinguishes the act of selling. For, as our partnership with a stock, selected from among thousands and bought in the bloom of innocence, grows older, a parade of psychic complications—guilt, greed, potency, paranoia, anxiety—start marching across the tape of the mind. Investment in the stock market can also be investment in the ego. Turning money into inner work is an old trick of psychiatry: if the price of treatment is high enough, the patient will waste no time in coming to the point. In the stock market, however, the participant is not sent a bill for his mental travail. That day of reckoning comes only when shares are sold and converted back into money, more of it or less of it than when the contract was entered into. No wonder many people don't face their losses until it is too late! How much pleasanter life would be if we never had to face an ego loss.

But, unfortunately, the market as a mirror of life shows us such crises to our faces. It has its ups and downs, a suspect past and an uncertain future; it reminds us, every day, what the latest price measurement is, pumps up our hopes that the next day will be saving or rewarding. Thus the agenda on every page of this text has been how to make the selling decision as objectively as possible.

Can it be done at all? We think so. There are indicators that tell us when the general run of emotions has gotten beyond reasonable limits, which means we should count ourselves out. There are indicators that remind us of our own emotions so we can check them against the facts. We have emphasized the special mental conditions wherein hope can be modified by practicality, dreams can be superseded by reality, and fear can be translated into action. And short of being able to wire yourself to a listener who would make more objective judgments, we've detailed the basic methods whereby you can handle your stock ownership in an objective, and thereby ultimately profitable, manner. Anyone who repeatedly uses the market as an arena for an emotional contest is destined to lose, because that is the definition of neurosis itself: a means of repeating failure in a socially acceptable way. Loss in the stock market is, please note, explainable to one's peers, a socially acceptable means of gambling, a place where ego can play the game and shrug if defeated.

No matter how we may try to relate to it, the stock market is a "thing" and things do not listen. But if it will not be a party to our desires, as a thing it can be measured, weighed, and analyzed. As a game, it has odds and strategies. As mass psychology, it can be tabulated. All these are significant ways of keeping emotion at bay and thus creating some sort of order out of what seems to others chaos.

Yet emotional shackles are not readily broken. Our minds do not come equipped with doors to lock out hopes and dreams, even if we identify them as such and have charts and graphs to help us. So we must make allowance for their presence. For most, the hardest mental conditioning will come in admitting to losses. "What won't go up must come down" is a sensible slogan, so learning to recognize positions which show little prospect for gain must be accompanied by the ability to dispose of such positions with the least amount of fuss. Hand in hand with this goes the discipline of not berating oneself for honest mistakes, for doing what seemed objectively sensible at the time, even if the future produced something different.

Interestingly, we play the stock market because, although other games may have close to even odds, in the stock market risk and reward ratios heavily favorable to the player are often available. If they are not, the bets can be modest, hedged, or ignored entirely. And if the bet turns sour, the bulk of it can be retrieved. (Try that at the blackjack table!) And the stock market is capable of huge variation. If we don't like, or are baffled by, today's game, we can come back next week or next month when the picture is different. Also, the bets can be placed at any given time, even on a "horse" that has already proven itself far ahead of the field. And whatever the players know can be observed, because they must buy and sell to profit on what they know, so that everyone's cards are always on the table. This paean could go on, but let's interrupt it with these words once again: All these attributes will do you no good unless you know when and how to close out your position.

The buying is easy, and there are plenty of people willing to help you. But when it comes to selling, you are on your own. No excuses, no apologies, no injuries or "bad luck" or house odds against you. The decision, including the decision to do nothing, is entirely up to you. Tomorrow's game will start where yesterday's left off, and it will be the solitary burden of the seller to call his own shots.

Weekly bar charts are available from R. W. Mansfield Company, 26 Journal Square, Jersey City, New Jersey 07306; daily bar charts from Daily Graphs, P.O. Box 24933, Los Angeles, California 90024. The application of the indicators in this book is a regular feature of *The Professional Tape Reader,* P.O. Box 96, Wall Street Station, New York, New York 10005.